6 95
C+ 7¢

THE PEKING PAPERS

The Peking Papers

Leaves from the Notebook
of a China Correspondent
by
JACQUES MARCUSE

NEW YORK
E. P. DUTTON & CO., INC.
1967

To the memory of

Dr. Pavlov's dog,

*this book is humbly dedicated
by the Pekinese who wrote it*

FIRST EDITION

CONTENTS

Part Three   THE FORBIDDING CITY

PREFACE

AFTER one has been an honest working journalist all one's life, it's difficult to write an honest book. It's like switching from a snack bar to a great kitchen as a self-appointed chef. A vast experience of sandwiches has not taught you how to cook. One has not the skill. One faces raw material of a subtler sort and of much greater variety. One deals in different truths.

There's truth in sandwiches. The bread, for instance, must be freshly cut and not curl up at the corners like old-fashioned Chinese roofs. But they are made to be quickly consumed and, one hopes, digested, and then forgotten. The only sandwiches one remembers are the bad ones. A meal is another thing altogether—another reality.

The trouble is that the fare one serves is also the fare one tends to feed on. Why else should a butcher look so different from a cheese-monger—and even think differently? Why should an author, slaving as he may be in his own literary kitchen, have so little in common with the agency correspondent, that maker of news sandwiches?

In the long run, an exclusive diet of sandwiches is good for neither the stomach nor the palate. It leads to ulcers and a blunting of the sense of taste. In the case of the agency man who has just completed a long assignment in Peking, both symptoms are acutely present, and they may be misleading. They point, not so much to a permanent surfeit of dough and cold ham, as to malnutrition and lack of exercise.

By contrast, the special correspondent there—as distinct from the permanent one—is often given more than he can take: he is crammed like poultry, in the hope, often gratified, that the proof will be found in the reading. He will generally agree that China is strong meat.

Of China, the permanent man gets his basic ration in the form of official literature. No press conferences for him, no interviews with national leaders or prominent personages, no trips around the country. If his hunger is not sated, he can turn, figuratively speaking, to the dung heap, as do, literally, Peking's innumerable destitutes who are no longer permitted to beg but can be seen nightly rummaging among the unspeakable refuse that piles up in the *hutungs*. Should he ever as much as mention their very existence to Chinese officialdom, it will be emphatically denied, and he will himself be accused of slandering the regime.

The special correspondent is given the V.I.P.P. (Very Important Potential Propagandist) treatment. He is not made to feel that he is rationed at all. He is taken straight to the marketplace, so to speak, there to make his choice and do his professional shopping. He does not always realize that it is a *special* market and a sham market. He can take his pick of whatever he is shown. What his eye does not see, his conscience will not grieve over. The use to which he later puts his basketful is his own business . . . up to a point. Another Chinese visa is not so readily available. He generally endeavors to give satisfaction.

And he may in fact often succeed, in perfectly good faith. I'm not thinking of those professionals who have made China their stock-in-trade, who write about nothing else and are the regime's blue-eyed Foreign Devils, who turn up again and again to be pampered, cajoled, bamboozled, and put to their appointed use. They will be mentioned, unkindly, later in this book, *passim*. But, by and large, the shorter the stay, the more favorable the report. This became most patent in 1964, when the Pakistani airline inaugurated its China service, with a load of special correspondents aboard its American aircraft, who were ferried to Peking from the Shanghai terminus and back again before re-embarking, Karachi-bound. They spent two days in Peking and two days in Shanghai, being made much of, and the stories that some of them wrote, who had never set foot in China before, were among the most dithyrambic I have read.

But then, the Chinese are very good at making a first impression. They are great illusionists and jugglers, and the inventors, after all, of the shadow theater and of the paper kite that looks so deceptively like a real bird.

No doubt the average visitor is shown much that is admirable on a rather materialistic and economic plane. But if China's present claims to greatness are to be analyzed, one finds little difference between them and those that were made thirty years ago by Mussolini's Italy and Hitler's Third Reich. Trains run according to the timetable. Guns come before butter. And, of course, intellectuals are *gleichgeschaltet*, the Press is all-official, and even the children praise the Party and worship the Leader.

Still, the V.I.P.P., whose visit may last from three weeks to two months, is hardly ever left to himself. He goes on being shepherded and chaperoned about to the point of bodily and intellectual exhaustion. He has to take in all the showpieces, and is made to believe that, could he but have stayed longer, he would have seen even more, in fact anything he could have asked to see. True enough, he does not always accept the unceasing propaganda as Gospel, but after being politely bowed out of the country by his smiling hosts, his mind is so full of unverifiable facts that he is bound to write in something of a postprandial mood.

Not so the permanent correspondent, useless as a propagandist and therefore ignored, who is there by virtue of one of the reciprocal arrangements that allow the New China News Agency to have its own men abroad. When his time is up, he does not leave with a full belly but rather with a bellyful.

If he is a Westerner, he has done the usual two-year stretch.* He is looking forward to a new assignment in another part of the world and does not necessarily expect to visit China again. He does not cultivate a special interest in Chinese affairs, in the country or its people. Soon the taste of frustration is washed away. Pleasant memories remain: he has made friends in Peking

---

* Soviet bloc journalists stay longer and seem better conditioned to stand the strain. Also, they usually live in the compounds of their own embassies.

among the hospitable, essentially diplomatic, foreign community, enjoyed their frequent cocktail and dinner parties, and drunk their whisky with gratitude.

China, he has not seen. The Chinese, apart from a handful of official underlings, he has not met. These underlings, if he remembers them at all, he would rather think of as comic characters of a somewhat fantastic nature than as the insufferable obstructionists they truly were. If his professional life has been mostly a dreary tedium strongly laced with exasperation, his social life has been fun. The two together have provided him with an occasional something to write home about, but certainly not with the makings of a serious book on China.

One can of course write a personal book, and, in fact, that is precisely what most visitors have done. Informative as their works are, they remain essentially travel books. Permanent correspondents travel little. They can write about Peking, to which the scope of their experience is limited, but to them, even Peking is limited, for it bristles with *Verboten* signs. Still, very soon, I thought I should make an attempt of some sort.

Perhaps I had an excuse, and I knew I had an idea.

The excuse was that, of all the thirty-odd correspondents then working in Peking, none but myself had known prewar or even pre-Red China. I was the only one who could indulge in comparisons of a legitimately odious sort.

The idea was that, as a resident, I had at my disposal a great deal more printed material than would ever come the way of any passer-through. All official, all propaganda. But I could afford to pick and choose, leaving aside the statements of policy from authoritative sources that were already known the world over and concentrating on less publicized but more revealing items culled from the daily and periodical press and originally meant for home consumption only. By means of accurately translated quotations, I proposed to picture the Chinese as they saw themselves, or as they should have seen themselves, had they been fully as mentally supine as was expected of them, and to show the Party-State's attitude to the West as it really was, not as speeches on public and polite occasions were making it out to be. I began collecting such material as, for instance, articles on fictitious "heroes" and "letters to the editor" which I strongly suspected had been written in the editorial rooms of the various papers that printed them. That was to be the most important and the only irrefutable part of the book. The rest, based on my own observations and (perhaps ill-considered) opinions, would remain disputable.

Actually, my personal contribution was not intended to amount to anything like an account of Communist China. It was to be a goldfish's-eye view of the country, as seen through the frosted glass of the Peking bowl in which I swam, feeding on crumbs of information. The earnest student of Chinese affairs would find few hard facts of unquestionable prophetic significance, the economist few figures—but no less inaccurate, I prided myself, than those he could glean in more didactic fields of writing since, perforce, they would come from the same and only source.

I had the choice of two approaches: the jaundiced approach and the lighthearted one. I decided in favor of the latter. It seemed logical. After all, in Peking we were joking all the time. The more frustrated we became as journalists, the more we had to laugh. Newsworthy developments, in so far as they were revealed to the foreign press or could be guessed at, we dealt with to the best of our ability in our daily dispatches. We tried to make sense of and to boil down to readable stories the verbiage of the *People's Daily* and the *Red Flag* fortnightly. But, personally, what we saw in it was no more than the repetitive clumsiness of clumsy indoctrination set down in clumsy language. The major campaigns which the Party machinery launched periodically on a variety of subjects were so unconvincing as to border on the farcical. The perpetual boasts of the regime, its over-Victorian prudishness, the palpable untruths which the people (and ourselves) were expected to swallow without demur, the childish propaganda, the purposeful isolation and ignorance in which we were kept, in fact everything that we most disliked and held in contempt made us roar with permanent mirth. At the same time, it all became unreal. The whole picture. It was like watching a film version of Orwell's *1984*, starring the Marx Brothers. The more frightening the incidents in the plot, the louder our guffaws. It was, I suppose, a form of mental self-protection.

That in itself was worth recording, briefly and in a humorous vein that would set off my many newspaper cuttings to advantage. To do so was my happy purpose when I left China. Then I began to write.

At first, all went well. I still had the feel of Peking and a reasonable supply of that bottled atmosphere we had been breathing under our oxygen tent. Peking, in a way, remained more important than China. That preposterous but perfectly authentic man we had nicknamed "Fishface," with whom the reader will soon become acquainted, was someone for whose existence I could vouch, which was more than I was prepared to do for Mao.

But perspective alters as distance varies, and the place one has left is never quite the place one has lived in. China, oppressive but invisible to Peking residents, gradually acquired a sharpness of focus which I had not known it to possess since the days one could tour it and speak to its people without hindrance.

The sense of freedom was, of course, life-giving. I had just rediscovered it in India where I had spent a fortnight feeling like a sailor on a spree and perhaps, intellectually at least, behaving like one, drunk with intelligent human contacts and unrestricted conversation. But I was to discover that it was not doing my work any good. My original plan now seemed flat and unprofitable. Who, I wondered, would bother to read anything so superficial? I had lost my own taste for it. The gilt was off the goldfish.

I still had my notes and most of my Chinese press cuttings, and I went back to them with a will, and over them again and again. They no longer made such humorous reading. The farcical aspect was still there, but it had all become a grim farce. I suppose it was a matter of surroundings. Now that I could speak and move as I pleased and argue the point—any point!—I no longer had to pretend that things were funny when they were not. And China was definitely *not* funny. At long last, I could admit it to myself. I had made good my escape from escapism.

It should have pleased me. It did not. More than ever, I wanted to write my book. But not the same book. I dug up from my trunk another set of notes which had been jotted down out of sheer professional conscientiousness and which I never expected to put to any literary use. To my astonishment, they fully tallied with my jocular ones. I retrieved more ancient personal documents from other trunks with now creaky hinges, looked up my old textbooks and history books and documents and found myself confirmed in a theory which I had formed in Peking and rejected because it was too depressing. Was I to write a serious book? After all, I had spent more years of my adult life in China than in any other country. Perhaps I could do it. On the other hand, why should the truth be acceptable in its dullest form only? I knew I had stuck to it to the best of my knowledge, not just scrupulously, but, during my last Peking assignment, desperately, no matter what mood I wrote in. It was too rare and precious and too short in supply to be treated lightly or tampered with. Moreover, having had to buy official untruths for thirty months, I thought it would be fun and poetically just to settle my bill in that illegal tender.

Finally, I gave up writing the book. I let it write itself. As a matter of fact, I had no choice. It had run away with me. I just sat well down in the saddle, so to speak, and concentrated on staying there. It followed a course all its own, often erratic, occasionally turning back, unpredictable always, over a strange country that was pleasant enough at first and grew increasingly dismal and forbidding and barren as one rode deeper into it. Perhaps it was China.

Part One

WESTERN APPROACHES

I

MINOR KEY

HE BOARDED the train before it had come to a stop at Canton station. The China Travel Service had sent him. He was to be my
interpreter and guide during my overnight stay and put me on
the plane to Peking on the morrow. There his responsibility
would end. He made that meticulously clear as soon as he had
formally said: "Boochoo, Mossou Ma Cuss" and we had exchanged civilities. He had the round head, the protruding eyes,
and the tapering body of a tadpole, and a bandage around his
neck, and he looked ill. He said he was overworked, but a willing
slave to duty. There were several French businessmen, sometimes
very rude to him, attending the Canton Industrial Fair. They
taxed both his patience and his strength to the utmost. Nevertheless, he had been told to meet me, and there he was, all grimness
and dedication.

"And where," I asked, "did you learn your French?"

"Canton University," said Mr. Liu, "where we are taught all
foreign languages."

"All?"

"Certainly."

"Do you know them all?"

"No. Only French. I am a specialist."

"No English?"

"I cannot speak English. I cannot understand English. But I can
read it."

"Then you can translate it?"

"No. But I can read the characters."

"The characters?"

"The letters, I should have said. *Les Anglais se servent des*

17

*lettres françaises.** I can spell the words. Their meaning, how-ever, escapes me. Russian, I cannot read at all. The letters are different. But we do study Western languages and culture very thoroughly."

"And are you taught Latin?"

"Some of us are. Even though we have, of course, no diplo-matic relations with the Fascist Franco regime."

"What has that got to do with it?"

"Well, after all, we cannot expect all our friends in Latin America to speak Chinese," said Mr. Liu magnanimously.

(Canton, April 20, 1962)

---

*I have purposely left this sentence in the original French. In English, it would have assumed a fortuitous and totally irrelevant significance. (author's note).

2

NO PRIMROSE UP THE
GARDEN PATH

THE FIRST thing I did when I arrived in Peking in the spring of
1962 was to look for Peking. It did not seem to be where I had
left it. It was not. It could not have been. I had never seen
Peking.

What I remembered was a provincial town to which I had paid
my last visit fifteen years before. It was then named Peiping, and
it had become something of a ghost town. The embassies had
finally moved to Nanking, and the Legation Quarter, stripped of
its status and privileges, had lost much of its glamour. Mere
consuls now dwelt in the huge legations and roamed their vast
compounds which garden-party guests could no longer fill.
Madame Chiang Kai-shek's "New Life Movement" had done
away with horse racing and gambling and opium, and everyone
agreed that Puritanism and Peiping didn't mix well. Still it
retained some of its decadent dreamlike quality, even though the
decadence had already become chiefly that of foreign prestige in
China.

A very long time ago, when I had had my first look at it,
Peiping had been a merry place. Unlike Shanghai and nearby
Tientsin, it wasn't a business center. It was delightfully idle. The
diplomatic corps had not yet condescended to follow the Nationalist government to its uncomfortable, unhygienic, and un-
westernized seat on the banks of the Yangtse. The legations, just
about to be raised to embassy status, still ran the Quarter, with its
motley garrison and its iron or wooden gates and its glacis dating
back to the Boxer Protocol. No Chinese had the *right* to live
there, but the foreigners (Western and Japanese) could reside

wherever they chose and the whole of Peiping was their playground. They rode little Mongolian ponies, played polo on the glacis, went to the Western Hills for weekends and picnics. There was the race course, and there was golf, and the Chinese farmers were quite used to the sight of foreigners paper-chasing over their land during the season. One went about the city's narrow *hutungs* in one's private rickshaw. One collected "curios." One read the *Peking and Tientsin Times*, or the *Journal de Pekin*, still owned, published, and edited by old Albert Nachbaur, who could have made a fortune in Paris as a *chansonnier*, but who preferred Peking where, in his sarcastic editorials, he claimed that Dr. Sun Yat-sen's "Three Principles of the People" (*San Min Chu Yi*) were the very same one could read on the weighing machines in any French railway station, namely:

1. Whoever weighs himself regularly knows himself;
2. Whoever knows himself keeps healthy;
3. If the machine is out of order, kindly apply to the station-master.*

Life was an endless string of parties. Everything was cheap because labor was cheap. Peiping was simply heaven. Whether the Chinese thought so, too, was quite immaterial.

Now, it was something altogether different. It was so unlike Peiping that I could not bring myself to say that I had come *back* to it. Nothing whatever looked or felt familiar, except of course such world-famous sights as the Imperial Palace and the Temple of Heaven and so on. These I remembered distinctly having seen somewhere, possibly on post cards. I recognized them just as I had "recognized" the Acropolis on my first trip to Athens. Anyway, they were still where one expected to find them, defying time. In comparison, most of the new structures looked jerry-built and already semi-decrepit, ambitious as they were. Much of the beauty of ancient imperial Peking was gone, as was almost all its charm. From the top of Coal Hill, instead of a sea of billowing gray-tiled roofs, one beheld (unless you looked at the preserved magnificence of the Forbidden City) a vista of abortive sky-

---

* In the original French:

1. *Qui souvent se pèse, bien se connaît;*
2. *Qui bien se connaît, bien se porte;*
3. *Si l'appareil ne fonctionne pas, adressez-vous au chef de gare.*

scrapers and low, square barrack-like structures. In the middle of huge (and new) Tienanmen Square, in front of the Imperial Palace, there was, and still is, the Monument to the People's Heroes; the official Guide Book says that it "commands the respect of all who see it." Be that as it may, one cannot help wishing that it did so elsewhere and not spoil the noble perspective of Chien Men. Bordering on Tienanmen Square was Peking's pride, the Great Hall of the People, built in just 300 days, and covering more ground than all the Imperial Palaces put together, but less attractively. Facing it squatted a museum in the same arid style.

Peking's big new thoroughfare, 240-foot-wide Changan Avenue, running from east to west, failed to impress me, as did its elaborate system of traffic lights, all worked by hand by policemen sitting in small wooden huts, regardless of the scarcity of motor traffic. The policemen always seemed to be picking up their telephones when you drove by. The avenue itself was curiously un-urban. It suggested the middle stretch of an important highway linking two major hypothetical towns. Actually, it still leads nowhere and, at both ends, becomes a primitive country road with a bad surface.

Then I had a look at the streets, the unrecognizable streets of old—Morrison Street, now Wangfuching; Hatamen Street, newly dubbed Chungwenmen Tachieh—with their pavement in bad need of repair and unattractive shops. Everything, old or new, reeked of squalid abandon, and the new was by no means modern but might have been both conceived and built a quarter of a century ago. There was, for instance, the State department store in Wangfuching, with its gray, unimaginative façade, its rickety counters made of bad wood and worse windowpane glass, its tasteless window display. This emporium of modern China was certainly worth an inspection, for it sold nothing imported and gave one a fair idea of national ingenuity, which remained great. Every article it sold was strictly "made in China" and ranged from tinned fish and beer to television sets, tape recorders, and grand pianos. It also offered old-fashioned clockwork gramophones (which I identified as a copy of the "Columbia" portable of 1932) and 78 rpm. highly breakable records. The store was always crowded, but, as things were either very expensive or could only be purchased on the production of "industrial coupons," the atmosphere was that of a museum rather than of Woolworth's.

The famous *hutungs*, narrow and unpaved, the elaborate doorways and inner courtyards of their traditional one-story, street-blind houses, were doomed, and with them whatever remained of individual privacy. But there had been a stay of execution. Building had practically stopped in Peking, and therefore demolition also. Whole districts, sentenced to death under the "Great Leap Forward" of 1958, were reprieved when the "Leap" collapsed; and the *hutung* dwellings might be left for a few more years to crumble of their own accord.

Such was, as I saw then, the setting in which six million people were living their daily lives, doing as they were told, consuming their meager rations, watching their tongues and their neighbors, and thinking their silent thoughts under the eye of the ubiquitous Street Committee.

Such was the capital of China. The capital of the People's Republic of China. The capital of the largest, most populated country in the whole shrinking world. Reborn? That was the word most commonly used. Young again. A phoenix of a city. A monstrous baby phoenix, misshapen, unhealthily overgrown here, stunted there, alive indeed, but showing signs of unsound heredity and of both attentive, if incompetent, nursing and shocking neglect, an infant city, only half groomed for the first prize of the show, with a clean face and dirty diapers.

What the truant Russian nanny had left behind was not nice to see, and her strict Maoist successor had not yet effectively taken over, or fed the child, or silenced it. That was still to come.

Of course, in 1958 (a Leap Year, according solely to the Party calendar), Peking's old city wall had been breached and in some sectors completely pulled down. The venerable bricks that had lined it (the inside being raw mud) were used for the building of new houses, but the destruction remained more striking than the construction. Authorities pointed out that Peking was expanding. It was not true. The ancient city was dead. Something else was coming to uncertain life where Peking had once breathed. Perhaps some day it would achieve the stature and character of another imperial city. At the moment, it was a village, unsmiling, unshapely, and desperately self-assertive, the result, it seemed, of an experiment in modern slum-planning. And grim, as all villages

must have been at the very beginning, before age had given them
beauty, and while they were still strictly, unmercifully utilitarian. Still, the biggest village ever.

Peking's uneven spread looked to me cancerous rather than
healthy. Perhaps I was wrong. Perhaps my approach was wrong.
I am an Old China Hand with too much of a memory. The first
view I took of Mao's Peking (even though I had once watched
the encouraging birth of New China in Nanking and Shanghai)
was not a happy one. Newcomers, on the other hand, real newcomers, often felt differently. They could neither see the China
that had been nor miss what was lacking in the image which was
before them. They did not know that the Chinese, for all their
misery, had once been a cheerful crowd, humorous and quick-
witted, Chinese women beautiful and well dressed, the nation one
of incomparable craftsmen. While I deplored, so to speak, the
decadence of needlework, they were admiringly conscious of the
progress of the sewing machine, a poor copy, as it was, of the
Western models of the Twenties.

They noticed that nobody was visibly starving. I noticed that
very few people looked as if they were eating their fill. I was
struck by what the individual had lost, and they by what the
community had achieved. This, in due time, struck me too, as I
watched, month after month, steady, if modest, improvements in
the people's *material* standard of living. I could not but acknowledge a dynamic element. But whether the driving force actually
sprang, as it was claimed, from the people itself, became more
and more doubtful. Was not China's reconstruction, Peking's
metamorphosis, entirely due to a masterly technique of mass
mobilization? The question became the more momentous as one
gradually realized that China, far from breaking with the past,
had picked up the threads of an ancient (and extremely arrogant)
Imperial tradition. Wouldn't this clash with militant left-wing
Communism, as actively preached and practiced here? Why
should it?

Absolute authority was the common denominator. That, at
least, was, from the very first, quite plain. And even before I
entered into my professional duties, three more things had
forcibly struck me: the general secrecy in which everything was
shrouded, the distrust in which the Chinese held all foreigners,
and the distrust in which all foreigners held the Chinese.

Perhaps I am overgeneralizing when I say that all foreigners distrusted the Chinese, and I should have been nearer the truth had I said that official China distrusted all foreigners. As for the latter, it was certainly true of most of them whose experience of Peking had been of more than a few weeks' or months' standing, who were almost without exception diplomats or journalists, and who had already had dealings with the officialdom of the regime, generally with the Ministry of Foreign Affairs. There were others.

Most of them, one seldom saw. They included the faithful retainers, the old Western friends of the regime. Very few in point of numbers, most of them had acquired Chinese citizenship and put their long foreign noses to the grindstone. They were people of great virtue and dedication, but not perhaps of great discernment, for it would seem—and it already seemed then—that they were serving and defending an imaginary cause in which no one but themselves believed, and that the Chinese used them because they were eminently usable rather than eminently useful. The Western deserters of the Korean War—I met a few of them—seemed keen to convince one that they had come over to the Chinese camp out of sheer idealism. Still, they seemed mostly concerned about securing a free pardon from their respective countries and going back home. Several succeeded—and recanted in a manner that did no good to their colleagues still in China. In fact, as it turned out, they had ratted in and ratted out again.

And then there were the Drujbas. They were so dubbed because they lived in the Drujba (Friendship) hostel, once built by the Russians to house the many technical advisers whose services remained available to China until they were recalled in the summer of 1960. Later it became the home of the milder kind of foreign so-called "technicians." They were mostly young people recruited in Western Europe by the Chinese recruiting services, which are very active. Their jobs were comparatively minor jobs, and I am mentioning them only in connection with the foreigners' attitude to the Chinese. They were hard to get hold of because the Drujba is situated in the western suburbs, some six or seven miles from the center of Peking, and transport is not so readily available for the inmates, while admittance is difficult to secure for outsiders. Briefly they were divided into two distinct clans: those who felt they must help the Chinese as a matter of professional duty, and those who cared little about their professional duty and could barely stand the sight of the Chinese.

And, of course, there were the griffins. I am using the word griffin (which no longer really applies) because I find it convenient. It is an old Anglo-Indian term which once described both a European newcomer to the East and a pony that had not yet been raced. At the same time, in those days, the human griffin, like his equine namesake, was young and starting out on an Asiatic career, usually commercial. No man, visiting China for the first time in his middle age, would have been called a griffin. The difference between the man I still call a griffin and the man who was a griffin in bygone days is great indeed. It lies chiefly in the fact that the former griffin had no other ambition than to become an Old China Hand in due time, whereas his present equivalent proposes to become a China expert in no time at all. The modern Peking griffin—generally a youthful member of the diplomatic corps—has already, and by his own obscure choice, spent several years of his life learning Chinese at home. He fancies himself as a sinologist. He does not claim to know China, but only her language. And that, he admits, up to a point only. But already, if it has been worth his while to study Chinese at such trouble and expense, then it stands to reason that things Chinese as a whole are also worthwhile. And so indeed they are, and always have been and will be. What the new griffin fails to see is that China is no more above criticism than any other country, which is perfectly normal, legitimate, and understandable.

It does not imply a political bias. On the contrary, it often encourages a political aloofness that will save much trouble. And this is certainly not a dishonest attitude, for the griffin would have been just as sincerely enthusiastic about China if China had been living under a regime drastically different from the present. If the griffin of the late Twenties or the early Thirties was ever required to learn Chinese, he would do so in the country itself, at the bidding of his employers and for a very definite, practical, and businesslike purpose. His China was that of the Foreign Settlements and, eventually, the Treaty Ports. It never occurred to him that he might someday become a luminary on Chinese affairs—unless the firm which he had joined as perhaps a junior

clerk would require him to become one and that strictly in connection with trade. The new griffin is an official. He is a civil
servant of a particular kind and of a rare and specialized training.
He is a well-organized bohemian who looks toward the future
with a shrewd eye, if a shortsighted one, which is by no means
incompatible. His future however depends on that of China and
he trusts that both will be prosperous.

His attitude is not very different from that of the average
tourist who comes to Peking. The price of the conducted tour
has now come down considerably, but only two years ago it was
roughly one thousand pounds ($2800) from London to the
capital of China and back, including visits to such "open" towns
as Wuhan, Nanking, Shanghai, Hangchow, possibly Canton if he
went out by way of Hong Kong. A thousand pounds is hardly
chicken feed, and no matter what one spent it on, one hated to
admit even to oneself that one had been overcharged. The griffin
has spent much effort by the time he reaches China and the
tourist has spent much money. They are both more inclined to
praise than to criticize. And so are of course all these periodic
visitors to whom a re-entry permit is professionally essential.

The old-timer who runs into them in Peking will find conversation sometimes difficult. He will forget the reasons that make
them look at things so benignly and will unreasonably blame
them for basing their judgment on the compulsory bits of China
which they are shown and for not having seen the China they
were not shown, and had no means of seeing; for believing
blindly that China begins *now;* for being unaware of its true con-
tinuity. For *knowing* of changes that have taken place—political,
economic, social—but having experienced none of them. For
being unaware of what they could not possibly be aware of; for
not having noticed the unnoticeable; for being either insufferably
matter-of-fact or gratuitously sentimental. For having nothing to
be nostalgic about. For being "observers." For believing in obvious "achievements" and for making up arbitrary statistics and
also, at times, for mistaking their own blindness for objectivity.
For having come to China for a limited period, as part of their
Chinese studies and in preparation for a Chinese career to be
spent outside China. For being impressed by the new steel plants
and the bogus communes and the fact that the Chinese can no
longer be tipped.

What impresses the Old China Hand is altogether different, and the Old China Hand does not so readily draw conclusions. The railway bridge on the river Yangtse means little to him. He will notice, though, among many other things, that the Chinese no longer laugh or spit in the way they used to.

3

ON LAUGHING AND SPITTING

A GOOD many years ago, the three typical noises of China were the shuffling of mahjong dominoes under my window at night, constant laughter by all classes of society, and general spitting with preliminaries.

Mahjong was suppressed long before the Communists took over, and I never missed the sound.

Laughter was everpresent, and if it might have been found irritating at times in the comfort and peace of Shanghai, it was certainly heartening on most occasions. I remember finding it particularly so on the various fronts of the Sino-Japanese war which I visited and where the Chinese, soldiers and civilians alike, were keeping up a wonderful morale and laughing in the face of the worst possible adversity.

Spitting, I never really took to—neither actively nor generally, as a member of the audience. It often went together with nose-blowing, which was done without handkerchiefs, through one's fingers. I remember a very formal reception at one of these old-fashioned *compradoric*-style mansions built at the turn of the century, when I saw a high Kuomintang official, coming down the stairs, blow his nose and wipe his fingers, not on the wallpaper as etiquette commanded, but on the banister. I watched for the next guest to come down. It happened to be the wife of a European ambassador. To my disappointment, she had gloves on and, anyway, did not touch the rail. I watched on. Finally, my patience was rewarded.

"And what is your first impression of New China?" asked Israel Epstein a few weeks after my arrival in Peking. "Eppy," although an old resident, does not think like one, for he has become officially Chinese and is a Communist and a "retainer" and he thinks accordingly.

"Not a very cheerful one," I replied. "It seems to me that the Chinese no longer laugh."

"What do you mean?"

"Well, in the old Peking there seemed to be laughter everywhere. Even the poorest rickshaw coolies, ill fed and in rags, sitting on the curb and waiting for fares, used to swap jokes and roar with laughter. Nowadays, people are sullen."

My old friend (we have known each other for a quarter of a century) looked puzzled for a moment. When he spoke again, I realized how truly Chinese his mind had become.

"In the old days, you see," he explained, "the masses were so miserable that they had to laugh all the time in order to forget their plight and to muster up enough courage to go on living. Now, they are content and need no longer worry about the future. As you have said yourself, they don't laugh any more. They don't have to, they are happy."

This set me wondering. It had never occurred to me that laughter, too, could be the opium of the people.

Yet the laughter of the Chinese kept on impressing newcomers. Of that I had further proof some time later when I dined, foreign style for my sins, with a visiting correspondent who had only just arrived and was new to China, at the Hsin Ch'iao Hotel, where tourist-journalists are usually billeted. He told me that what had struck him most about the Chinese was that they were laughing all the time.

"How so?" I said, quite taken aback.

"But of course. They laugh when they meet you, and when they explain something to you, and when they are apologetic, when they tell you sad news and when they tell you good news. They laugh out of respect when they speak of Chairman Mao and out of contempt when they speak of the Americans. My room boy, who had been away for two days, was in stitches this morning when he explained that he had had to go to his mother's funeral. They even laugh when I tell them funny stories. That is, they always did, but once."

"When was that?"

"When I forgot to tell them that the story was funny."

And, of course, he was right. It was only that I had been expecting just the very kind of laughter that no longer existed.

Also, I realized, just as there are, in the Chinese spoken language, several tones, each giving the same syllable a different meaning, so there must be various tones in the laughter of the Chinese, one of which, the merry unpremeditated one, once so familiar, had now disappeared, a thing my colleague would not have known.

The dreadful thought crept on me that maybe cheerful individual laughter had been banned and that, next to the Thought Police, there was a Laughter Police whose ever-watchful ear was busily listening throughout the land for off-key merriment.

Very much later, the consensus among foreign correspondents in Peking was that the only time an Information Department spokesman had been known to break into a genuine guffaw was when he was asked to produce a photograph of the first Chinese atomic blast only three days after it had taken place, in October, 1964.

A young European diplomat and his wife had just arrived in Peking and, as is usual, their ambassador had given a cocktail party to introduce them to their various colleagues of the Western community. They were new to China and had just flown in through the back door, that is, by way of Moscow, missing the gentle introduction to the country which the stopover in Hong Kong and the ensuing overnight stay in Canton provide.

They were quite charming and they were absolutely delighted with Peking as griffins will be. The Chinese, they pronounced, were wonderful people. "However," said the young diplomat's young wife, "I wish they didn't spit so much."

I had already heard many remarks of that sort and I felt I was getting slightly deaf, like a veteran gunner whose eardrums, blunted, not to say altogether calloused, by the sound of heavy artillery barrages, are no longer attuned to the more delicate music of sporadic small arms fire.

I simply could not hear the Chinese spit or clear their throats with that mixture of thoroughness, abandon, and voluptuousness that had once been so characteristic. If I could no longer trust my ears, at least I could trust my eyes. The Chinese were no longer visibly spitting. Also, spittoons had become scarce.

In the old days, spittoons were everywhere. There was an incredible variety of them, from the humblest, in cheap eating places patronized by coolies, to the very expensive spittoon of rare and delicate porcelain which one saw in the mansions of cabinet ministers. In the very modern air-conditioned offices of American-trained Chinese businessmen in rimless spectacles, there were brass receptacles, highly polished, with bellies as round as that of Mi Lo Fo, the laughing buddha, yet looking so very un-Chinese and indeed so totally un-old-worldish that one could only think of them as cuspidors. Had you ventured to call them mere spittoons, the odds are they would have spat back at you.

There was something about spitting in China in those days. It was a national trait and a national bond—like the Chinese script which knew of no difference in dialect—only it was more widely used. When it came to the lengthy process of expectorating, you could not tell a dock laborer from a warlord. Upon returning to Peking, I had noticed, with no particular sadness, the decadence of spitting. In the offices of the Press Department at the Wai-chiaopu, there were no spittoons visible and the officials, the press officers to whom I spoke, spat not at all.

Spittoons can still be found in public places and in restaurants, but they no longer gape invitingly. The standard variety is a humble porcelain bowl covered with a round lid from the center of which a long pole sticks upwards so that you can remove the lid without having to bend. In the better places, the spittoon is enshrined in a sort of wooden cabinet, usually painted white or pale green, which gives it the look of a miniature lavatory of a primitive model, and the lid can be lifted by means of a pedal. Pre-liberation spittoons had no lids, but people spat in them. Now, spittoons in restaurants are used almost exclusively for emptying ashtrays in and, by small Chinese children only, to urinate in.

In my days, there were roughly two types of spitters: the slow, careful yet determined, strictly *vertical* spitter and the quick-on-the-draw crack shot who could hit the target from any angle. Careful planning and execution with the former; brilliant improvisation coupled with superb precision with the latter. Two schools, in fact, and within each, tremendous scope left to individual style and stance. And so there remains a doubt in my mind as to the reason which caused the authorities to discourage spitting both in public and in private. Was it hygiene, or was it just that spitting became frowned upon as a means of self-expression?

4

EAR TROUBLE

He was busy packing. From the courtyard, I could hear him whistling merrily to himself. I climbed the two steep flights of stairs. As I walked into his room, he looked up from an already half-filled suitcase and switched on the radio. It blared. He said something.

"Microphones," I lip-read.

"Where?" I shouted.

"Everywhere."

He had "done" his two years and had not enjoyed Peking. Now at last he was leaving for good. He had microphones on the brain.

"I always make a point of warning people when they arrive," he said.

I had already been warned. In Hong Kong, to begin with. Then in Peking itself, by other foreigners. Some seemed to think that the whole city was wired for sound and that the secret police were desperately keen not to miss a word one uttered. It was rather flattering.

"They hide them," he went on, "in the most unlikely places. Not just in your office, as you might expect. But in your dining room, in your living room, in the kitchen and the servants' quarters, too."

"Why in the servants' quarters?"

"To make sure that your cook and your amah and your driver do not lie to the Street Committee when they report you."

That seemed farfetched.

"You'll see," he said.

33

At that very moment, the radio became silent. He looked at me and nodded ominously. He put a finger to his lips. There were footsteps on the stairs. The door opened. An amah came in, brandishing an electric iron.

"Fuse, him blowed," announced the amah, who spoke some English.

We went down to the basement in a procession and changed the fuse. The loudspeaker resumed its loudspeaking. As we made our way upstairs once more, he whispered: "That was not an accident. It will happen again in five minutes. You just wait."

I waited. Nothing happened. He looked peeved.

A few days later, I saw him off at the airport. His departure coincided with the arrival of a young diplomat who was new to China, but whom he knew of old, and the first thing he did was to take him to the very middle of the spacious waiting room, away from possible eavesdropping devices, and breathe words of caution. "All over the place, my dear fellow . . ."

Later, I heard that he had once warned a newly arrived honeymooning couple that there would be "at least one" microphone in their bedroom. They had separated soon afterwards, their married life an utter failure. Some usually unreliable sources even assured me that he had mentioned an invisible telescreen. But then, very soon, Western residents in Peking become obsessed with Orwell. The Chinese might, too, were they but given a chance to read him.

I still have to meet someone who has actually discovered a microphone in his Peking home or office. The only one I ever saw during the whole length of my stay was produced by an African diplomatic courier who said he had found it in the base of a table lamp in his room at the "Love-of-the-Masses Hotel" in Canton. It was a neat and very compact little gadget, clearly marked "Made in Japan." I suspect to this day that he bought it in Hong Kong himself to impress us.

Still, the presumed myth of the microphones was there throughout. From the first I thought it indicated that the foreign community was not habitually lavishing praise on China in private conversations and also that being actually under constant observation soon told on one's nerves. Both proved perfectly true, and I rapidly found myself taking part in the innocent pastime of running the regime down and at the same time laboring under the strain of isolation without privacy.

One's telephone was of course not safe, and it may well be that even when not in use it was not altogether disconnected—but there was not a telephone in every room. One's mail was carefully watched and there was ample evidence of that, not only to be found in clumsily re-stuck envelopes whose flaps would often stick to the enclosed messages, but in that it took letters from Europe or Hong Kong two times longer to reach Peking than it took newspapers. Outgoing letters were also slow in reaching their destinations abroad. Either way, some simply went astray.

That one was being spied upon by one's servants was no mystery at all, and one felt that when one moved about in the city, one's whereabouts were always known. After all, there were at most five hundred foreigners in Peking; the numbers of their cars were listed, and it was easy to keep track of them. One also gathered that most of the officially "visible" Chinese were informers: their speech was often clumsily provocative and the complaints they whispered in your ear, pledging you to secrecy, bordered at times on the unbelievable.

Yet, unexpectedly, an unauthorized Chinese would turn up—and sound surprisingly genuine.

5

INTRODUCING FISHFACE

❧❦❧❦

CHINA used to be the country where an introduction was never performed without a formal exchange of visiting cards. Foreigners, and those once numerous Chinese who were in habitual contact with them, had their names printed in characters on one side of their cards and in Roman script on the other. At night, the newcomer would empty his pockets of all the pasteboard he had collected in the course of a busy social day. Now, there are no busy social days, and the Chinese one meets, either in their offices or at official receptions, are just introduced under the first character of their names, that is, under their family names, and since there are only roughly one hundred such names in the country, one ends up with a nodding acquaintance with a large number of Changs, Wangs, Wus, Lis, Tsaos, etc. Or else an introduction is altogether dispensed with, and one smiles and shakes hands without a word. No card is ever produced, and one is generally left guessing as to what the man one has just met does for a living—even though one may safely assume that he works for the government, which mostly means for the Party as well. It is disconcerting at first, but one gets used to it.

This was explained to me at the first reception I attended at the Great Hall by an obliging correspondent from Eastern Europe. Gesturing with his empty mao-tai glass, he drew my attention to a Chinese in Party uniform, who was excitedly chatting in a group near us and whose features were not unlike those of a fish.

"Look at that man," he said. "I have known him for years, but I know neither his name nor his official position."

"Nonsense!"

"You just try to find out. If you succeed, I buy you one bottle real Russian vodka. If you fail, you buy me one. You can get it," he added for safety, "at the old Moscow Restaurant, even though it is now Chinese-owned."

"It's a bet."

I first tried my luck with the affable first secretary of a Western embassy.

"I cannot tell you his real name," he said, "but we call him Fishface. I daresay you can see why."

"Will you introduce me?"

"With pleasure. But it will be rather a one-sided introduction. I cannot very well call him Mr. Fishface to his face. I'll have to make vague noises. He won't mind, though. He's used to it."

No introduction was necessary, however, for as soon as Fishface saw me, he came forward, all smiles, and greeted me as if we had known each other all our lives.

"Mr. Marcuse!" he exclaimed. "How nice to see you in Peking."

I mumbled delightedly.

He went on: "And why, if I may ask, have you neglected us for so many years?"

I mumbled apologetically.

"You are," resumed Fishface, "such an old friend. You were in Shanghai in 1932 . . . in Hankow in 1938. . . ."

He had the story of my professional life at his fingertips, and it rolled off his voluble lips without a moment's hesitation. Not just the story of my China days. All the rest of it. He knew I had lived in India and in Egypt and in Singapore. He could barely have been out of his swaddling clothes thirty years ago, I thought (or could he? A touch of gray at the temples, an unlined face—ageless . . .), but he made it so plain we had practically grown up together that it would have been nothing short of rude to tell him that his name had momentarily escaped me. Finally:

"Ah, please excuse me," he said. "I see someone is calling me."

Over his departing shoulder, he gave me a last smile. I got hold of some chargé d'affaires or other.

"Do you know what that man does?" I asked.

"Which man?"

"The man over there . . . er . . . Fishface, I understand one calls him."

"Oh, of course. I'll tell you. He's *not* in the Protocol."

"Yes, but what *does* he do?"

"I'm afraid I don't really know. But I'll find out for you."

He beckoned to another diplomat, who came over obligingly.

"You know Marcuse, don't you?"

"Of course!" said the other, whom I had never seen before.

"He wants to know what Fishface does."

"He's with the Protocol."

"No, he's not."

"Yes, he is!"

"No, he's not!"

"Well, he certainly was six months ago!"

"That may be so. I only came out in February. But I am positive he is not now."

"Are you?"

"Definitely."

"I can't believe it."

They drifted away, still discussing, and I was left alone. I put my question to other guests. Nobody could answer it. And nobody knew what Fishface's real name was, not even my old friend "Eppy" Epstein, himself a naturalized Chinese, who could only say that Fishface was "always around."

And so Fishface proved to be. Later I told him he had cost me a bottle of vodka, but I did not explain how, and he did not press me. He laughed and, implying I was being cagey, said he liked an occasional drink himself.

6

CURIOS

Iᴛ ɪs a well-known fact that, in pre-Liberation days, the Imperialists used to plunder China. Not only wholesale, but also piecemeal. Any foreigner could buy antiques and take them away. They were mostly very clever copies. Curio merchants in China—they were not all Chinese—were reputedly crooked. Now, they are without exception scrupulously honest Chinese officials. They will sell you nothing that does not bear a certificate of authenticity and no attempt is made to cheat you. The whole trade is in the hands of the state.

You may still buy anything you like, no matter how old or precious. The only snag is that, if it is more than fifty years old, you may no longer take it out of the country. When you do your final packing, if you want to avoid serious trouble with the customs, you have to summon government experts to supervise it. They will draw up a list of the Chinese works of art which they allow you to export and tell you what you must leave behind. They are more thorough than actually competent, and I know of an English couple from the British chargé d'affaires' office who were prevented from taking back with them some perfectly genuine pieces of Scottish earthenware which they had themselves brought in. No amount of argument could persuade the Chinese experts that they were not priceless specimens of early Chinese craftsmanship that had, moreover, been acquired fraudulently in Peking.

Whatever articles one has bought locally and is not allowed to take away can however be returned to the official dealer who will refund in full the money paid for them.

During my last year in Peking, when the curio shop in

Morrison Street known as "Marco Polo's" was catering to foreigners only—no Chinese could buy anything there—payment in
foreign currency was demanded. English pounds or Hong Kong
dollars. Notes or travelers' checks. But no U.S. dollars in any
form. People's China did not want anything, not even money,
from the "arch-enemy of the peoples of the world," America.

The restriction on curio exports was explained by China's un-
willingness to see her art treasures pass into foreign hands. That
seemed sensible enough until you met some of the professional
antique dealers who come to Peking regularly twice a year from
various European countries and buy Chinese "art treasures"
practically by the ton, and of the very oldest, most valuable, and
perfectly authentic varieties, and with no questions being asked
about their final destination, which is usually the U.S.A., as
everyone pretends not to know. They deal direct with the Chinese Arts and Crafts Corporation, of which Marco Polo's is just
the retail branch, and you always know of their presence in town
by the fact that the genial Mr. Wang, the shop's manager (I
knew him decades ago when he actually owned it, and he is a
charming man, who speaks fluent French and English, and greets
you and bows out again with old-fashioned courtesy, and gives
you the very best tea to drink out of the thinnest and most
translucent porcelain possible), is not to be found behind his
counter. He is away at headquarters, dealing much more important deals with much more important customers than you or I are
likely to be, and on quite different terms. He is the Corporation's
interpreter and wholesale salesman.

I have met several of these regular visitors, even though they
are not encouraged to advertise themselves, and they were
certainly not complaining about business. According to them, the
looting done by foreign troops in Peking in 1860 and again in
1900 was quite negligible compared with what the Chinese
Communists had done themselves.

"Can you still describe it as looting?" I asked of one of
them.

"Not technically," he replied, "since after all it was theirs by
right. But they did go through the Imperial treasures and hoarded
it all up in huge warehouses, through which I have been shown,
for the purpose of selling it abroad. So, after all, what's the
difference?"

"The difference is perhaps that it is not being stolen from them and that they are getting money for it."

"They are, of course," he admitted, "but not one tenth of the money it's worth. They don't seem to know how valuable most of their stuff is. Only old Wang knows. But we can beat him down easily, because *they* are so keen to sell."

I had taken him out to lunch at a small and pleasantly old-fashioned restaurant (not completely state-owned) in a *hutung* off Hatamen Street, and he was particularly pleased because, that very morning, he had acquired some invaluable authentic Sung vases "for next to nothing."

"What's more," he added, "they have it all crated for you themselves by people who really know the job, and nothing hardly ever gets broken, and they ship it as far as Hong Kong *at their own risk.*"

"That sounds pretty good."

"Yes and no," he reflected gloomily. "If anything is damaged in transport—which, mind you, is most unlikely to happen—you get your money back, but not the actual *value,* of which they have no idea."

"What about the fifty-year clause?" I asked naïvely.

"What's that? Never heard of it."

I explained. He shrugged his shoulders.

"They never mentioned that to us. As long as we pay cash, they're happy."

"In what currency?"

He looked at me commiseratingly.

"Why, in American dollars *of course,*" he explained. "They won't take anything else."

7

THE ABC OF CHINESE RAILWAYS

❧❧❧❧

SHORTLY AFTER my arrival in Peking an attaché in one of the Western embassies asked me whether I had come up by air or by train. I told him I had flown and that my experience of Chinese trains so far was limited to that unavoidable but brief Shumchun-to-Canton run. He had been in China for two years already and was about to leave for good. He told me that I should soon find out that there were two kinds of Chinese trains. I asked him what they were and he said:

"There is the train that takes you north toward Peking and the train that takes you south, away from Peking and in the direction of Hong Kong. Some people will tell you that they are identical, but you must not believe them. They are completely different."

I asked him what the difference was.

"The difference is," he repeated, "that one takes you north toward Peking and the second south, away from Peking, toward Hong Kong. Also the northbound train is very much faster than the southbound one."

"How much faster?"

"I don't know," came the puzzled answer. "By the clock, it's forty-eight hours either way, and the trains run on time. Of course, in this country, you can't trust even the clocks. After a while, you find you cannot trust your own wristwatch. Perhaps," he added apologetically, "I have been here too long. But you will see for yourself. Meanwhile, watch your watch."

I thought the man had indeed stayed in Peking too long. What he had meant, I thought, was simply that, hating Peking, he always arrived too soon for his liking, whereas, on the train that bore him southwards, he counted the hours, and time seemed to

42

lag. Nevertheless, his words stuck in my mind and I began to watch, as he had suggested, my watch. I found that it was fast for a few days on end, and that, for another few days, it was slow. It gave me quite a turn. I wondered what evil influences could be at work. Then I remembered that it had not been working properly since, shortly before leaving for China, I had taken it to a Swiss watchmaker at Geneva who had kept it three weeks and charged me outrageously for cleaning, oiling, and regulating. So I took it to that big shop in Wang Fu Ching, where they sell Chinese-made clocks and watches of all sizes and description and where they also undertake to repair them. I gave it to a very ancient Chinese who looked himself like one of those masterpieces of clockwork that used to be manufactured by skilled craftsmen in past centuries. He sat in a glass case to keep the dust out and opened a tiny wicket through which I handed him my timepiece. He opened it under my very eyes and took a quick look at it through a magnifying glass, whereupon he said that moisture had got into it, that it wanted cleaning, oiling, and regulating all over again, but that it had not been seriously damaged. He gave it back after two days and asked for three yuans. It has kept perfect time ever since. Such is the power of exorcism.

Later, having traveled on the Peking-to-Canton line back and forth many a time and having found that the trains always ran with the greatest punctuality, it occurred to me that this man was merely mending watches in his spare time for the sake of a little pocket money, high government officials being notoriously ill paid, and that he was in fact the Chinese Minister of Railways. I cannot vouch for this, however; official sources whom I approached refused to confirm or deny.

As to the train itself on that particular line—I have never used any other, having had little opportunity to travel—I can perhaps offer some useful information to the newcomer who enters China by way of Hong Kong and Canton.

The first thing you will want to know, as you board that slow train into China at Canton station, is where to find the switch, and you may indeed wonder whether there is one. It is there all right and, what is more, it works.

You will find it cunningly concealed beneath the small table under the window. You press it and the strains of "Socialism is good" are suddenly cut off even, if you are quick enough, before the word "good" (*hao*) can be blared forth by the loudspeaker and you will be left wondering for the rest of the trip about the nature of socialism. There is an individual loudspeaker for every soft-class compartment. If you have Chinese fellow travellers, they will of course know where the switch is, but they won't tell you or touch it themselves. But if you find it by your own ingenuity and switch off the noise, no one will mind. Much goodwill indeed can be gained thereby.

The train then begins to move with a jerk, but at the very moment the timetable says it should move. That it should do so at all may surprise you, not that the Chinese railways are inefficiently run—in fact they are not—but simply because "soft-class" compartments are furnished like miniature bed-sitting rooms and look as if they were meant to stay forever in one spot. There is a small table lamp with a pink or pale blue silk shade, and glass beads and tassels, and there is a real flowerpot with real flowers growing in it. The window is screened by dainty muslin curtains. Gay porcelain mugs of steaming tea await your pleasure, and there are on the floor, next to an enameled spittoon in which one is not supposed to spit, a large Thermos full of hot water and four pairs of grass slippers. Each soft-class compartment has four berths. Hard-class compartments have six. The price of a berth is as much again as that of an ordinary ticket. Still, you can travel from Canton to Peking in the comparative luxury of your sleeper for the equivalent of seventeen pounds ($47), a forty-nine-hour, one-thousand-mile expedition.

After having picked up the suitcase that fell from the rack when the train got into motion and wedged it more securely into place, you compose yourself for the journey.

The train is usually packed. There are also carriages, both soft and hard, that have no berths and are of a very rough Pullman type, with no separate compartments and a central aisle cluttered with luggage, suitcases, boxes, parcels, and bundles. On the high-backed seats, the poorer passengers, men, women, and children in very large numbers, chat or eat in their shabby blue cotton clothes sitting bolt upright or, at night, sleeping with their heads on each other's shoulder. No one has to know the owner of a shoulder before using it as a pillowcase, and there is a fine example there of Chinese forbearance, kindness, and mutual help. You will find everyone cheerful and pleasant at all times. If you have been told that a look of sullen hostility is all the foreigner can expect, you will soon find out that is not so. As you move about the train, a friendly nod and a smile are almost invariably returned. There is always a high percentage of soldiers, most of them without arms and perhaps on leave. They are more reserved than the civilians and may give you a suspicious glance. There is nothing personal in this: the expression on their faces rather seems to be part of their uniform. But they will promptly discard it if you need help, which they are always ready to render.

The trains are understaffed, and whatever staff they have is overworked. Guards and attendants will nevertheless do their best to make you comfortable. The latter toil ceaselessly with mops, rags, and buckets full of very dark water, trying to keep the carriages clean. There is no doubt that Chinese trains are often cleaner than European trains, at least at the beginning of a journey. They are perhaps less so toward the end.

Peking trains leave Canton station at three P.M. You will have your first meal in the dining car around six, when a waiter in a more or less white coat comes to your compartment to inform you that a table has been made ready. You cannot look forward to a leisurely dinner and you will be asked to leave as soon as you have finished, for many hungry passengers are awaiting their turn and the dining car operates on an almost round-the-clock basis. You will not want to linger because, in the dining car, the loud-speaker cannot be switched off. It continuously blares forth Party songs and propaganda speeches, and it is deafening enough to make conversation impossible. When you are better acquainted with China, you will discover that private exchanges of views are not encouraged.

If you wish to eat foreign style (which I do not advise) you may order in advance. A bill of fare in Chinese, Russian, and English of a sort will have been brought to you. It is a venerable document, very greasy. You will find, however, that the cleanest available tablecloth has been laid out especially for your benefit. No matter how crowded the dining car may be, you will eat in splendid isolation. The Chinese food that is served is simple, but well cooked and generally of good quality. On one of my trips up from Canton, halfway through the voyage, I saw a large amount of fish being unloaded at a small station and thrown there on the rubbish heap. I was told it was not fresh.

You can get a bottle of Canton beer, seldom iced, which used to be quite drinkable in 1963, but has since deteriorated considerably. If you are lucky, there may be some Tsingtao beer on board, and it is indeed excellent by all standards. It is advisable to carry one's own paper drinking cups, due to the peculiar Chinese custom of washing glasses in oil. They may not actually do so, of course, but that is how it feels, and looks and tastes. (A wiser thing still is to purchase a glass on the English train before you reach the border. The glasses they have there are very thick and convenient and almost unbreakable. You can buy one or several from the boy who peddles drinks. He has of course no right to sell them, but he will, and with pleasure, nevertheless.)

The staff takes great pains to keep the toilets clean. It is an almost impossible job, largely because of the many soldiers who like to dwell there for a long time, often leaving the door ajar. You will notice with dismay that their markmanship is not first class. There are no showers, but there are small washbowls, with running cold and occasionally hot water, where you can wash your hands and face, if you don't mind getting your feet wet. In your compartment, the thoughtful China Travel Service will have laid on an assortment of Party literature, in many languages, with which to wash your brain.

At every stop, and stops are frequent for there is never such a thing as an express train in the Western sense, the train empties itself with remarkable speed and its passengers crowd around the open-air stalls on the platform, where peasants from the neighboring collective farms come to sell the products of the small individual plots of land which are now allotted them and on which they are allowed to grow and breed whatever they like. What they can offer is an interesting indication of the degree of prosperity of that particular district through which you are passing. Traveling on the same line over a period of two and a half years at a few months' interval each time, I could not help notice a steady rise in the standard of living. On my last journey, vegetables, bananas, apples, bread, and even fried chickens and sweets were being sold practically everywhere, in much bigger quantities and greater varieties than I had seen before. At a small station two hours out of Canton, I saw an old woman selling soap, probably a local industry. It was being snapped up.

Then the stationmaster blows his whistle and waves his wand,

and the train fills up again in a matter of seconds. The journey is resumed with yet another bone-shaking rattle.

It is still a single-track railway. Attempts that were made in 1958, at the time of the Great Leap Forward, to lay a parallel track have been given up. There is still evidence of that effort at many points, and as you cross various waterways, you will see concrete piles stretching upwards with no bridge to support. The Yangtse, of course, the train will cross on the new perfectly completed bridge, of which the Chinese are rightly proud. But just before that, there is the unfinished Wuchang railway station with its brick walls and no roof over them.

As night falls and you turn in, you find that white sheets, clean but not ironed, have been put on your bunk with a neatly folded woolen blanket. The small light fitted over your berth was meant to house two electric bulbs, but only one is there for reasons of economy, and it makes reading difficult. Better let yourself be rocked to sleep by the motion of the train and the steady tempo of wheels over rail. The pattern of that particular rhythm in every train all over the world finally suggests words. On the Canton-Peking line, they are "down with modern revisionism, down with modern revisionism, down with modern revisionism." Over the points, it alters to "Mao Tse-tung, Mao Tse-tung, Mao Tse-tung, Mao Tse-tung." There is also the distant music from the loudspeaker in the adjoining compartments, where no foreigners dwell and where, therefore, no one has dared to silence it. You need not put your wallet under your pillow. New China is a law-abiding country where there are no thieves. Which is just as well, for there is also no communication cord on the train. The socialist way of life does not approve of communication cords. Not anywhere, not in any respect. The unexpected simply cannot happen. Everything has been perfectly cleaned, oiled, and regulated and runs smoothly, ticks just like clockwork, just like your own watch: you can sleep on both ears.

8

HERE TODAY AND
GONE TOMORROW

❧❧❧❧

"Je voudrais parler à M. Marcuse," whispered the hesitant voice on the telephone.

"Speaking," I replied in the same language, minus the slight Chinese accent.

"My name is Wang," said the voice. "Surely, you remember me."

"I have known many Wangs in China, including several French-speaking ones."

"Anyway," the voice sighed, "Wang isn't really my name. I have to be careful, you understand."

"Then you shouldn't ring me up. Why don't you come to see me?"

"That is quite impossible. I would be stopped at the gate and questioned. But I want to meet you."

"If you can't come here or even give me your true name over this obviously tapped telephone, I don't see how you can safely make an appointment."

"Tapped!" he said in a hushed voice, and hung up, leaving me to wonder whether I had been dealing with a particularly naïve specimen or one altogether different.

He was back on the line the next day, however, speaking rapid English with a Chinese-American accent and saying his name was Liu. He had everything figured out. Would I meet him at half past ten tomorrow morning in Tien An Men Square, in front of the memorial to the Martyrs of the Revolution? Had I a car?

Make, color, number plate? Right. Could I park as close to the Monument as permitted? Good.

"I shall wear a fur hat," said Wang, alias Liu.

"At this time of year?"

"So you'll know me."

I thought I would not be the only one to notice him. What I had not foreseen was that, turning up at the appointed time in Tien An Men Square, from Chang An Avenue, there would be, hanging about, six or seven Chinese in fur hats—a rare spectacle in Peking on a bright May morning. Instead of stopping, I drove around to the old Legations Street and thence to the other side of the square where I parked by the curb and watched the fur-hatted comrades sauntering toward me with well-calculated nonchalance. Then someone wearing the normal blue denim, but hatless, suddenly opened the door and sat down next to me. I drove on without a word, much in doubt as to the identity of my passenger. He was a man in his early forties, as far as a Westerner may guess the age of a Chinese, and he was smiling.

"Gee," he breathed, "that was neat."

There was no mistaking the voice or the American accent.

"What was?"

"Me taking off my hat," he said, producing a well-worn Mongolian rabbit-skin cap with earflaps from his bulging breast. He added: "I took it off as soon as I spotted them. They were there ahead of me. You were right. The telephone is tapped. I suppose all telephones are. It never occurred to me."

Then, lapsing into French, he went on without a pause: "Are you a Communist?"

"No."

"Are you a Catholic?"

"No. Are you a policeman?"

"No."

We drove on in silence for a while, with him stroking his headgear as if it were a cat. It may well have purred but the engine of my antiquated Volkswagen was very noisy.

I turned off Nan Ch'ih Tzu into a maze of narrow *hutungs*, and that is the wise thing to do in such cases, because motor traffic is practically nonexistent there and you will know at once if you are being followed.

"Why did you want to see me?" I asked, sticking to French.

"I saw your name in the *News Analysis* and I looked up the number of your office in the telephone book. You see, I am so lonely."

"Do you live by yourself?"

"You haven't been in Peking very long."

"Only three weeks."

"I thought as much. Nobody stays by himself in Peking. I have a wife and five children. We all live together in the same house with another family. Three rooms for the lot of us. But of course I am out all day, working."

"Do you work alone?"

"Of course not. There are about twenty of us on the same job in the same room. So many people all the time! No one to talk to! That is why I am so lonely."

"You mean that you are never alone?"

"That is," he said with great simplicity, "the same thing."

He suddenly added, perhaps as an implied proof of his good faith: "My real name is Chow."

To this day, I do not believe that it was. It doesn't matter since, anyway, it is not the name I am quoting now.

For quite a few months, I saw Mr. Chow at fairly regular intervals. At the end of every meeting, we arranged where and when I should pick him up next. At first, we just drove around the *hutungs* talking of this and that, but later, after I had found out from my foreign neighbors in Wai Chiao Ta Lu that you could bring Chinese guests to your flat without any risk of their being stopped or questioned by either the watchman at the gate or the elevator boy as long as you never left their sides, he even agreed to come for dinner. His appetite was enormous and his taste for foreign beverages rather on the eclectic than the discriminating side. As he drank glass after glass of whisky strongly laced with crème de menthe, or of a mixture of port and apricot brandy with a dash of calvados, he would grow redder and redder in the face, Chinese fashion, but it never affected his speech or his composure or loosened his tongue to the point of indiscretion. He never told us where he lived or worked. About the actual nature of his work he was not altogether so secretive and he made no mystery of his background.

He came from a Chinese Catholic family and had been edu-

cated at one of the Shanghai French convent schools, then at
"Aurore" University, later moving on to an American university
in Peking. He described himself as a biologist and his present
occupation as "research." At all times, he seemed to know or
sense exactly how far he could go in his confidence, without
involving anyone but himself. He was certainly not devoid of
courage but, as he put it, "everyone in China is afraid, and nobody precisely knows what of." Often, when I went to fetch him
at some street corner, he would turn up, holding, neatly wrapped
in paper, some present under his arm: a scroll, a small vase,
which, he said, had "long been in the family." These, for the
most part, proved to be rather valuable (which to me definitely
established his bona fides, since no police spy has ever been
known to squander antiques on his quarries), and I had the devil
of a time getting them smuggled out.

He would never agree to bring his wife along. When mine first
suggested that he should, he replied uneasily: "She is not even
aware that I know you. I wouldn't dream of telling her."

There was a brief embarrassed pause and then he hastily went
on: "It isn't that we don't get on well together, but, you see, her
work is quite different from mine, and so, apart from the weekly
Street Committee meetings which we attend together, she has
political activities of her own."

He explained apologetically, gulping down another large swallow of slivovitz and maraschino, one of his favorite after-dinner
mixtures: "Compulsory activities, of course . . ."

"What do they consist in?" I ventured to ask.

"Oh well, you know, it's always more or less the same. There is
some chap from the Party who keeps us informed of current
affairs . . . some of them . . . and explains points of policy,
and asks us to ask questions. And then, of course, we all ask
questions, not those we really might want to ask, but those we
know we had better ask. And then, we are all very satisfied with
the answers we get. And then, So-and-so will be asked whether
he or she has something to report about someone else, and then,
he or she had better report something for fear of being accused
of shielding a guilty person. And, of course, it is only natural that
one should be expected to make reports mostly about those one
lives closest to and knows best. So that, in the end, it is better to
know as little as possible in order that it may not be proved that

one has been aiding and abetting anyone in anything. It is all quite simple, really."

"And the children?"

Chow said: "Was any man, ever, of the same generation as his children?"

Then I remembered he had been brought up by the Jesuit fathers. I said: "I have never heard such an argument from the lips of a Chinese before. You talk like a Communist."

He smiled thinly. "You don't *really* think so. You know we must be careful of everything we say before our children. They do not just report us once or twice a week, like everybody does, but every day, at a moment's notice, quite honestly, just because they are taught that it is their duty. In fact, it is their chief duty, for we, the parents, are by definition untrustworthy."

"How is that?"

"Because, unless we happen to be of a working-class or a peasant family, we are still bourgeois reactionaries. Also, we have known other days which, to us, were better days, and we have a memory and the means to compare. You will soon find out that what the regime is most afraid of is the memory of the people. We, the actual witnesses, will of course die out. *They* know it. It saves them the trouble of killing us. They think the future is theirs. They are sure they can afford to wait."

Chow was very critical of the regime and deeply hurt in his religious faith, one reason being that, even though freedom of worship was being officially proclaimed, auricular confession was out. That was perhaps why he unburdened his soul to me and why he felt so lonely. I thought him a man of great honesty. His antagonism to the regime was devoid of anger, if not of bitterness. He deplored the ideological trend, not only because it was entirely materialistic and ran against his deepest convictions but because he thought it backward and sterile. He said: "The children and the young do not learn as fast as we did. Even in high school, they are now made to memorize, never to think. I see that in my own children with whom I have little human affinities, but whose work at school I am still able to check, to some extent."

Another night he said, looking particularly gloomy: "What gets me down is this perpetual spying. You know, they have revived that centuries-old system that made every household responsible for the behavior of both its right-hand and left-hand neighbors. I suppose the only man who can be fifty percent happy nowadays is the one who lives on a street corner. He only has one set of neighbors to watch him and to watch."

Chow was nevertheless prepared to give credit where credit was due. When I pointed out to him that the man in the street looked to me, if not better clothed, at least better fed than under the Kuomintang, he admitted this to be true, but added: "Have you visited one of the rural communes? No? What a pity. I hope you will soon. Since you knew China before, you will notice that living conditions for the cattle have improved. And—you are right—so have ours. But *they* have not yet managed to milk the cows mechanically."

One day, and I think that was our last meeting, I asked Chow whether he would like the Nationalists to come back from Formosa and take over. He raised his hands in horror. He shouted—and I had never heard him shout before: "What! Those bastards who turned us over to the Communists? Never!"

I have of course done my best, without altering anything of what Chow told me, to disguise his identity as far as I ever knew it. I have not put his confidences in writing without some precaution. Mr. Chow, however, is *not* a figment of my imagination, and I cannot say that any resemblance between him and any living Chinese is purely coincidental, for, indeed, I have known Mr. Chow, as reported here, and several other persons, equally lonely because of the crowd, and equally genuine. Perhaps my reference to "any living Chinese" may verge on the optimistic for I cannot be certain that Mr. Chow is still alive. One evening, he failed to turn up at one of our appointments. I drove up and down the *hutung* and round the block and then round the block again for over half an hour, but still there was no Mr. Chow. I thought perhaps he had got the day wrong, and I tried again on the morrow. But there was no Mr. Chow and I have never seen Mr. Chow again or heard from him.

Here, I see no reason not to tell another, much simpler and later story exactly as it happened, or even to alter a name, since everything that took place did so in public and the Chinese personality involved, as will appear, behaved in the strictly approved manner in front of the proper witnesses.

In the spring of 1964, the Experimental Ballet Troupe of the Peking School of Dance staged a production of the Soviet ballet "Esmeralda," based, as the program said, on "Victor Hugo's novel *Notre-Dame de Paris*." The diplomatic corps and the foreign press were invited. The honored foreign guests sat in the front stalls. There were not enough of them to fill the auditorium, and a large number of Chinese officials had been detailed to pack the house.

When the curtain came down for the interval, I made my way to the foyer where the customary cup of green tea was being served.

Class distinctions are very sharp in China's classless society and the Chinese audience were sitting in the pit, which was separated from the stalls by the customary alleyway. As I walked down this, I heard my name called and I turned around. A Chinese wearing the formal Party uniform rose from his seat and practically embraced me, baring in the friendliest of smiles a once familiar set of buck teeth.

"Do you remember me?" he said, shaking me warmly by the hand.

"Of course I do, Lin Chi-han," I said, returning his grasp.

And Lin Chi-han it was. I had first met him, I believe, in 1938 in Hankow, in the Foreign Ministry (for, Nanking having fallen to the Japanese, Hankow was, in those days, China's first wartime capital), and I believe he was then head of the Protocol Department. He had been educated at a good Belgian university and spoke French. I saw more of him later in Chungking and again, after the war, in Paris, where he held a fairly high post in his country's embassy. That was before the Communist takeover. Then I heard that he had forsaken the Nationalists and gone to Peking to serve the new regime early in 1950. Since then, none of his many foreign friends had heard of him.

I can still see Lin Chi-han sitting in that front row of the pit between two equally uniformed Chinese, shouting "Marcuse!" and standing up to greet me. We walked into the foyer and sat side by side in the inevitable stiff armchairs with their white cotton cloth covers, exchanging platitudes and reminding one another that it had been "long time no see," or French words to that effect. But we were scarcely alone, and those two types who had been flanking him in the auditorium were most definitely within earshot.

"Lin," I said, "now that we have met again, we must not lose sight of each other. Do ring me up soon."

His face froze. He said: "You know our discipline. We are not permitted to see foreigners. If you wish to invite me to dinner, then you should write to the Foreign Ministry, asking permission for me to see you."

"Can't you do that yourself?"

"No. That is not allowed."

"Are you still in the Waichiaopu?"

"No. I work for another department. I travel a lot."

"Abroad?"

"No, no. There is much to be done in China."

Then the bell rang for the next and last act, and we agreed to meet after the show, I using the pretext that I wanted to introduce him to my wife who had remained in her seat throughout the interval.

True to his word, as we all filed out, he was there, waiting for the Marcuses to turn up. But he was certainly not alone. Standing at a polite distance were the usual Party witnesses and we all shook hands and the proper unintelligible introductions were made, but no further reference to future meetings.

Needless to say, the letter was never written. One has a heart.

It may be inferred from the two cases I have mentioned that there is strictly no intercourse, barring official ones, between Peking's tiny foreign community and the Chinese population. This is of course not strictly true. A number of Chinese are in daily contact with foreigners, but they all, without exception, must have special permission. They include one's own clerical staff and servants, shopkeepers, and, naturally, some officials.

There are even a few Chinese of both sexes who seem at liberty to visit alien acquaintances. Beyond the fact that they have all had a foreign education (which does not mean that all foreign-educated Chinese are permitted to meet foreigners), it is hard to discover what criterion such permissions are based on. What is absolutely certain is that those Chinese who do not enjoy such a privilege will only cross your threshold, if they ever do, in fear of their life. And, if not of their lives, of whatever modicum of freedom they are still able to cherish.

During the year 1951, still remembered in China as the "Year of Fear," some three million people at a very conservative estimate were sentenced to death—and duly and publicly executed amid scenes of carefully engineered mass hysteria—by People's Courts that based their verdicts on no text of law whatever, but on a decree promulgated on February 21 regarding the "Suppression of Counter-Revolutionary Activities." There was, of course, no question of an appeal in any form. There never is, even now.

Nowadays, to the best of my knowledge, very few capital executions take place in China—that is, in that skeleton China which foreigners can view—and those people who disappear are likely to turn up again a few years later without having suffered any apparent bodily harm, but thoroughly re-educated and as totally acquiescent as if they had undergone lobotomy. It is common knowledge that people who express undesirable thoughts are sent "to the country," not just to till the land, but to see that it is properly fertilized.

Not so long ago, I met in Hong Kong a Vietnamese girl who had lived for a long time in Peking and had committed the unforgivable sin of becoming the mistress of a foreigner. The foreigner suffered no harm apart from being expelled from the country, but the girl was whisked away and not heard of for quite some years, after which, having succeeded in proving to the satisfaction of the authorities that she herself was a foreigner too, she was allowed to depart. When I spoke to her, she would not elaborate upon her experiences, but merely said with sweet simplicity:

"*La merde n'a plus de secrets pour moi.*"

9

ABRACADABRA

THE DAY Mrs. Chen mentioned to me the "Three Red Banners of the People's Communes, the Great Leap Forward, and the General Line," and assured me in a matter-of-fact tone of voice that the Chinese people, including herself, were constantly "holding them aloft," I could hardly keep a straight face. This cliché I was accustomed to see in print several times a day, but it was the first time that I had heard it actually spoken in perfect earnest by a supposedly responsible official in the course of a serious conversation. The absurd thought that Mrs. Chen was trying to pull my leg crossed my mind and was at once banished. One look at Mrs. Chen's face was enough to convince me that it had been uttered in all sincerity and there would have been no point in asking her whether she actually believed that she was in fact physically keeping the three banners flying aloft round the clock, one in each hand and the third possibly balanced on the tip of her blunt nose. She would have thought my question stupid and she would have resented it since it would have implied that I was doubting her word.

Later I became used to Party slogans, no matter how hackneyed, meaningless, obscurely symbolic, or just plain ridiculous, being quoted as part of small talk. There were also frequent quotations from Marx, Engels, Lenin, Stalin, and of course Mao Tse-tung, as well as ancient proverbs, but in that latter respect nothing was new to me. There was simply an old Chinese custom with which I had been familiar for many years. Foreign correspondents, with a little practice, could become very good at capping quotations from the classics, once they had seen that the quoter was unaware of their contexts or their sources.

57

I remember once mentioning an old Chinese proverb to Fish-face: "Cherish the truth that lives in your heart and beware lest it should escape through your lips," it went. Fishface digested this and said: "Yes, yes, this is an ancient proverb, but today, we find it a little cynical." I admired his composure because I had only just thought it up.

It was my first Chinese proverb. After that, I invented many more and I used to try them on Waichiaopu and other officials and interpreters from the Travel Service whenever I had the chance. They never admitted that they did not know them. On the other hand, it did me no good because it convinced them that I only pretended not to know Chinese and that actually I was not only well versed in the spoken language, but could read the classics, a thing they did not do themselves, because studying the classics was no longer encouraged.

"When the dragon whispers, the shouts of men are drowned," was a great success. My audience would absolutely gape. "Confucius?" ventured a man from the Ministry of Foreign Trade at one of the official receptions. "It doesn't sound like Confucius," I said, thinking hard. "I should think it more likely to be Lao Tze. Because, you know," I added confidently, "of the dragon element in it."

"Possibly," he said, "possibly Lao Tze, yes indeed, possibly Lao Tze."

"But," I said, "perhaps prophetic."

"Ho ho," he said as it dawned on him.

"It seems to fit," I said obsequiously, "into a very contemporary context."

He beamed and I saw him no more that evening, except from a distance, and he looked puzzled but greatly interested and deep in thought. For a long time, I expected my proverb to be quoted in the official press. It never happened. Perhaps they are still busy checking.

It was the total lack of any sense of humor in the properly indoctrinated that gave one such pleasure, perhaps unfair, in mystifying them. Their minds were completely literal and they spoke their ready-made metaphors, even the most fantastic, without ever changing a word or adding one of explanation. The Three Red Banners were always before their eyes, happily waving in the East Wind that Prevailed over the West Wind. And everything they said, no matter on what subject, was said with fervor, recited almost, and one was expected to accept it as Gospel—even when it was a palpable untruth.* They were in fact just human gramophones, all honorable, dutiful, truthful liars. They would eventually admit that their truth was different from ours, but not that ours might perhaps be as good as theirs. They would never elucidate their meaning or elaborate. They spoke the word dictated from on high, whence all verity came. It was so real, this verity, so illuminatingly obvious, that if you questioned it, you exposed not so much your imbecility as your wickedness. It was indulgently hoped that in time you would undergo a change of sentiments rather than a change of opinion, a change of heart that would in turn bring about a change of mind.

* The defunct Great Leap provides an example of this blinker-blindness. The Chinese, better than anyone else, know for a fact what a fiasco the Leap was. But they will not admit it, not even to themselves, and so the "G.L.F. banner" goes on fluttering "aloft," signifying nothing.

10

INVESTING IN DOG FLESH

❧❦❧

EARLY in 1962, the Chinese were paying greater attention to their food ration than to their thought ration, and they were quite palpably encouraged to do so by the authorities. This attitude was the result of two successive failures: that of the liberal "Hundred Flowers" movement of 1957 and that of the "Great Leap Forward" of the following year. On top of them had come three years of "natural calamities."

The meat ration was two ounces per head per month, the "cereal ration," mostly dried vegetables. (An "invisible" Chinese told me that he and his family had suffered from malnutrition to the point of dropsy in 1960 and had spent their meager savings in restaurants, which "gave them a bad name.") People were now trying to grow whatever they could on whatever bit of ground they could use. Citizens were urged to show initiative and submit ideas. And so it was that an article appeared in the columns of the Peking evening paper of July 19, 1962, under the signature of Ma Lan-chun, a well-known columnist and a member of the Party, the reading of which would scarcely have encouraged Dr. Pavlov to bring his kennel to China. It went thus:

"For well over two thousand years, dog breeding has been a tradition among the Chinese people. The usefulness of dogs has always been acknowledged. They faithfully watch over the house at night, keeping prowlers away. They can also be slaughtered and eaten. In the south, people still eat dogs and, in North China, dogs used to be eaten as well. Therefore, my idea that dog breeding should be revived will not, I hope, meet with the opposition of many comrades.

"Still, criticism may be leveled at one in quite unexpected

fashion, and sensible suggestions are sometimes unfavorably received. In the present instance, I expect certain people to say that dog breeding is not practicable because dogs are hard to keep in order and they run everywhere and relieve themselves where they shouldn't, which is not hygienic. Other people might be unreasonably afraid of dogs, even of those bred by themselves. That is why, before I encourage people to breed dogs, I must urge them to look upon the matter from an ideological point of view, and now, in order to get them to see my purpose, I have to explain things in details of fact and reason."

The author then proceeds to quote the classics and to demonstrate that, from time immemorial, dog flesh has been considered a delicacy throughout China. He does not hesitate to go back to the Chow dynasty, which flourished in the eighth century B.C. and to the "Book of Rites," written then (so Ma wrongly claims), which says that "during the autumn months, the Emperor himself used to eat dog and even sacrifice dogs on the altars of the gods."

"Many legendary heroes used to be dog-butchers in their youth," Comrade Ma adds, "which shows that there was nothing dishonorable in the breeding and butchering of edible dogs." Moreover, he recklessly opines, "what was good enough for the gods must also have been good enough for men.

"It is difficult to ascertain at exactly what period the profession of dog-butcher entered decadence in North China.

"Of all edible meat," Ma Lan-chun goes on, "dog flesh has the highest nutritive value and its consumption can heal many diseases. That is why our forebears were so fond of dogs."

The authority of the Medical Dictionary of Li Shih-chen, of the Ming dynasty, is then brought to bear. That venerable monument clearly states that "there are three breeds of dogs and each answers its own purpose. In the countryside, dogs are bred for hunting. Barking dogs make good watchdogs at home. The edible dog provides extremely beneficial food, for dog flesh is a tonic for the stomach, makes the body lighter and generally keeps people healthy. It is essential that a dog should not be bled when slaughtered, for the meat would lose much of its nutritious value."

"But that," the author says, "is not all. The most important thing, according to Li Shih-chen, is that the excrement of the dog is almost a panacea. It will cure many diseases, if properly used. It is a very effective antidote against many poisons. Moreover, when absorbed by mouth, even in small quantities, it will cure smallpox, cholera, and diseases of the heart."

The author of the article regretfully admits that dog manure was nevertheless mostly used to fertilize the fields. In South China, farmers preferred dog manure to that of pigs, oxen, and sheep.

I thought, when I read the story, that it would mark the beginning of a dog-breeding campaign. I constantly expected a nation-wide following, but there was none. Also, the Ma Lan-chun byline unaccountably vanished from the columns of the Chinese press. I was later given the explanation. Ma had been a little too bold and had overreached himself. First, there were strictly no dogs left in North China, outside the diplomatic corps, and therefore Ma's suggestion was impractical. Dogs would have to be imported, and in spite of Ma's cheerful reminder that "dogs cost nothing to feed because they eat only filth," it was felt that perhaps the breeding of dogs would be an extra burden on an already very restricted budget. That was bad enough, but there was worse. In his quotation of the classics, Ma had made the mistake of saying that what was good for the gods was good enough for men. The notion that the gods were above man was simply not to be entertained. And who had given Ma permission to look up the classics?

Ma's signature has vanished from the Peking papers. Perhaps for purposes of political re-education he has been sent to the countryside to conduct comparative studies in fertilizers. The eat-more-dog movement was doomed from the first. And human Pekinese still have to go down to Canton in trains for a decent dish of puppy stew.

II

A PEKING ORGY

WHEN special correspondents are taken to Shanghai, it is customary for them to be introduced to a capitalist. For a long time, it was always the same capitalist, and I thought there was only one in Shanghai, a sort of human showpiece, a living monument to Red leniency. Now it seems that at least two were recently interviewed by reliable V.I.P.P.'s and that many more are extant on the banks of the Whangpoo. They live, one is told, in comfortable houses, and have a car and a driver each. I cannot imagine why none was ever shown to correspondents in Peking, because there are capitalists there also. I know. I met one, and, through him, others. But the Information Department had nothing to do with it.

It sometimes pays to have lived in the country before.

I ran into him one day in Peking's Foreign Languages Bookshop and we had some difficulty in recognizing each other. Twenty years is a long time.

I had met him occasionally in prewar Shanghai when he came down from North China where he already lived and pretended to work. But he thought life dull up there and he liked to come down for a spree in what he called the Paris of the East. I got to know him because he happened to be a distant cousin of the comprador of a foreign bank whose nephew worked on the staff of an American evening paper published in Shanghai and was an acquaintance of mine. We spent many a happy evening together. It usually began with a very lavish Chinese dinner, briefly attended by shrieking singsong girls, and then we made the tour of the cabarets until the small hours of the morning. He was then quite a man about town and would have been a member of the

best clubs, had they taken in Chinese. He was always dressed in
the latest fashion from across the Pacific. Once he got going, you
could hardly get him off the dance floor. He used to buy twenty
dollars' worth of dance tickets at one go and only make brief
appearances at our table to order another round of drinks. He
had a magnificent set of gold teeth. He still had them now and I
suppose that's what I recognized him by. Otherwise, he was
much changed.

"And what do you do now?" I asked.

He said: "I do nothing. I still live in Tientsin. I still belong to
the leisured classes."

So I had another look at him.

He was dressed in the padded blue cotton suit which is China's
winter uniform, but it was old and shabby. He wore a dirty cloth
cap of the same material, the kind Chairman Liu Shao-chi
sported. However, he seemed well and his complexion was florid,
and he certainly had not become thinner. I extended the usual
invitation to come and see me but of course he, too, would not
accept. He laughed apologetically: "They don't keep too much
of an eye on me," he explained. "I am too insignificant and too
old. As long as I attend the meetings and make no trouble, I am
all right. But still, I mustn't make myself conspicuous or carry
things too far. That is why I come to Peking for an occasional
fling. But even here I must be careful."

A fling? As we walked out onto the broken pavement of Wang
Fu Ching, I was once more struck by the drabness of Peking's
busiest street, the shabbiness of its shop windows, the all-
pervading sadness of the place. I thought of the theaters and
cinemas with their moralizing programs, of the old Bridge of
Heaven, the last remaining amusement center in the "Chinese
City," * now cleansed of all forms of vice and shrinking yearly in
area, of the virtuous sterility of it all, the community singing of
Party songs and the ubiquitous Mao, and my mind went back
with regret to the fine old days of social inequality when at least
some people could have a good time, including my friend here. A
fling?

"Well," he said, "I have an ailing uncle here, and family
reasons are always a good excuse for a trip, even today, and there

---

* As traditionally distinct from the much larger "Tartar City." As to the
Bridge of Heaven, it has been done away with by the Red Guard.

is more freedom, after all, in Peking than in Tientsin, because the town is bigger. Also, if one is not known locally, one is not so easily spotted even though, as a stranger, one may arouse a certain amount of unwelcome curiosity. Still, one must chance it."

"But what do you mean by a fling? Girls? Gambling? Opium? No can do."

His hands went up in horror.

"No, of course not. Nothing like it. I never used to smoke, anyway. But a quiet meal with a few friends. There are no foreigners in Tientsin, and the restaurants are not so good or so numerous. Here, in different surroundings and comparative anonymity, one may chat with less restraint."

There would really be nothing wrong, he decided, in our having dinner together, in a public place, of course, for the Wai Chiao Ta Lu was sure to be watched. He said he would ask some of his friends as well.

"But," I said, "won't you get into trouble, being seen with a foreigner?"

"Not if there are several of us," he said. "It will be assumed that we are all spying on one another. Also if you are there, we shall get rice and bread."

"Who are your friends?"

"Oh, just people like myself," he said, "ordinary citizens with a private income. Mostly from Tientsin, here on some pretext."

So it was arranged there and then, and for the same evening; he'd rather not postpone it, even for a day—safer so, he said. He would order dinner in a very good restaurant, but not, as he pointed out, one of the completely state-owned eating places. There were still a few that were part-owned and the old proprietors and the old cooks were still there and they had an interest in the business. "You get much better service in those," he said, which I already knew to be true. "Brother capitalists," he explained.

Three of his cronies turned up and it was quite a feast. They were all as shabbily dressed as he, but we ate shark's fins and Peking duck and he apologized for the absence of bird's nest soup, which wasn't available these days any more, except to Party officials. Had I not been there, he pointed out, he could not have ordered rice or bread, for they all had already exhausted their meager cereal ration and were not sure anyhow that Tientsin ration tickets were valid in Peking or should even be shown in the capital. But with a foreigner present, no difficulty arose. Such, he said, was face. Between mouthfuls, he told me his story, occasionally turning to the others for approval. They gave it, nodding, with long streams of noodles hanging from their lips like the beards of ancient Confucian sages.

The factory he owned in Tientsin had been taken over by the state and he had not even been retained on the staff, unlike the Shanghai capitalists I had heard of. He, too, nevertheless, was still being well paid, doing nothing. He was getting what he described as "handsome royalties." He had been allowed to keep his house in Tientsin, because it had fewer than fifteen rooms, and there he still dwelt with his aging wife and, he sighed, his even older, naturally, mother-in-law. But they were no longer alone in the place and other families had moved in.

"Of course, they pay rent. But very low rent."

"I assume," I said, "they pay it not to you but to the state."

"You're wrong there. They pay it to me: four yuans a month per family."

"And how much income tax," I asked, "does it cost you?"

"Not a *mao*, not a *fen*," he said. "There is no income tax whatsoever in China."

"Well, that is something the regime can be congratulated on."

"There has never been income tax in China," he stated.

I reminded him that, in the old days, in some provinces, taxes had been levied on the peasantry as much as twenty-seven years ahead of time. To this he replied that that happened indeed under the rule of the warlords and that anyway it had nothing to do with one's income. One must not, he pointed out, confuse the legal revenue of the state with sheer exaction. Also, when the Kuomintang government had extended its control over these remote provinces, things like that stopped. The Communists now took the credit for much that had been achieved before their time. But nobody remembered anything.

He gave a quick look at our commensals. They were paying no attention to us, they were flushed with *huang ju*, they were in a kind of happy trance and exchanging, between bursts of uproarious guffaws, ancient jokes in a jargon that at first I could not quite understand. Then I realized they they were abundantly and very happily quoting Groucho Marx and Eddie Cantor in that particular brand of pidgin-American that was so fashionable in Shanghai in the middle Thirties.

"Let us have a private *kampe*," said my host, filling our cups with yellow wine again.

We toasted each other and drained them and then he said with great solemnity: "I shall now make a pun. You do not forget it!"

He made it. Then another dish appeared and we had more drink, and I shall never again believe in the old saying that *veritas* is to be found *in vino*. Up to that moment, he had been happily treading the primrose path of escapism at an ever faster pace. But suddenly, under the influence of the wine, he ceased to be uninhibited. He stopped being himself. And all the propaganda that he had swallowed in the course of years came out of him like an enormous postprandial belch. It may to some extent have been due to the fact that the comrade waiter had just re-entered the room, bearing more *huang ju*.

"Who am I to be sitting here, talking to you as I have been?" he nearly shouted in a determined if somewhat thick voice.

I had an unpleasant feeling that he would have looked me straight in the eye, had either of us at that juncture been able to see straight.

"I," he went on, "have been for many years an oppressor of the people. I have been an exploiter of the working class. I have been a running dog of the imperialists and you are, I know, a foreign spy in the pay of the Americans. I shall report you, I shall report myself, I shall report us all. Look at this wine!" he commanded, pouring it out. "Do you know what it is? It is rice wine, they call it Shaoshing. But it is not real Shaoshing. It is only *Peiching huang ju*. Peking yellow wine. The people of Shaoshing have not enough rice to make wine. They have not enough rice to eat. I, myself, have no rice coupons left. I can no longer eat rice. I am reduced to drinking it."

After this outburst, we all got up and moved unsteadily to the other end of the room which was furnished with armchairs shrouded in the usual white cotton. There we ate apples and drank tea and we all became reasonably sober almost at once, for such is the virtue of rice wine that its effects soon leave the head and are kind to one's stomach, if less so to one's legs.

Then I asked my friend to tell me more about himself. He said he was not doing so badly. In the first place, he had no children. This made him happy for two essential reasons, one temporal, the other spiritual. To begin with, he could speak freely to his wife, as long as he did not raise his voice and his neighbors could not hear him, without fear of being reported to the authorities on the very next morning by his own flesh and blood. And then he said he would rather die without any sons to worship his spirit than with sons who would not feel like worshipping it under the present system and the education they would get. Not, he said, that he believed in such nonsense as the spirits of the dead, but still . . .

He was receiving about fifteen hundred yuans a month from the state as "royalties." But since he was not actually earning his pay through work, he wasn't entitled to "industrial coupons" and couldn't therefore buy such things as woolen cloth or leather shoes. Practically all consumer goods were out of his reach.

Industrial coupons based, oddly enough in this socialist country, on the salary drawn by each individual at the rate of one coupon for each twenty yuan earned monthly, were definitely on the way out by the end of 1964. But they were still essential early in 1963 when this dinner party took place and there was even a black market for them, the only black market I knew in China throughout my stay. As it was then, his life being that of a "social parasite," as he put it himself, his food and cotton rations were the absolute minimum. Still, he could eat well as long as he didn't try to do it at home on his monthly quota of two ounces of meat. The cereal ration, as it was called, was also insufficient. It was thirty pounds and included rice, flour, and dried vegetables in varying proportions, according to the harvest and the state of the market. At the time, it was still mostly vegetables. In restaurants, however, everything except rice and bread was off ration. He could gorge himself day after day on choice delicacies, and since he had always been a gourmet, he would spend most of his time and money eating and drinking. In that respect he said it was very much like old times. The food was no longer quite as refined as it used to be, and he missed the jolly company of yore; on the other hand, he no longer had to dress for dinner, which was extremely fortunate. Lacking industrial coupons, he could of course not order himself a length of woolen material, or a foreign-style suit. His cotton ration being so scanty, a new blue denim suit even, especially a thickly upholstered one for the winter, was pretty well out of the question, and the problem of shirts and underwear rather insoluble. However, if one wore a regulation suit, no one could tell whether you had any underwear on or not. The loose cotton padding he could get—two ounces each winter —was just enough to provide a warm lining for a pair of slippers for everyday street and house wear.

In the summer, he went to Peitaho beach—once Peking's resort for foreigners—and stayed at a good hotel and did himself proud. Or else, if he felt energetic enough, he could take a trip to Shantung province and climb the Tai Shan mountains by means of the ten thousand steps that lead right up to the top—the only civilized form of mountaineering I have ever heard of.

In spite of all this extravagant living, he never managed to spend all his money, and what remained he put in the People's Bank, in a sort of long-term savings account which paid five percent yearly. He could not take his money out again until twelve years had elapsed and he had no illusions about it. He was convinced that the present toleration of capitalist saving-up could not last and that whatever money he and others were encouraged to put into the bank would be confiscated before long. Still, there was nothing else he could do with his capital, and he would have become a suspect had he not thus invested in future poverty.

At this point of his confidences, somebody woke up and went around the room unsteadily, looking under the scrolls that were on the walls and finally lifting the wooden lid of the spittoon by means of the pedal with which such conveniences are now equipped in the best places. He peered into it so long that I was afraid he was going to be sick. But he was merely making sure that the room was not wired for sound.

Then someone walked in to tell us that the place had been kept open for us well past the legal closing time—it was nearly ten—and the party broke up. I asked my friend whether we should meet again, but he said it was hardly possible. One such dinner could be explained away but not two, and he would go back to Tientsin soon. I was worried lest I should have led him and my fellow-guests into trouble, but he said no. Of course they would all have to make a report.

He said: "Everyone will be questioned separately, in a friendly manner, mind you. Of course, we shall all make different reports."

"Will that be wise?" I asked.

"Well," he explained simply, "if we all told the same story, it would sound extremely odd. So we shall get together and compare notes and decide what each man will say. That is quite customary," he finished, dismissing the whole matter with a breezy wave of his pudgy hand.

And so we parted. I did not find it too easy to drive home through the *hutungs*. I found it even more difficult to write down the gist of what had been said that night, fresh in my mind as it should have been. What I could not recall was the pun he had been so keen I should not forget. It only came back to me in the middle of the night, and I got up in a hurry and grabbed pen and paper before I forgot it again. It went like this:

"I am going to paint the town red!"

And I could almost swear that, when he said it, he gave a sly look over his shoulder at the large picture of Mao Tse-tung that was hanging upon the wall. I wished him luck, from the bottom of my heart, and went back to bed.

12

A SINOLOGIST

His was the last remaining Western compound (Western both
geographically and politically) in the old Legation Street. It held
vast lawns and a well-kept garden around which stood a number
of brick houses built, I should imagine, some sixty years ago, just
after the Boxer affair, in a style that conjured up placid canals,
windmills, and tulip fields. He himself bore the title of chargé
d'affaires because his country and China had established diplomatic relations at that level and kept them there. He knew China
well and the Chinese and Chinese, which he spoke, read, and
wrote, and it was well worth your while to discuss the news of
the day with him because he would not be carried away or jump
to conclusions, which many of his less experienced colleagues
were prone to do, but put it in its proper perspective. People like
him are very useful to journalists who live from story to story
and whose very process of thought is hampered by the subconscious obsession of speed wordage, cable charges, and the *Kansas
City Milkman*.

"Well," he said, "now that you have been here three months,
how do you see it all?"

The Peking summer was rather fierce that year, as it is most
years, but this old-fashioned office with its high ceiling and thick
walls remained cool, a welcome change from my oven of a flat in
the Wai Chiao Ta Lu.

"I do not see it clearly at all," I confessed, "but I think the
explanation is to be found in the history of China rather than in
that of Marxism."

"I am inclined to agree," he nodded. "But why do you say
that?"

"Because Mao and his contemporaries seem to be laboring under four complexes. There is the Great Wall complex: keep the barbarians out. There is the Middle Kingdom complex: China cannot be wrong. There is the Forbidden City complex which one might also call the Mystery complex: nobody ever knows what goes on, what is being discussed or decided in the higher Party and government spheres. Finally, with Mao Tse-tung, we have the Son of Heaven complex."

He lit a fresh cigarette, inhaled a lungful, and observed: "You have left out the fifth complex, which is at least as important as the others."

"And which is?"

"The loess caves of Yenan complex."

At the time, this remark struck me as only clever. Later, I came to think that it was perhaps the most penetrating one I had heard in Peking.

Part Two

FOOD FOR THOUGHT
IS NOT SERVED A LA CARTE

13

WORDS

Po Lo-niu: *Ni tu shen mo,*
   T'ai-tzu?
Ho Mu-lei: *Tzu, tzu, tzu.*
   (Shakespeare)

It was over one single word that the Information Department and I first came to words.

I had already been summoned to the Waichiaopu once or twice before and mildly reprimanded by Mrs. Chen, and the smile on her rather full lips had gradually become thinner and thinner. But she had never got down to cases. She had merely mentioned that I ought to be more "careful" in my stories and had hinted that, perhaps, I had been misinformed. To which I had replied that my complaint was that I had not been informed at all.

"What about?" she had asked.

"Generally," I had answered, adding: "What have I been wrong about?"

Her reply had been: "Generally."

It was like a nursery game. But now she stopped beating about the mulberry bush.

"You have said," she said, "in one of your articles that Radio Peking's commentaries in Hindi, beamed on India, had become lately 'more and more subversive.'"

"So they have," I confirmed.

This was taking place in October, 1962, at the time of the Chinese aggression.

"They have not," said Mrs. Chen, flatly.

"But has not Radio Peking been urging the Indian people to 'shake off the yoke of the imperialist Nehru regime' and to oppose 'the American-dominated policy of the New Delhi government'?"

"Certainly."

"Well, wouldn't you call that *subversion?*"

"Certainly not. We were telling the Indian people what they should do for their own good. That is friendly advice, not *subversion.*"

I pondered that.

"Your tea is getting cold," said Mrs. Chen, always the perfect hostess.

"What," I asked, "is your definition of subversion?"

"Maybe," said Mrs. Chen nasally, "you do not understand English very well."

"It is a fact that, unlike you, I have not had the benefit of a California college education," I confessed, my back now definitely up.

She bristled all over and her next line came in Chinese. Her interpreter, who had so far confined himself to taking busy notes, now became vocal.

"My English is excellent," he said in English, interpreting for Mrs. Chen.

"*Je n'en doute pas, cher monsieur,*" I said. "*C'est seulement l'anglais de Mme Chen que je comprends difficilement.*"

"Please, speak English!" said Mrs. Chen through her interpreter.

"*Mais, je le parle si mal,*" I apologized. "*Je m'exprime beaucoup plus facilement en français.*"

"*Mon interprète ne comprend pas,*" said Mrs. Chen to my astonishment.

The interpreter then spoke sharply to her in their common language, and she looked quite abashed, and I understood who was boss.

"Please, speak English," she repeated in Chinese, and the interpreter, quite unnecessarily, translated.

I retorted: "*Cela me paraît inutile, puisque vous parlez si bien le français. Nous n'avons pas besoin d'un interprète.*"

Mrs. Chen was silent.

"Please, speak English," said the interpreter, entirely off his own bat.

"Subversion," explained Mrs. Chen through his good offices, "is something the Chinese government never indulges in. Subversion is beneath us. We never interfere in the affairs of another country. That is where we differ from the Indian government. I understand that you receive the so-called news bulletin put out daily by the Indian embassy."

"I do. So does every correspondent in Peking."

"That shows that we do not interfere. We could easily prevent its being distributed."

"Why don't you?"

"Because we are above that. The dogs bark, but the caravan moves on, as the old Chinese proverb says."

"I thought it was an Arab proverb."

"They may have taken it from us. The point is: do you read that bulletin?"

"I do."

"Daily?"

"Daily."

"In that case," said Mrs. Chen, "you are unforgivable if you have not grasped the meaning of the word *subversion*."

"But," I objected, "doesn't the Chinese embassy in New Delhi also put out a daily news sheet, equally widely distributed?"

"Possibly. It is our duty to make the truth known."

"May I suggest that, if you stopped the Indian bulletin in Peking, the Indian government might likewise stop the Chinese bulletin in New Delhi?"

"They may have done so already, for all I know," said Mrs. Chen grandly. "If they have, it means that they fear the truth. We will not ban theirs because we are not afraid of lies. Or *subversion*."

As an afterthought, she added: "Still, we may. Have some more tea."

"You may?"

"Well, if they interfered with ours . . ."

The interpreter cleared his throat peremptorily. Mrs. Chen was cut short. After a pause, she went on: "I suppose you also listen in to All India Radio?"

"Whenever it is not jammed by Peking."

"Then you ought to know what the Indians say about us."

"What they say about you is not unlike what you say about them."

"It would be wise," said Mrs. Chen, "for you to keep on listening to the lies broadcast by All India Radio. Then you would perhaps know what subversion is."

She rose upon these words. The three of us rose, the interpreter scattering the pages of his notes and reminding me of Buster Keaton in the final scene of Chaplin's *Limelight*. At the door she said, shaking hands somewhat reluctantly: "We shall judge you by your deeds."

She said it in English. I already knew it to be one of her stock phrases.

Words. Phrases. Slogans. They all meant something different according to who happened to be using them.

Clichés. A political form of calligraphy.

Some months later, when the Soviet-Chinese conflict became open, the slanging match between Moscow and Peking produced numerous examples of the subjective character of the Marxist vocabulary. The two sides spoke different tongues but the same language, which is the Party jargon, and they hurled the same abuse and the same accusations at one another and branded one another with the same iron, both growing increasingly indignant, feeling increasingly maligned and wounded and remaining totally incapable of recognizing their own words when spoken by the other camp. The subjectivity of words, implying the subjectivity of thought, automatically made one aware of the subjectivity of truth. It further followed that truth was not to be found in facts but in beliefs and faiths. Which, all things considered, looked sensible and above all practical. For, once you have taught a man how to think, it may become difficult later, when circumstances make it important for you that he should change his mind, to persuade him that his logic has so far been at fault. If you succeed, you make him look a fool in his own eyes. If you merely teach him blind belief, then it can be altered for him painlessly. Total anesthesia, entailing somehow total amnesia. How it works, I do not know. But I have seen it work. We all have, who have watched the switches of Soviet popular loyalties.

I remember, in point of fact, a conversation I had some years ago with a German Communist. He is a man of integrity and courage, with a fine war record—on the side of the Allies—and the more meritorious since he only joined his Party after the collapse of the Third Reich. It went like this:

"What do you think of Stalin?" I asked.

"I think he was a very bad man."

"What did you think of him before he died?"

"I thought he was a great man."

"What made you change your opinion?"

"The Party."

"How so?"

"Conclusive evidence was produced."

"What do you think of Khrushchev?"

"He is a great man."

"What would you think of Khrushchev if, someday, the Party told you that he had been a bad man?"

"This is an absurd question."

"What if the Party produced conclusive evidence?"

"There could be no such evidence."

"What would you have said if, on the eve of Stalin's demise in 1953, I had suggested to you that Stalin might be a bad man and that the time would come when the Party would give you proof of it?"

"I should have urged you to have your brains examined."

He said all this quite honestly. At the same time, he saw the humor of the situation and answered my very leading questions with much laughter. No conversation of that type could be conducted with a Chinese.

Studying the Party phraseology in the Peking press, and keen as I was not to offend Mrs. Chen more than I had to, I compiled a small manual of words that were not to be used in a Chinese context. I often referred to it when writing my stories. It enabled me to avoid the objectionable expression, to turn it into a paraphrase that did not weaken it or affect clarity but also did not offend, simply because it was not "classified." Thus did I keep out of much superfluous trouble. Taboo or not taboo was the question.

"Ulterior motives" are unknown to China. Only her foes and those of the people (they are undistinguishable) have them. China has "lofty aspirations."

The enemies of the people work together "hand in glove." The friends of the people work "hand in hand." Criticism of China is "filthy abuse" or "slander." China's criticism of others represents "unanswerable arguments," or "the plain (or, as the case may be, unvarnished, shameful, sad) truth." China's enemies indulge in "underhand dealings," while she practices "revolutionary strategy in the light of Mao Tse-tung's thinking." The Imperialists, or the Modern Revisionists, are forever "plotting," while China is being "farsighted." Their "sinister designs," their "high-sounding utterances" and "two-faced dealings" are contrasted with China's own "high purposes," "fearless vindication of the truth," and "straightforward policy." Hostile governments are made up of "brazen opportunists." Chinese statesmen are "brilliant tacticians." The Chinese Communist Party is "enlightening the People." The Communist Party of the U.S.S.R. is "hoodwinking the great Soviet People." Any improvement in the living conditions of the Chinese masses is "revolutionary." Any improvement in the living conditions of the Soviet people is "reactionary." Lack of improvement in the living conditions of the Chinese people is not due to the inability of the state to improve them but to the "spontaneous, selfless devotion to duty" of the people themselves who are paradoxically made to look (but not to believe) that, should they but give up building socialism, they could lead a life of wealthy idleness. Reported lack of improvement in the living conditions of the Soviet people points to the inefficiency of modern revisionism and the present leaders of the U.S.S.R. Where others "take illegal action," China is "fully justified" in whatever she does. When China attacks one of her neighbors, she is "acting in self-defense." When that neighbor fights back, it is guilty of "unprovoked aggression."

During the Sino-Indian fighting of 1962, which the Peking press played down, for the Chinese public was simply *not interested,* the actual Indian frontier guards were described as "invading armies" and the large Chinese forces that had been waiting for D-Day for months on the border, and indeed already beyond it, were "Chinese frontier guards acting in self-defense against overwhelming odds." The Chinese vastly outnumbered the Indians in fire power as well as in men. But it is always the written word, the official record, not the actual facts, that counts. Actually, it works both ways. The Chinese worship of the written word robs China and her officialdom of all sense of proportion—and so, of humor. The literal side of their minds makes them immensely vulnerable to flattery, much, and often grossly, as they use it themselves. It may occasionally lead them to a mortifying loss of face.

In the early morning of December 31, 1962, foreign correspondents were summoned by telephone to the Waichiaopu for a press conference. The conference, we were told, was to be presided over by Madame Kung Peng, head of the Information Department.

Since briefings were unknown in Peking, it looked as if really something serious was about to be disclosed.

Madame Kung Peng I knew reasonably well. In the days before Liberation, when the Chinese Communists were keeping in close touch with the foreign press, we had all seen much of her. We were rather fond of the Communist Chinese Party in those days. To us, the Chinese Communists stood for courage, righteousness, honesty, and disinterestedness. It may have been just snobbery. But I can still very distinctly remember that many correspondents from the corrupt, rotten imperialist press in Shanghai went to the greatest trouble to provide Madame Kung Peng with Hong Kong-bought stencils and other stationery, duty free, to help her put out her propaganda handouts. These were still legal then. It was before the final break with the Kuomintang, and Chou En-lai was still in Nanking.

I had not seen Kung Peng again until she came to Geneva, together with Vice-Premier Chen Yi for the opening of the Conference on Laos, in 1961. She had then held at the Palais des Nations a daily and remarkably frank and informative press conference. Some months later, in Peking, soon after my arrival, she had invited me to lunch at the Szechuen restaurant with quite a large number of people and it had been a lavish, delicious, and friendly meal, and a completely informal one, which made it the nicer, but that had also been the first occasion when I had heard it said that my "mission" to China was to work for the cause of Sino-French friendship. I had taken it then as a mere show of courtesy, for it is indeed polite to give people more importance than they have and more face in the Chinese sense of the word than they deserve.

However, on that particular morning, we all rushed to the Waichiaopu, and indeed there was Madame Kung Peng. She looked livid and there was no doubt at all that she was suffering from shock. She was not acting. Had she not been in unquestionable good faith, the occasion of a press conference would still be worth mentioning for its very rarity.

So there we sat, waiting for her to begin, and she did so querulously.

The English press, she said, had disgraced itself in a body. In order to slander China it was no longer above forgery. A London weekly called *Tribune* had just published a "letter" allegedly signed Chou En-lai and which of course Chou En-lai had never written. It had all been done with "ulterior motives."

We were extremely puzzled and remained fully as puzzled after a half-page mimeographed communiqué was handed out to us which did no more than paraphrase her spoken statement. We took it in dutifully and then I asked her what it was all about.

She replied: "I could not possibly tell you. My dignity as a Chinese official forbids it."

We then all pointed out that her communiqué, as it stood, was perfectly useless to us and that it was not news and could not be news until we knew what the *Tribune* had printed that was so objectionable to China.

Madame Kung Peng then said that she fully realized that journalists had to know the facts and that, therefore, she would make arrangements for us to go straight to the Hsinhua News Agency and read the text as it had been received.

There we all drove in a sort of motorcade and were received at the door and taken to a room upstairs and shown the text and indeed left alone to read it.

The *Tribune* story was by no means a forgery but an end-of-the-year hoax which every reader was expected to take as such. As did our colleagues from the East European press, Russians included, for it simply could not be read with a straight face. The Prime Minister of China was assuring his Portuguese friends that China would not rest until Goa had been wrested away from Indian imperialism and restored to its rightful owner, Portugal, and the British government was in similar fashion told that China would never rest until Calais had been wrested away from French

imperialism and restored to the proper ownership of the U.K.
There was a lot more in the same ludicrous vein. It was rather
well done, and the official Chinese style had been used by a hu-
morist of no mean talent. It was extremely funny. Only the Chinese were not amused, except, I was told later, Chou himself. This,
however, is hard to believe, for he could easily have called off the
ensuing official protest that was made in London and added
nothing to Peking's prestige. *Unless* the decision was not, and
could not have been, his.

However, there was a *demarche*, which Whitehall played
down, and *Tribune*, in its next issue, made it clear that what
everyone of its non-Chinese readers had rightly taken as a joke
had indeed been meant as one, and of the most harmless kind. No
other civilized country besides China would have had to be
reassured. Not even Stalin's U.S.S.R., for, well before the death
of the Russian dictator, amusing stories about the regime were
being widely circulated in Moscow, and I got them, not from
Westerners, but from perfectly loyal Soviet-bloc journalists or
officials who would not have criticized the regime in earnest but
thought that laughter was still permitted.

Mao's China does not laugh at itself. The only "Chinese" jokes
I heard, I could trace to one or another of my East European
colleagues, and, sometimes, to myself. Mine usually came back
after some weeks from diplomatic, often Communist, sources,
who swore they had heard them at the Waichiaopu. Which
would show that, at least in the Protocol Department, if they are
no longer inventive, they remain healthily malicious and not
quite as quiescent as they are expected to be. But I have my
doubts.

The Protocol, however, was not involved in the *Tribune* affair.
It was handled in different and much higher quarters, possibly
higher even, as I have suggested, than the Premier's office, and in
so parochial a manner as to suggest the imperial chop of the
untraveled Mao, to whom a joke about China could not be devoid
of "ulterior motives." To him, who never speaks, the spoken
word can be disrespectful, even insulting, but the written word,
the material stroke of the brush or the pen, or the impact of the
printing press, becomes an *act* and, eventually, an unfriendly one.
Fun for fun's sake does not and cannot and must not exist.
Cartoons that appear in the Chinese press, together with their

captions, are never humorous or unpolitical. And they are more often cruel than kind, for one is supposed to be righteously angered, not amused.

Cartoons are mentioned in this chapter about words because originally the Chinese ideogram was much more clearly figurative than it is today—a symbolic drawing, a cartoon. Even now, the *written image*, blurred as it has become to the many, remains essential. An official guidebook of Peking published in 1956 states that the Monument to the People's Heroes, then in the process of being erected in the middle of Tien An Men Square, is to bear, carved in Mao Tse-tung's calligraphy, the inscription: "The People's Heroes Are Immortal." Even to the most fervent adepts of Maoism, that phrase would in itself hardly bear the stamp of genius, or even of modest originality. At the same time, its very insignificance would prevent anyone from describing it as hackneyed, gratuitous, meaningless, and banal. What counts is the Leader's own *handwriting*. What also counts is that the written word should be put down in the proper old script, as opposed to the new romanized—"latinized" is the approved expression now—Chinese on which the regime has been at work for years. The personal magic would then disappear. When we, Western barbarians, find it necessary to carve into stone some quotation from one of our great men, we do not find it necessary to reproduce his handwriting. It is the spirit that matters (in so far as it matters at all), not the letter, and certainly not the penmanship. If it were, the typewriter industry would go bankrupt.

The cartoon as it now appears in the Chinese press carries therefore far more weight than it does in ours, for it is a throwback to the ideogram of thirty centuries ago.

Up to the initial stages of the Great Leap Forward of 1958, political cartoonists had been encouraged to satirize some of the bureaucratic aspects of the regime. No sooner did it become plain that the Leap—the result of Maoist bureaucratic planning—had gone wrong, than the Chinese bureaucracy, now on the defensive, banned all criticism of itself from the newspapers in whatever graphic form. Artists who had so far done their honest duty were severely dealt with. Henceforth, only the reactionaries, domestic and foreign, had to be held to ridicule. Never the Chinese Communist Party, which was to become increasingly infallible with every one of its failures. This taught the people a useful lesson, for it became clear that whatever was legitimate today could become subversive tomorrow and, in a country where no proper courts of law existed, there was nothing to prevent arbitrariness from being retroactive. This may explain the phrase already quoted: "We are all afraid and we do not know what of." When I first heard it, I thought it only meant "of what punishment we may incur." It also meant "for whatever crime we may have committed in the innocence of our law-abiding minds."

When President Kennedy was assassinated, the news was briefly reported by the daily press on the inside pages in small characters and was not mentioned in editorials. The only comment appeared on November 24 in the *Workers' Daily* only as a cartoon, a caricature showing the dead President wearing a necktie with dollar signs on it, a bullethole in his temple from which blood was dripping into a pool. The caption was "Kennedy bites the dust" (and this is a mild translation). Soviet-bloc circles in Peking were fully as shocked and nauseated by this official display of gross lack of human decency as were the Westerners and indeed many Chinese. (The caption involved a particularly unsavory pun on the President's name.) Local foreign reactions gave rise to considerable puzzlement, I heard, among Chinese official circles, where it could not be understood that the death of an enemy, no matter by what means, was something that had not to be rejoiced over. The murder of President Kennedy deserved no more than a cartoon in the cheapest Peking newspaper. As long as he was alive, the head of the North American republic was worth attacking. Once dead, he could only be made fun of.

The traditional cult of the dead never applied to dead foes. No posthumous honors, to the best of my knowledge, were ever bestowed on a fallen enemy. Indeed, why should the spirit of an enemy killed in battle or otherwise be feared? No one defeated in this world can be victorious in the next. That stands to reason. Only "the People's Heroes Are Immortal." This bold assumption that the dictatorship of the proletariat, lagging as it may on earth, has already been established in Heaven (and indeed what thought could be more Christian?) and that the enemies of China are by divine, if atheist, justice deprived of eternal salvation, implies that the sacred word—and the word, provided it be *written*, is sacred—need not be spent on the unworthy. Therefore, if a minor hurricane hits Cuba we have a catastrophe that is to be deplored in the columns of the Chinese press under banner headlines. If, at the same time, the collapse of a dam in Italy (where even the Communist Party, yielding to Togliatti's revisionist leadership, has betrayed the cause) kills several thousand people, that is not worth mentioning at all, and the Chinese press will ignore it. If the whole town of Skoplje is shattered by an earthquake it is likewise not considered newsworthy, and it is only after foreign correspondents in Peking have pointed out Chinese callousness that it will be casually reported, together with the sending of some paltry relief. What Peking will hesitate to spend is not the money, but rather the all-important word, especially at a time when the rate of verbal exchange is not quoted on the local market, when the value of the foreign word is, as the *Tribune* incident has shown, unknown in China, and that of the Chinese word uncertain abroad, especially on the Western side of the Iron Curtain.

As unexportable as the "Jen Min Piao," * the Chinese word has a fixed value at home. It must be spent wisely and, above all, used "correctly" (which does not mean grammatically but arithmetically), for the ideologically wrong word will lead to the ideologically wrong thought. (We should naturally think that subversive thoughts might lead to subversive speech, but to the Chinese, a "train of thought" is really like a train—running over rails of words and in danger of taking the wrong line if the points are not properly set.) Thus Peking's former Tartar City and Chinese City have been renamed the Outer City and the Inner City respectively. The reason is simple to understand, twofold as it is.

First, how could there be a city in China named the "Chinese" City, since by definition all cities, towns, and villages in China are Chinese? But then, how could there be a Tartar City as distinct from a Chinese City and yet part, together with the latter, of the capital of the country? It would tend to remind people that the last dynasty had been a Manchu (Tartar) dynasty, that barbarians from the north had once overthrown the truly Chinese

* China's national currency.

Mings, and that China had been ruled by foreigners for three centuries.

Secondly, if it was so, and these aliens, the Manchus, had once invaded China, then how could their country, Manchuria (or Tartary), be and always have been, as was claimed, an integral part of China, in fact the northeastern provinces of it, not even an "autonomous region" like Inner Mongolia, Sinkiang, and now Tibet? Awkward question indeed, and such as to lead one into the most dangerous of heresies!

However, in China, when a question proves awkward, you don't make matters worse by attempting to answer it. You simply make sure that it is not asked. This is not achieved by forbidding it, which would make it the awkwarder and give it substance. Instead, you *remove* the question by the simple process of removing the reason that suggested it. In the case of Peking's two cities, the trick was done by means of a double misnomer. The Inner City is not an inner city because there is no outer city around it and the Outer City is not an outer city because there is no inner city inside it. The so-called Inner City, in fact, lies south of the so-called Outer City from which it is very clearly separated by an ancient wall—now in the process of being torn down. But as I write these lines, I realize how wrong I am. There is no such thing as a misnomer. There are only *misfacts*. The Word is always right.*

I was once sharply rebuked by the Waichiaopu representative in Shanghai when I happened to mention that I was staying at the British consulate. There was, I was informed, no British consulate at Shanghai. There was only the Shanghai branch of the British chargé d'affaires' office (of Peking). Its small staff performed normal consular duties in the old British consulate, set in the old and vast British consular compound, still officially acknowledged as British property. But it was not a consulate and must not be called one. No exception was taken to my enjoying the hospital-

---

* Actually, the terms "inner city" and "outer city" were already used by the Ts'ings. It was understandable that these Tartars should call their own city the "inner" one and where the pigtailed Chinese lived the "outer" one. What is hard to understand is why the supernationalistic Chinese Reds should have returned to this distinction, thus verbally ostracizing themselves from their own capital.

ity (and I enjoyed it very much) of the Spankies, but I must not refer to Mr. Spankie as "the British consul." His name I was free to look up in the Peking Diplomatic List. I should thus convince myself that his real title was: "First Secretary (absent)." The terms "British consulate" and "British consul" were wrong, inaccurate, and therefore tendentious, for, if permitted to be used, they might encourage the British to get above themselves.

On February 3, 1966, an American friend in Hong Kong who is very well informed on developments in China wrote to me that the office of the British chargé d'affaires in Shanghai had been "cut down to one official, given a title about a paragraph long, and authorized to concern itself with nothing but British nationals' affairs. The omission or misplacement of a single word in the new title brings the letter back with a huge chop stating *'Cette organisation n'existe pas.'* " *

What's in a name? This is *not* an awkward question. The answer is: everything!

---

* French, to Communist China, has remained the international postal language uninterruptedly, even though there were no diplomatic relations between Paris and Red Peking until 1964.

14

THE BANQUETING HALL

THE STATE BANQUETS to which members of the diplomatic corps
are invited and the correspondents also, the latter without their
wives (which puts the press in its proper place), are worth attending, dull, repetitive, and uninformative as the speeches may
be. They are held in the honor of government guests mostly, and
there are three standard menus. According to the one that is
served, you can assess the esteem in which the visitor is held.
They can be surprisingly good—surprisingly because there may
be as many as five thousand people partaking—and they can be
execrable, consisting of a few courses only, of which the first are
Chinese and the last two Irish stew and vanilla ice cream. When
the occasion is a visit from such a trusted friend as, for instance,
Prince Norodom Sihanouk, the best fare is produced, and a silent
Mao Tse-tung himself may be brought in, supported under both
armpits by respectful underlings and hoisted onto the proscenium
(for there is actually a stage, bristling with microphones, from
which addresses are delivered) like some fat *omelette surprise*,
precisely as the meal is thought to have come to an end, and
promptly brought down again amid roars of applause and then
whisked off so fast that one expects apologies from the cook. The
luscious dish is not to be sampled. The soufflé deflates away. The
surprise remains. And, in that carefully prepared atmosphere of
replete frustration, the party breaks up.

In the view of the Chinese hosts, a great honor and privilege
has been bestowed upon all present, and (even though they are
not so precisely conscious of it) a demonstration of classical
Chinese culinary art at its best has just taken place. The feast is
over and general thanks are being belched (this is a mere figure

of speech, for belching, while still permissible, is no longer etiquette, and the foreigners are hopeless at it, especially their womenfolk), and one feels one could not eat another bite, and then, quite unexpectedly, there is set upon the table yet another delicacy so enticing that the appetite, dead to the world, is stirred again into a fleeting semblance of life. This comparison was thought very poor by my Soviet bloc colleagues who said that the appearance of Mao was much more like that of the traditional bowl of rice put before his guests by a self-deprecating Chinese at the close of a modest fifteen-course dinner with the words: "You have had nothing to eat; won't you sate your hunger with this humble nourishment?" and which they push away, equally politely remarking that they just cannot face it.

15

THE ANALECTS OF FISHFACE I

IN THE brightly lit Banqueting Hall, where we were drinking maotai as an apéritif, Fishface came to me with hand outstretched. He looked even more delighted than usual.

"Good evening, Mr. Marcuse," he said, beaming.

"Good evening, Mr. F . . . I mean, good evening to you."

"Very soon, now," he remarked.

"Ah, good," I replied, assuming that he, too, was getting hungry. But he was thinking of the establishment of diplomatic relations between France and People's China, now definitely in the offing.

"You should be happy," he went on, "to see your tireless efforts in the cause of Sino-French friendship so gloriously rewarded."

I thought my leg was being pulled, but Fishface was merely at his own exquisitely polite best. I bowed and looked self-deprecating.

"The Chinese and the French peoples," said Fishface, "have always had much in common."

"Certainly."

"They share an unconquerable love of freedom. The French Revolution! The Paris Commune!"

"And an unconquerable love of good food."

"Good food. No doubt. It delights the palate. But it is the company that makes the feast."

"You know," I said, not to be outdone, "I think the Chinese and the French are the only two nations in the world that understand anything about food at all. Look," I warmed up, "at the variety of dishes, at those regional delicacies. . . . But, of course, Chinese cooking is even better than French cooking."

Fishface flushed with pleasure. "You are too kind. But no, no. I must contradict you, if I may. French cooking is the better of the two. Much, much the better."

"No, no. I insist. Chinese cooking is best. Think of shark's fins!"

"Hamburgers!"

"Peking duck!"

"Ham-and-eggs!"

"Canton snake soup!"

"Irish stew!"

"Wusih live shrimps!"

"Beef stroganoff!" said Fishface, with great finality.

Then we returned to our comparisons.

"The Chinese and the French," I said, stretching a point, "also share an admiration for beautiful women. . . ."

". . . taking part," he interrupted hastily, "on an equal footing with the men, in the work of national reconstruction."

"They worship the dead."

"You probably," said Fishface testily, "think of the China of pre-Liberation days. We have done away with superstition. Our people are enlightened. They no longer worship the dead, or burn joss sticks, or spend money on funerals. Guided as they are by Chairman Mao's thinking . . . "

"What about those tombs that dot the fields in the Peking countryside? You can see them on both sides of the road, as you drive to the airport."

"Remnants of the feudal past!"

"Why don't you remove them? They take up a lot of space that could be cultivated and bear crops."

"The people wouldn't like it," said Fishface candidly. And went back to his subject:

"Another thing that should draw the peoples of China and France even closer together is the fact that they both have great leaders. Despite the different social systems, we are well aware that General de Gaulle did liberate France just as Chairman Mao liberated China."

"And they cultivate bureaucracy."

Fishface's fishlike face froze.

"Again, you are thinking of the old China. In those days, the people were oppressed by the bureaucrats. Now they are no longer oppressed. It shows there are no more bureaucrats."

"Still," I objected, "I have never had to fill quite so many forms or write quite so many letters about quite so many trivial matters as now. Nor have I seen so many officials engaged in so much paperwork anywhere else, except perhaps, as I was saying, in France."

"That is not bureaucracy. It is efficient administration."

"It does slow things down, though."

"We are in no special hurry. We know that time is on the side of the Revolution."

"But you seem to be. What about the Great Leap Forward?"

"It has been misunderstood in the West. You believe that it has failed, because, to you, a leap must be fast, sudden, rash even. Experience has taught us that it is better to do things thoroughly and well than too quickly and with no proper foresight. Is it not an English saying that one should look before one leaps?"

"How long will you go on leaping?"

"Forever," said Fishface, proudly. "We shall always hold aloft the three Red Banners of the People's Communes, the General Line, and the Great Leap Forward! Besides," he added irrelevantly, "the East Wind now prevails over the West Wind, as chairman Mao has repeatedly pointed out."

"Is that kind to France?" I asked.

He looked as if I had hit him below the belt. He was speechless. I felt awful.

"Sorry," I said. "I apologize. I was only joking."

"Joking?" he said, greatly relieved, and proceeded to roar with laughter.

"Another thing yet," he said, "that brings the peoples of China and France so close together is that they can always enjoy a good joke."

"Besides, as the old Chinese proverb says," I said, making it up with great presence of mind: " 'What is a change of weather between friends?' "

"Exactly!" said Fishface, as if he had heard it at his amah's knee.

He was happy again. At that moment, Chou En-lai walked in with the guest of honor, followed by the diplomatic corps, and we all went and sat down at our appointed tables and were served menu number three, the one that carries Irish stew.

16

FOREIGN CORRESPONDENTS
AT WORK

❧✦❧

CHINESE communiqués are distributed by the Foreign Ministry's Information Department, usually at dead of night or in the very early hours of the morning. The telephone rings and you wake up and rub your eyes and reach for the receiver. You pick it up and a Chinese voice, speaking English with the usual touch of American accent, asks whether you are you, and then speaks invariably as follows: "This is the Information Department of the Ministry of Foreign Affairs. We shall be releasing a communiqué in twenty minutes. If you are interested you can come and get a copy." If you are still new to Peking, you will ask what it is about. The voice will then repeat: "This is the Information Department of the Ministry of Foreign Affairs. We shall be releasing a communiqué in twenty minutes. If you are interested you can come and get a copy." You will think that you have not been heard properly and put your question again and hear the same sentence once more. This indicates no ill-will on the part of the man at the other end of the line; it is just that he is not there to answer questions.

You will then put on your clothes and start your car, if it will start. If you live in the Great Diplomatic Building, you will drive for half a mile down Changan Avenue, empty of traffic at that hour except for the vegetable carts which are coming in, drawn by tiny emaciated ponies; the odd procession of two-wheeled, man-drawn, night-soil carts on their way to the fields; an occasional mysterious military convoy, and the inevitable very modern motor-powered sprinkler that waters the precious asphalt, irrespective, it seems, of the weather. You will then turn right into

94

the narrow street which faces the new railway station and then left into the Waichiaopu *hutung*. The Ministry's old Chinese-style gateway is brightly lit and you drive in without any formality. The sentry on duty, who knows the number of your car, simply presses an electric bell to announce your arrival. You drive right up to the wing which houses the offices of the Information Department and you climb a few steps into the vast reception hall. It is in semi-darkness, but in a corner by the door there is a small table with a desk lamp. A minor official from the department rises, shakes you by the hand, and formally says, *"Ni hao."* You reply, *"Ni hao"* and are handed a copy of the communiqué in the language of your choice. They come in Chinese, English, French, Russian still, and sometimes Spanish. You shake hands again and depart. Not another word is exchanged except an equally formal *"Tsai tien."*

Then you go home and read the text you have been given. It may be quite short; it may run to a number of pages. If you find it of little news value, you simply file it away for eventual reference; if not, you take the cover off your typewriter and do a commentary. You seldom trouble to cable it as a straight piece of news because, by the time it is handed to you, it has already been put on the air in various languages by the Chinese News Agency and by Peking Radio and monitored in Hong Kong, Tokyo, Manila, and even London, Paris, and, of course, Moscow. If it contains important news, it has already received world-wide publicity. You are always the last informed of what the Chinese government wishes to make public.

Should you nevertheless feel bound to do a story at so ungodly an hour, you will again leave your flat-cum-office, and this time cross the whole breadth of Peking to the main telegraph office, which is open round the clock. There is a branch at the Wai Chiao Ta Lu, but it shuts at eleven P.M. So you find yourself driving along Changan Avenue for the second time in the same night, but much farther now, breathing the effluvia from the honey-carts once more and watching the water carts still at work steadily sprinkling the macadam in perhaps the now outmoded hope of seeing a hundred flowers shoot forth on its uneven surface.

At the telegraph office your credentials will be scrutinized and your story gone through word by word by the sleepy night shift (who claim to know no foreign language), and finally accepted. Back to bed you drive.

During office hours at the Wai Chiao Ta Lu branch, where no accreditation and cable cards need be produced by the well-known inmates, your copy is also pored over by several people. They, too, understand no English, no French, and, I was told, no Russian. Still, no mistyped word will go past their eagle eye. It may be that they only know the *look* of the vocabulary, like the typesetters of foreign language newspapers in pre-Liberation Shanghai. The individual officially in charge is seated at a desk and armed with a pencil, but the others will crowd him from behind and look at your text over both his shoulders and point excitedly, offering comments and suggestions. The sight of three or more people doing the job of one is not uncommon in Peking. The regime has thus done away with unemployment. Having understood this, you will not write, like the *Neue Zuercher Zeitung*'s special correspondent Lorenz Stucki, that you were particularly struck by the general laziness of the Chinese.

Transmissions are unpredictable and you will not find it strange if the last take of your story should reach its destination first, even though all takes were "filed" in their proper sequence.

There is officially no censorship on outgoing press messages and it is generally accepted that there is none, which I would still believe myself but for one incident that occurred in the autumn of 1964. I had sent a very harmless story in which I mentioned President Liu Chao-chi. The phone rang a few hours later in my office and I was asked whether I would care to reread my cable because they thought there was a mistake in one take. Before doing anything of the sort, I asked whether my cable had been duly forwarded and was assured that it had. Then I read the story over again and found no mistake, as I informed whoever was calling from the cable office. Then a few more hours went by and the phone rang again and it was again someone in the telegraph office who said my cable could not be sent unless the missing word was added, for there did happen to be a missing word, so they said. I told them there was no missing word and my cable should go as handed in. They said they couldn't do that because I had described Liu Shao-chi as "Liu Shao-chi, President of the Republic of China," and I should have written, "Liu Shao-chi, President of the *People's* Republic of China." My story simply could not be forwarded unless I added that word. I complied and then wrote a letter of protest to the Information Department of the Foreign Affairs Ministry, pointing out that there was after all a cable censorship and that it was unthinkable that: (a) my story should have been thus delayed without my being informed sooner; and (b) that no one could reasonably suspect President Liu of having gone over to the Formosans. I then proceeded to wait for a reply from the department but it never came.

A fortnight later, at one of the state banquets in the Great Hall of the People, a woman in the Foreign Section drew me aside and said: "Mr. Marcuse, we have read your letter about that cable. We wish you to understand that there is no censorship in China." Then I asked her to explain to me how, in that case, a correspondent's cable could be stopped and its text objected to. She said: "This was done by an overzealous official, not a censor, mind you, just an overzealous official in the telegraph office. He meant well, but we agree that he should not have done it." And then she added: "Of course, he will not do it again."

Little shivers ran down my spine.

With personal interviews practically out of the question, press conferences nonexistent, speechless official "spokesmen," and human contacts with the population strictly banned, the foreign correspondent in Peking has three main sources of information: the official handouts, the English service of the official NCNA, and the official daily press. One's work, almost entirely paperwork, consists essentially in interpreting written documents. Of the three sources, the last is by far the most interesting because the newspapers publish not only their long editorials—also generally broadcast before they appear in print and so, paradoxically, known to the foreign public before they are to the Chinese reader—but also a great variety of small articles and commentaries which provide revealing sidelights on the daily life of the population and the political trend at the local level. The provincial newspapers, however, are scarcely available in Peking.

The editorials of the Communist Party organ, the *People's Daily*, are of course to be treated as gospel and analyzed as such. One manages to work out a new angle occasionally by comparing the day's lead with another the paper published on the same subject several weeks or months ago. The two are usually almost identical, but a change of word here, a different turn of phrase there, may provide the ghost of a hint. From such tiny variations on well-worn themes one sometimes draws conclusions that are not necessarily well founded, and occasionally thinks one has discovered intentions that are not there at all. Still, it makes copy. But it is exegesis rather than journalism.

That at least is how things were when I took up my work in Peking. They became a little livelier as Sino-Soviet relations deteriorated increasingly overtly. After the "Open Letter" of the Soviet Communist Party of July 14, 1963, strongly criticizing China, Mao's Central Committee decided to hit back, and both the *People's Daily* and the Party's fortnightly *Red Flag* started publishing at irregular intervals a series of articles, allegedly written jointly by the editorial departments of these two organs, refuting point by point the Russian charges, revealing much that had secretly passed in recent years between the two fraternal Parties. With each editorial, bitterness could be noticed to increase and anger to rise. Every time, there was really something new. But still, to us it was paperwork, if of an exceptionally exciting kind, and technically still routine.

So had been the first weeks of the Lei Feng campaign and so were to be the reform of the Peking opera and the ever tighter thought control and the back-to-the-country drive. Every development had to be followed through the medium of Party prose and no questions could be asked, for no one in a position of authority, however modest, would ever dare listen to them, let alone answer them. Our own observations were limited to the visible repercussions of new trends on the daily life of the Peking population. Private Chinese comments, few, rare, and laconic for obvious reasons, were seldom very revealing, since the rank and file were no better informed politically than we were ourselves. They were of course much more carefully watched, as no foreign plenipotentiary, however hostile to China and outspoken in his own circle and in his reports to his government, could be such a potential menace to the serenity of the regime as the most insignificant laborer who would speak his mind among his equals after making it up unchecked. No tares must be sown among the Party wheat, for they tend to prosper in preserved furrows.

Of course all foreign correspondents had their own Chinese translators and these did a remarkably conscientious and honest job. But it was sometimes difficult to make sure that the original meaning had been correctly conveyed, especially when the foreign rendering seemed to exclude all possibility for the original text to hold any meaning at all. At first I had no doubt that my translator, the venerable Mr. Ma, a scholar of the old school, well versed in the classics and a Moslem to boot, had understood it correctly, but later doubts arose when Mr. Ma confessed that there were many things in the editorials and other political or technical articles of the daily press that he himself could make no sense of. He said there were many new words and the simplified characters which the regime had introduced in order to make reading simpler for the masses made it more difficult for him because he was used to the old ones.

Every morning he would produce for me a summary of the day's press. Then, from the headlines which he had translated, I chose those items of which I wanted either a digest or a full translation. I remember asking Mr. Ma one day *not* to translate for me one of these huge editorials that had appeared in the *People's Daily* since the official English translation had already come over the teletype, but merely to tell me how long it would take him to read it.

His answer was: "Between two and three hours."

"I said· "But, Mr. Ma, you are a very learned man, and if you can read this editorial from end to end in two to three hours, how long would it take the average reader, the man in the street?"

Mr. Ma said: "From five to six hours."

"But," I asked, "how many people in busy Peking can spend five to six hours a day reading a newspaper story?"

Mr. Ma raised his hands in a helpless gesture, gave me one of his thin-lipped smiles, and said nothing, and I felt that it would have been unfair to press him further. After all, he had to report it all to the Service Bureau and presumably to his own Street Committee as well.

Apart from the reading matter which we were given and on which we worked, there were also the official receptions where speeches were made—we were given the texts in various languages. There were the state banquets in the Great Hall of the People, which can accommodate up to five thousand guests, and more speeches; and there were frequent so-called mass meetings, also at the Great Hall of the People and sometimes at the People's Stadium (which correspondents could only enter when duly invited), when no texts were distributed. However, earphones and simultaneous interpretation were provided. These meetings were mostly held in honor of foreign state guests and, on the Chinese side, the speaker was usually the Mayor of Peking, Comrade Peng Chen, now in disgrace. He was extremely long-winded and vociferous and, as a rule, the lectures on such occasions were scarcely worth remembering. In the end, we gave up attending, except when we felt that Peng Chen might become so abusive and condemn modern revisionism in such terms that the Soviet Ambassador and the other Soviet bloc envoys would get up as one man and walk out. This was at least straight news.

Until the collapse of the Great Leap Forward of 1958, even permanent correspondents had enjoyed a wider choice of conducted itineraries in China. Afterwards, such tours were reserved for visiting journalists. Still, we could, without too much difficulty, visit the Wuhan cities, and Nanking, Shanghai, Hangchow, and, of course, Canton which is the gateway to Hong Kong. When it came to traveling elsewhere, one's requests were politely ignored. Things were easing up a little by the time I left China, but nevertheless, my successor had to apply nine times to the Information Department in writing before he obtained permission to visit such places as Chungking, in Szechuan, and Kunming, the capital of Yunnan, a province which borders on North Vietnam. Permission was only granted after the several correspondents of NCNA in Paris had found their freedom of movement through the length and breadth of France, a facility which had never been questioned, suddenly restricted in a manner quite unprecedented so far, even though the French correspondent in Peking had never been able to cross without special permission the fifteen-mile perimeter within which foreigners are confined.

Whether they hail from the West or the East, foreign correspondents are very much on the same footing. Some privileges, such as occasional, strictly prearranged discussions with Chinese journalists and comparatively greater, but still supervised, traveling facilities, used to be enjoyed by Communist correspondents, but such favors were gradually abolished after the Moscow Congress of 1960.

As a result, correspondents of all origins and political hues were brought much closer together, united as they were by bonds of common frustration. Ideological controversies were tacitly avoided among the press corps, and if Marxism was mentioned at all, it was agreed unanimously that Maoism had nothing to do with it. By such tactful devices, the Communist correspondents came to believe that we, of the West, understood what Marxism meant. We formed the opinion, hastily perhaps, that *they* did not, which helped promote the development of those reciprocal blind spots that are so essential a part of mutual understanding.

As to Chinese affairs, they were soon made banal by the very banality of one's sources. Indeed, I am even more convinced now than we all were then that since it was policy to keep the foreign resident "out" of China, it was policy also to make him lose interest in it. It may have been meant kindly, in an effort not to add temptation to frustration. Thus, I remember looking forward with much keener interest to the periodical film shows at the British chargé d'affaires' office than to the yearly First of October parade, lavish as it was and which we used to watch from Tien An Men, with Mao Tse-tung taking the salute from the rostrum. The point is that the British chargé d'affaires' office would show a new film every fortnight and the Chinese National Day march past was the same, year after year.

This may surprise the reader who could rightly claim that the British film show had no news value. My answer to that would be that the National Day Parade also had none and that, in reporting it, most correspondents simply used to paraphrase either their own story of the previous year if they had been there, or that of their predecessors if they hadn't.

During the first month of one's stay in Peking, one had occasional pangs of professional conscience. One felt that one was not seeing enough, not hearing enough, not participating enough, that therefore one might give not only an incomplete account, taking things as a whole, because of sheer lack of knowledge of what was going on both outside and inside the capital, but also an unfair picture, and one that would be biased out of sheer exasperation. However, the mood one was in, this mood made up of enforced ignorance and soon of enforced indifference, was not exclusively experienced by the foreigner, but by the Chinese masses themselves.

It was not only for the Long Noses' benefit or detriment that everything *factual* was systematically minimized. If we were de-

liberately encouraged to *become* apathetic, the general public was
made to *remain* so. For apathetic it was and stayed, except for
those calculated periods when, for some reason or other, the mental diet was briefly changed from one of Party opium to one of
Party hashish.

Even in such circumstances, it is to be noted that interpretation
was played up and the bare facts played down. At the time of
China's foray into India, in October, 1962, there were no Chinese
war correspondents on the field of battle and actual war news
was reduced to a very brief daily bulletin issued by Hsinhua. Chinese correspondents—no foreigners allowed—later gave firsthand
accounts of how handsomely the Chinese frontier guards were
treating the many prisoners that had been taken from the "invading Indian forces" and of the latters' gratitude to their captors.

At all times, great care was taken not to arouse genuine popular
feeling. In any "campaign"—I shall come back to "mass demonstrations" later—the actual issue was put before the people in
terms of restrictive slogans that tended to blur rather than clarify
it, and this, made obvious by the radio and the daily press, contributed to the feeling that nothing was really important unless
watchwords made it compulsorily so. Since foreign correspondents were not supposed to react to Chinese watchwords, they
must not attach more importance to one given development than
to the next. Nothing bewildered the Information Department
more than to see representatives of the foreign press play up one
item culled from the *People's Daily* one day and ignore another
on the morrow, even though it appeared on the same page and in
the same column and was made up of roughly the same number
of ideograms and lines.

To have one's own scale of journalistic values was deemed im-
proper and applying it to one's work downright indecent. Personal comment was not appreciated, unless unreservedly lauda-
tory. Things had to be all one piece. One could not praise one
aspect of Chinese policy and criticize another. One was either a
friend or a foe, unreservedly, but one's attitude was never supposed to be a matter of individual volition.

Communist correspondents, being looked upon as officials,
were not thought ever to express their own minds but to write
upon orders, and that could hardly be held against them. The two
correspondents of the Yugoslav Tanjung agency who succeeded

one another during my Peking stay, Vasil Magdeski and Branko Bogunovic, enjoyed a paradoxically privileged position in that, representing as they did the press of the abhorrent Tito regime, nothing good could be expected of them and the worst would not have been a surprise. They were never in trouble and could have got away with murder. Indeed, they would have embarrassed the Information Department greatly had they lavished praise upon China. They tactfully did not.

The two simultaneously permanent Western correspondents— Reuter's and Agence France-Presse's made no sense to the Chinese at all because they were unpredictable. When I first displeased the Information Department, and Mrs. Chen asked me whether *this* was A.F.P. policy, and I replied that A.F.P. had no policy, she looked at me with that mixture of disbelief and queasiness with which one views freaks. When the establishment of diplomatic relations between France and China failed to turn me into a sycophant, fears were discreetly expressed on the Chinese side that General de Gaulle might have lost his grip. Freedom of the press, I was given to understand, could only be a sign of weakness at the Top.

During the early stages of the Franco-Chinese honeymoon, French correspondents flocked to Peking as V.I.P.P.'s. Their reports were not all unreservedly favorable, and this made the Chinese wonder. Now that the two countries had decided, apart from all else, on cultural exchanges, how was it that French journalists could find anything to criticize? What could cultural exchanges mean but exchanges of praise?

But if they surprised the Chinese, the Chinese often surprised them, too.

The visiting editor of a French provincial paper once came to see me, shaking with mirth after his first interview with the press officials. He had been advised to keep clear of permanent correspondents because they were "full of preconceived ideas."

"Preconceived?" he had asked unbelievingly.

"Yes," he had been told, "the longer they stay, the more preconceived their outlook becomes. They are extermely prejudiced."

As a matter of fact, Mrs. Chen was not altogether wrong. Everyone of us had arrived with a wide-open, kindly disposed mind, inclined to enhance rather than belittle. Later, after it had been made clear to us that we were negligible quantities, mere compulsory articles of import in China's human barter trade, much of that initial goodwill went and we soon began to take *Schadenfreude* in Chinese setbacks. Somewhere in his book *Dateline Peking*, the Canadian correspondent Frederick Nossal wrote something like "The Chinese obviously hated us and all we could do was just hate them back." * Actually, it did not go quite as far as that, but it certainly made us happy to find them at fault. When a Chinese-built freighter, the *Great Leap* (ha! ha!), broke in two on a reef in the Yellow Sea, we gratuitously put it down to poor shipbuilding and seamanship and we rejoiced at the inevitable loss of face. Had she flown another flag, we would have thought it all plain hard luck and very sad.

Of course, it was only after several months that we found ourselves in so negative a frame of mind. The special correspondents could not possibly have shared it. Still, even with them, all was not plain sailing, and the same French journalist once lost his temper with Mrs. Chen and asked her whether he should daub his face with black boot polish in order to be permitted to see any of the things he had come to see. Her obvious answer was that it would make no difference, and, here again, she must have been right. African diplomats and students—there were no Negro correspondents in Peking—enjoyed no special privileges but were on the contrary expected to attend Afro-Asian solidarity meetings, which they reluctantly but dutifully did.

To go back to the press, every correspondent from the free world, whether special or permanent and resident, is a bit of a gamble and a bit of a puzzle. It is impossible to foretell how he will react and how he will write. It has already been said that China could only be praised unconditionally, and to this I may add that China expects to be praised unconditionally *in the words previously used by the Chinese themselves.*† This, no foreign

* I am quoting from memory, not having the book with me, and, if I err, may the author forgive me.

† This strange rule of repetition—again the sanctity of the Word!—is one to which the Chinese strictly adhere, no matter at what level. Official speeches made by different personalities on the same subject are spoken by all in exactly the same phrases. Premier Chou himself, having once agreed to be interviewed by a persistent V.I.P.P., said to him: "I cannot imagine why you wanted to see me. There is nothing I can tell you that has not already appeared in the Peking press."

journalist is likely to do if only because the original Chinese text is generally too verbose, too exasperatingly repetitive for the general public to stomach, and because in its wording, it is often so oversimplified and childish as to verge on the farcical and to defeat its purpose rather than serve it.

"Why must you foreigners always opine?" Mrs. Chen once asked me. I knew better than to try to explain; whatever I said would not and could not be understood. To the Party officials and even to Mrs. Chen, whose tiny mind had lost none of its clamlike quality in the teeth of an American education, we were all inscrutable Occidentals from the mysterious West. There were times when I felt like a European version of Dr. Fu Manchu, complete with ulterior motives, unfathomable cunning, and an enviable position as a member in enviable standing of some deadly secret society.

To certain V.I.P.P.'s, very few in numbers, I have already alluded in my preface. They are China's fellow-traveling salesmen. When in China, they keep well away from the foreign community. They are periodic visitors, well received but without publicity. Peking being a village, sooner or later, and entirely by chance, one happens to learn of their presence. Their sources of information are strictly Chinese and their audience largely Anglo-Saxon. They are shown a greater area of the surface than others, it being understood that they will not ripple it or indulge in unseemly soundings. I shall certainly not suggest that they are insincere, that they do not believe what they write—I was about to say what they preach—but nevertheless they conjure up the conventional picture of the missionary, as painted by Communist propaganda, which is that of a man possessed of both blind faith and a shrewd sense of business. The difference is that they are trying to make neither converts nor sales in China, but spread the Chinese Gospel abroad at a considerable profit—to themselves.

With his *Red Star over China*, Edgar Snow was the first to put the Chinese Communists on the map. It is an informative book, and when it appeared, it served a useful purpose. It made the world aware of something that was very real indeed and of which it had so far been kept in ignorance. It certainly did not go either as far or as deep into the phenomenon of Chinese Marxism as Harold Robert Isaacs's *The Tragedy of the Chinese Revolution*, but precisely because it was less technical and much more personal, it reached a wider public. I do not suppose for a moment that if Isaacs today applied for a Chinese visa he would be granted one. His knowledge of the true political background of Maoist China is too great for him to be a welcome guest.

Following in Edgar Snow's footsteps is Felix Greene, a comparative newcomer, who writes with much greater ignorance of China's past and with greater advertising zeal. I had never met him or heard of him when I bought his book in Hong Kong on my way to Peking in 1962. It is called *The Wall has Two Sides* and it was supposed to be the latest thing about China and the most unbiased. The title I thought a little surprising and so I automatically turned to the bibliography printed at the end of the book. Among the works which the author had listed, I found not one single volume (with the sole exception of the *Analects* in the Arthur Waley translation) that had been published prior to 1944. Chiang Kai-shek's *China's Destiny* is not mentioned, which is a pity because it is a very revealing tome and several of its chapters might have been signed Mao Tse-tung. Of Harold Robert Isaacs's works, only *Scratches on our Minds*, published in 1958, and which I have not read, is mentioned. His concisely monumental *Tragedy of the Chinese Revolution* Greene doesn't seem to have read, and I suspect that he has no knowledge whatever of even the existence of Isaac's first book, *Five Years of Kuomintang Reaction*, which was published in Shanghai in the early Thirties at considerable risk to the author. I thought Greene's scholarly and literary background slim.

Greene himself I came to know when he turned up in Peking on one of his tours in the autumn of 1963. I must confess that I was thoroughly prejudiced against him because I had found his style of writing *sanctimodious*, if I may add a word to English lexicography. Now he was no longer preparing a book but had switched to television and was receiving full cooperation from the authorities. We dined together at the Danish embassy and had a long but not private talk over coffee. We discussed his book and I did not ingratiate myself with him by asking whether he had ever seen a one-sided wall. Then I tackled him about the V.I.P.P. treatment he had been given on his last trip and about his description of the new Peking railway station. I ventured to suggest that his good faith had been taken advantage of and that what he had written about the station was balderdash: about the station restaurant that stayed open day and night, about the tickets that could be ordered by telephone and were delivered promptly by messenger, about the TV rooms, and the "two nurseries for infants, where mothers can leave their children under the care of young trained nurses." He had added "in one of the nurseries I saw rows of little tots fast asleep in their cots."

At the Peking railway station, as far as I had been able to ascertain, there was only one nursery. It was there all right, there was no denying it—it had glass doors through which one could look in. But no one could *walk* in. Throughout my sojourn in Peking, during which I had gone to that very station at least once or twice a week either to see people off or to welcome others arriving, I had never known this nursery to be in use. Its doors were permanently shut and padlocked. There were playpens for everyone to see and rocking horses and toys but covered with dust.

When I mentioned that to Felix Greene he could not believe it. Others who were present and had been in China for some time bore me out. I asked Greene whether he had been to the station again by himself and he said he had not. I reminded him that by his own admission in his book his visit had been prearranged and that the deputy stationmaster was there waiting to greet him. I reminded him that the Chinese were masters at stage management, but that was something he did not particularly wish to hear.

After that session I saw no more of him, except from a distance when, for instance, he was filming Wang Fu Ching, which had been cleared of traffic and down which a sprinkler was operating, a thing never witnessed before in broad daylight.

People like Snow and Greene are not really V.I.P.P.'s, all things considered. They are V.I.P.'s—Vested Interest Propagandists. By which I do not mean that they tell deliberate untruths, but that, perhaps unconsciously, they know which side their North China *mien pao* is dollared on, and I wonder what would become of them (unless they have a tremendous private income) should Communist China suddenly fold up, which is not altogether to be dismissed as a possibility.

17

THE PEOPLE'S DAILY

❧❧❧❧

THE *People's Daily*, the official organ of the Chinese Communist Party, is a morning newspaper but not an early riser, even though it is "put to bed" before midnight. There is no such thing as stop-press news in its four or six pages. The paper is not for sale, nor is it delivered, before eight in the morning. On special occasions, that is, when it has to carry *in extenso* a particularly lengthy and important government or Party statement, it may not appear until ten A.M. or noon, or even later. The rest of the press follows suit on most of these occasions, for they have to print the same document. The *People's Daily*, like the other newspapers, has only one edition, and its circulation is comparatively small. Actually, this organ, perhaps one of the most influential in the world, is not very much read.

Among foreigners in Peking, it is known as the "Daily Bible," because it is handled and spoken of by the Chinese, at least by the officials, with the reverence one associates with holy writ and also because it usually offers, if not a prayer for the day, at least a watchword for the day. The general public does not read the *People's Daily;* it has neither the time nor, one should imagine, the inclination, but what the morning message is, it is not permitted to ignore. Loudspeakers blare it forth in factories, People's communes, universities, public or communal eating places, dormitories, indeed everywhere, and it is usually made the compulsory subject of a political discussion in the evening.

Thus does the *People's Daily* play a tremendous part, not only in the political life of China, but also in its daily life. Read or unread, it provides strictly controlled information, thought guidance, and, in short—private opinion being strictly banned—a form of prefabricated public opinion. In fact, what appears in the columns of the Party's organ is not necessarily supposed to be *read;* it is supposed to be absorbed through a semiconscious process, comparable to that of breathing.

A joke recently circulated in the capital's East European circles about a man who had gate-crashed the last People's Congress. His presence was known to General Lo Jui-ching's men, but apparently it was very difficult to identify him, and a new check of all the several thousand members' credentials would have been inconvenient. Then General Lo * himself hit upon the brilliant idea of having copies of the morning's *People's Daily* distributed to all present. This was done and the enemy spy was at once detected: he was the only person found to be actually *looking* at the paper.

The circulation figures of the *People's Daily* is a jealously guarded secret, as all secrets are in a country where everything is secret but what is compulsory knowledge. In 1960, when the blackout was not quite so strict and figures of production and other statistics were still made public, the Peking edition ran to about seven hundred thousand copies daily. In 1963, the Moscow *Izvestia* claimed that it had fallen to half a million, but no one I questioned in Peking at the time saw any evidence of this.

It is simultaneously published in other large cities, such as Shanghai, Shenyang in Manchuria, and possibly Chungking. It had for a long time a Wuhan edition as well, but when I passed through that city, late in 1964, I was told by my interpreter and guide that it had been recently discontinued, a piece of information I had no means of checking. The *Jen Min Jih Pao* was certainly available there, but it may well have been the Peking edition flown in, now that China had bought six British Viscounts to replace the much slower antiquated two-engined Soviet crates. It would of course not indicate a drop in the paper's circulation but an increase in the number of copies printed in Peking to cater to the needs of Wuhan.

Then, as in 1960, the various editions of the paper were believed to total one million four hundred thousand copies. In Peking itself, with its population of six millions, only one hundred and fifty thousand copies were sold daily, according to foreign

* Lo was still at the head of the General Staff and also, if no longer officially, the boss of Military Intelligence.

estimates. The same figure was quoted in 1960 when the remaining five hundred and fifty thousand were supposed to be sent to other places in Hopei province, of which Peking is the capital as well as that of China, and to the four surrounding provinces. The paper, or any other for that matter, is not sold in the streets Western fashion. Nor are there any newspaper kiosks. It is mostly sold in post offices. It can also be found in hotel halls, the airport, and the railway station. Subscribers make up the majority of its clientele. Its single-copy sale is small.

The immense and, so to speak, illiterate reading public of the *People's Daily* is nevertheless reached very fast. The more important comments of the Party's organs are carried simultaneously by other newspapers, in simplified form if need be, and on a country-wide basis. Provincial newspapers print nothing but Hsinhua News Agency Service, which automatically features a very adequate Peking press review for compulsory pickup by the local papers, from one end of the country to the other, from Canton to Manchuli, from Shanghai to the Afghan border. A *People's Daily* digest is discussed, clarified when required, at the constant political meetings, as already said, and the radio harps on the essential themes up to fifteen and twenty times in a single day, condensing, simplifying, and babyfying them down to playpen dialectics, using a language appropriate in style, expression, and accent to the local audience, until, in the end, the listener is urged to believe that it is his own thoughts and sentiments that the *People's Daily* has been expressing, which shows how close to the People the Party always remains. This involves much condensation but is warranted to retain its original properties and flavor, like coffee in soluble powder form. Not everyone is capable of brewing good coffee from the bean, nor read the *People's Daily*, which is in fact intelligible only to a very small, politically specialized elite, and one that is well above the average in literacy. The *Jen Min Jih Pao* uses over five thousand characters, as compared to the two thousand or so of the *Workers' Daily*, which, like all other newspapers, still has to front-page the *People's Daily* editorials in their original full texts, baffling as they may prove to possible readers.

The *People's Daily* is no less remarkable for its silences and omissions than it is for its assertions and its news, for whatever world event or development it abstains from announcing will also not be brought to the knowledge of the masses by any other newspaper or by the radio. Foreign news published in China in one form or another, it should be remembered, all bears the signature of the Hsinhua. During my last stay in China, the only Chinese correspondents abroad were from Hsinhua except toward its end, when, by virtue of a new reciprocity agreement, the *People's Daily* sent a couple of correspondents to Tokyo. Their reports, however, never appeared in the columns of their paper or were made public, but were apparently treated confidentially. It must never be forgotten that the control of information as a whole, and of non-information, is entirely in the hands of the Party, to which everything and everyone is subordinated, including the government, the latter being, in effect, its administrative and diplomatic wing. If Mao Tse-tung is now officially just the highest officeholder in the Party, he is still a much more important personage than Chairman Liu Shao-chi, who is the Head of the State, or Premier Chou En-lai. Liu Shao-chi and Chou En-lai, before being Chairmen respectively of the Republic and of the State Council, are both Vice-Chairmen of the Central Committee and what is more, members of the Standing Committee of the Politbureau. Chou, as Premier, merely heads a zombie cabinet.

The *Jen Min Jih Pao* building in what was formerly Morrison Street, now Wang Fu Ching Tachieh, is the working place of some four hundred people working in two shifts. There seem to be few reporters amongst them for reportage is almost unknown in the Chinese daily press and the agency holds a virtual monopoly of it. The *People's Daily* editorials and its commentaries signed "Observer," as those of the fortnightly Party "theoretical" publication *Red Flag*, are said to be written and edited, not behind the austere gray façade of the drab house in Wang Fu Ching, but at Party headquarters, which means nobody knows exactly where, and personally "inspired" by Mao. Occasionally, as in the case of the anti-Soviet "Polemic on the General Line of the International Communist Movement" series which ran from September, 1963, to July, 1964, totaling nine "comments," the editorial staffs of the *People's Daily* and *Red Flag* are reported to have joined forces and the articles appeared in both publications.

For over a month I spared no effort to gain access to the *Jen Min Jih Pao* premises and to meet either the manager of this newspaper or one of its responsible editors. I never succeeded. What I managed to contact on the telephone was an ill-named "Public Relations Department" through which I was told that due to "pressure of work" the *People's Daily* was not in a position to receive foreign visitors at the moment. My simple questions about the history of the paper, its circulation, and a few others, strictly professional in nature, could not be answered because the "necessary data" was lacking, which, it was pointed out, was very much regretted, for one would have been delighted to be in a position to satisfy my curiosity.

In those days, at official banquets, foreign correspondents were introduced to the editor-in-chief of the *People's Daily*, who hardly ever seemed to bear the same name or, for that matter, to have the same face. As for the general manager of the newspaper, Mr. Teng To, General Secretary of the Peking Section of the Communist Party, nobody seemed to have ever seen him. He was unapproachable and invisible. Still I remembered meeting him in Chungking during the war, when there existed an ephemeral truce between the Nationalist government of China and the Communists, who were no longer described as rebels. Mr. Teng To was then manager of the *New China Daily*, which by virtue of this truce was then being published in China's wartime capital. After Japan capitulated and after the American attempt to mediate between Nationalists and Communists had failed, Chinese unity was once more broken and Teng To took his presses back to Yenan, the capital of the Red districts where, until 1948, two official Communist Party dailies were published simultaneously. Later, there was a merger and they became the *People's Daily of North China*, with a circulation of some thirty thousand copies printed by hand in one of the loess caves which the Communist authorities were soon to leave for the Peking palaces. It was in March, 1949, that this newspaper established itself in the newly liberated capital and took its present name.

Even today the *Jen Min Jih Pao* is composed by hand, even though it is printed on rotary printing presses built in Shanghai. Each compositor deals with fifteen hundred characters an hour, which means that ten hours of individual work goes into a page of fifteen thousand characters. That is probably why the *Jen Min Jih Pao*, whose presses also print the fortnightly *Red Flag* and a good many brochures, needs such a large staff. Most of its members sleep in the paper's own dormitories and all meals are taken in its refectories, which are well-supplied from a farm situated in the Peking suburbs that is the newspaper's collective property.

In May, 1966, dispatches from Peking told the world that the trusted Teng To was no longer trustworthy and probably never had been. He seemed to have been dismissed from the *People's Daily*, while remaining a member of the Peking committee of the Party, which may look strange. What may look stranger still was that the *People's Daily* itself, managed for many years by the unfortunate Teng, and indeed founded by him, should emerge completely unbesmirched and so presumably totally unaffected in its righteous political thinking by the evil influence of a man publicly accused of having "sung the same tune as Khrushchev." Not so the *Peking Daily*, the *Peking Evening Daily*, and the local party section's fortnightly *Frontline*—all charged with "anti-Party" tendencies. Both dailies were also directly connected with Peking's municipal Party organization, but it would perhaps be farfetched to link these attacks against organs of the Peking Communists with the unexplained disappearance from public view of the capital's own Mayor, Peng Chen, concurrently Secretary General of the Standing Committee of the National People's Congress and a high-ranking member of the Central Committee, and to draw the conclusion that there was a "Peking clique," politically dangerous and against which measures had to be taken. In fact, apart from printed denunciations, no measures, so far as anyone knew, had been taken at all. The attacks against the three publications and against Teng personally seemed to have been launched by the *Daily Light* (*Kwangming Jih Pao*), which was supposed to be the organ of the intellectuals (when these were not away in the country doing the prescribed amount of manual labor), and did no more than follow the very recent lead of the Army newspaper's campaign against "bourgeois thinking," which itself came shortly after Kuo Mo-jo and the other intellectual leaders had beaten their breasts and indulged in an orgy of self-criticism. Not so very long ago the People's Liberation Army itself had been under political fire.

The notion that there may exist various and conflicting trends in the Chinese press is not to be entertained. No newspaper enjoys even a modicum of independence; all are owned and operated by the Party. The press, taken as a whole, is not unlike a restaurant that would serve different menus at different prices to suit the customer's purse. On each, the fare can be more or less elaborate, more or less plentiful. But the raw material comes from the same provider and the dishes, luxurious or humble, are all prepared by the same cook. The introduction of a new delicacy, the disappearance of another, may have something to do with the time of year and market prices and need no more indicate a crisis at managerial level than the demotion to the rank of dishwasher of a waiter caught once too often with his thumb in a plate of soup.

What happens in Mao's journalistic kitchen is probably even less important. All charges, no matter against whom they are leveled, boil down to that of having departed from the orthodoxy of Maoist thinking. Since it is difficult to discover what Mao's line of thought actually is, no one is in a position to condemn or absolve. What remains certain is that no newspaper editor has the possibility of not toeing it. None did any more, to go back to my metaphor, than carry the dishes from the serving hatch to the table. All newspapers constantly and simultaneously followed the same policy, as dictated from above, blindly, faithfully, insufferably tediously. The same applied to individual writers, and I am strongly convinced that the periodic minor upheavals were as artificial as they were carefully engineered. They were part of a policy according to which no one, outside the innermost circle, was ever allowed to feel safe or appear to be. They taught the frailty and the vanity of individual aspirations, confirmed the infallibility of the Leader alone, and were enforced through a meticulously worked-out rota of self-abasement. No hard feelings, all around. All in the day's work.

18

THE OLD RETAINERS

Red China's foreign Old Retainers are very different from the writers who periodically visit the country and describe its marvels. Although the latter are, in a way, shareholders, they nevertheless normally live abroad and in countries where Marxism is a rich man's hobby and the proletariat won't touch it.

Nor must the Old Retainers be confused with the Drujbas, for these work under contracts and stay no more than a year or two, are seldom encouraged to come back, have been hired abroad, are not necessarily connected with any Communist party, and are fellow-travelers only in the sense that Peking pays their return tickets.

The Retainers have made China their home. They work for the Party, not on a short-time basis or with much thought of ever returning to their respective native lands. Some have become Chinese citizens. Some have married in China and raise Eurasian families—most happily, it would seem. Their loyalty is beyond doubt. They are engaged in various activities. There are those who work in communes, those who teach, those who write. As a matter of fact, they all write, professionally or otherwise. They are China's most valued mouthpieces, if only because their foreign status or origin is thought to provide them with a wider and less skeptical audience abroad than any true Chinese could hope to capture. Their very Western names are believed to carry an assurance of at least some objectivity and also of a measure of intellectual freedom. These two things they are themselves convinced that they possess—in which they are as mistaken as any other zealots would be. The creed they preach is to them unquestionable, and they can contradict themselves endlessly without being aware of it, while they propagate untruths in unimpeachable good faith. They are unselfish, utterly dedicated people who expect nothing for themselves, and I have great esteem for them —morally, if not always intellectually. There is in most of them a strong missionary streak. They are, almost without exception, of British or American origin. The Americans predominate.*

The best known of them all is Anna Louise Strong, often referred to in the Chinese press as the "American journalist," who rose to fame in August, 1946, when she was given an exclusive interview by Mao Tse-tung in which the Chinese leader revived the old Chinese metaphor of the "paper tiger." This interview, verbatim, is part of Volume IV of Mao Tse-tung's selected works published in English by the Foreign Languages Press of Peking in 1961. It is true that, in the same tome, there also appears the text of a much briefer interview given also in Yenan, in September of the same year, to a perfectly genuine U.S. correspondent, A. T. Steele, who was never a Communist and who at the time still worked, I believe, for the *Chicago Daily News*. Its text is brief and, unlike that of Anna Louise Strong, carries no special "message." It takes up less than two pages in Mao's works and deals only with the abortive American attempt at mediation between Nationalists and Communists and the eventual future of the Chinese civil war. The interview totals three questions and three answers. The Strong interview contains seven questions and seven answers. The Strong questions are brief—fifteen lines of print. Mao's replies are elaborate—one hundred and ten lines. Arch Steele is just part of the setting. Mrs. Strong is a member of the set and of the staff. Steele asked to be received. Mrs. Strong was summoned.

I cannot think of her and her associates without seeing in my mind's eye a sort of Red baize door behind which they would have their quarters, and assemble and take their meals together, deeply united in their devotion to the great house in which they serve and their love of the Master.

I do not know the exact number of China's Old Retainers. In one of her *Letters from China* (letter number five), Mrs. Strong mentions a few who contributed to it. She writes:

* I have purposely left out those few who, for some reason or other, are staying in China because if they went home they might run into trouble for reasons other than their political opinions.

The friends who have helped me with this "New Year" letter are *Israel* and *Elsie Epstein*, formerly of New York, writers
and editors in Peking; *Sidney Rittenberg*, formerly of Charles-
ton, S.C., Palo Alto and Yenan, now in radio work in Peking
and father of three beautiful little girls; *Rewi Alley*, famous
New Zealand author and cooperator, my neighbour here;
Talitha Gerlach, for many years with the YWCA in the U.S.
and China and *Gerald Tannebaum* of Baltimore, both now
with the China Welfare Institute, Shanghai; and two other
Americans, *Joan Hinton*, working on a big livestock farm
outside Sian, and *Shirley Wood*, college teacher and mother of
six in Kaifeng. (Jan. 12, 1963) *

Israel and Elsie Epstein, the former Elsie Fairfax-Cholmeley, I
have personally known for many years, and I saw a good deal of
them in Peking. "Eppy" is the only professional journalist of the
whole team, but it is not quite true that he is "formerly of New
York." Even though he was in fact educated in the U.S., he was
never an American, which indeed I believed him to be until he
told me otherwise. When we first met in Hankow in 1938, he was
working for United Press. He is of Polish or Russian origin and
remained stateless until he took out Chinese papers. He happened
to be in Hong Kong at the time of Pearl Harbor and was interned
by the Japanese after the fall of the island. He escaped from Stan-
ley—no mean feat!—taking with him another internee, Elsie.
Once they had reached the mainland, enemy-occupied, of course,
guerrillas helped them make their way to Free China, after which
proceeding to Chungking was plain sailing. Later, they moved
on to Yenan. They were married in China. Sometime after Liberation, they went to Peking and have been working there ever
since on English language Chinese publications such as the pic-
torial *China Reconstructs*. Eppy has written a book, *From Opium
War to Liberation*, which is informative and contains passages
which he would probably not think of writing now; at any rate
they would not pass the censor and he, in his perfect candor,
probably does not even remember having once written them.
But, to the actual texts, Epstein's and other's, I shall come back
later.

Elsie Epstein is not, as far as I know, "formerly of New York."
She is English, and very English at that. She has kept her British

* *Letters from China* (Peking: New World Press, 1963), Vol. I, p. 28.

passport and has not let her national status go native. Occasionally, Chinese as Epstein now is, they take a holiday abroad and visit Elsie's very "county" family in England. From such forays, they return more than ever convinced that Mao's China is leading the way to the future happiness of mankind. They have never looked back. They have adopted two Chinese children to whom they are devoted and who are fully as charming and affectionate as Chinese can be—and I do not mean only children.

The family lives in a small flat in one of the comparatively new red-brick blocks beyond the old city walls, in the western suburbs where foreigners who work for the Chinese government are billeted as a whole, while the diplomatic body is being moved farther and farther east, on the other side of the capital's outskirts. They have retained—off duty, at least—a refreshing sense of humor, and I remember many a happy evening in their home. I disagree with almost everything Eppy writes nowadays, but, after all, the Epsteins have made their choice and stuck to it not with forced loyalty, but with their very hearts and conscience. They have accepted a certain discipline and become converted to a certain faith. When Epstein writes about the wonderful change that has happened in Tibet, I do not for a moment think him guilty of a conscious lie. Nor do I think that he is being truthful. But he certainly thinks he is, for he is unaware that he, too, in the employ of Peking, has been taken on a conducted tour, not to say for a ride—with blinkers on. If he is at all aware that he has not been shown everything there is to see, he feels that it has been withheld from him for honorable reasons, and it would be disloyal on his part to look further. There must have been moments when it hurt his intelligence—or perhaps not. Such things are beyond dispute as is any man's idea of his own conscience.

I cannot follow the Epsteins in their philosophy—but I can also not disapprove of them. They are immensely genuine, and I wish I had not hurt Eppy's feelings as I did when I mentioned that his friend Rewy Alley was already known in Chungking in 1940 as "Screwy" Alley. Members of this small body of initiates, these High Churchmen of Mao, take themselves extremely seriously and will perpetually quote one another as unimpeachable, authoritative, and impartial sources of information, experts and judges. They tend, with the exception of the Epsteins, to be solemn, and they will remain so even and especially when they wax lyrical or lapse into political baby-talk. In verse or prose, they are atrocious writers.

I made the acquaintance of Alley in Chungking in 1940. He was then working for the Chinese Industrial Co-operatives of which Mme. Chiang Kai-shek was the nominal head, and he was a very active sort of fellow, fresh from his native New Zealand, bustling about in khaki shorts and shirt, physically the very prototype of the scoutmaster, oozing cheerfulness yet lofty thought, sublimating China of which he knew little, with already something about him of the promising evangelist who has heard the Call without quite managing to identify the Voice. He still had to meet Mao.

His official position in Peking nowadays is vague. One knows that he teaches. His name does not appear on the list of registered foreign correspondents, nor does, for that matter, that of Anna Louise Strong, the "American correspondent," but both turn up at the yearly reception which the Chinese journalists give for their foreign colleagues. Whether they appear as hosts or as guests has never been made clear. Nor do they sit at the two or three tables assigned to foreign correspondents at the very back of the huge hall when state banquets take place. The Epsteins do, though, for Eppy is the officially registered correspondent of the *National Guardian* and Elsie that of the *New World Review*, two American publications which I confess I have never seen.

Alley has signed a translation of some of Mao's poetry. The actual translation, I was told, had been the work of a Chinese team and it took a long time and a lot of work, with the usual shuttling back and forth between author and translators, with the translated text being repeatedly translated back into Chinese by especially appointed scholars so that Mao could assure himself that his meaning, literal or implied or allusive or esoteric, had not been distorted. After this, Alley put it all in poetic English of a sort, and then the whole process was started again in reverse and the imprimatur finally granted. So at least the story goes. But Rewy Alley is a poet in his own right. He will occasionally pen stanzas under such titles as "United States Budget, 1963," a poem quoted by Anna Louise in her China letter number five. Here are some excerpts:

Rulers of the world's richest
state, look over their income
reckoning how best to spend in
the coming year; shall it be
      on rockets to the moon, space
      ships, or more napalm burning
      of Vietnamese villagers; blockade,
      subversion against Cuba; looting
      a prostrate South Korea; planting
      new bases in a re-armed Japan
      or putting new spy satellites
      into orbit; pouring new billions
      to ensure India help for an
      invasion of China; paying to build
      new bases up the Amazon to keep
      Brazil's poor, poorer, or for
      a nice new nuclear base in Paraguay?

Quite a few dollars, too
are needed to provide
cushy corners for party plugs
hangers on of the shiny, plastic
Kennedy Dynasty; then there
are new fascists to be nurtured;
decision made which of the dictators
to be paid in full, which
can be bargained with.
      In all, a wide selection;
      you pay your money, they
      make their choice; you, the
      pitiful taxpayers of this
      twentieth century whose
      Struggle finances all.
                  (Peking, Nov. 20th, 1962)

Mrs. Strong herself explains in one of those letters how and
when and why she came to China and what made her stay there.*
She was in her early sixties, she tells us, when she first saw Yenan
in 1946. The first thirty years of her life had been "spent in
Western America where we fought for better forms of democ-
racy, women's suffrage, labor's participation in politics, public

* Incidentally, Mrs. Strong joined the Red Guards in 1966. Another letter
from China quoted by Peking's *Global Digest*, Vol. III, November, 1966,
issue.

ownership of utilities against the 'Wall St. Octopus.' " She was a member of the Seattle School Board and later feature editor of the *Seattle Union Record,* "a daily owned by the Central Labor Council." With this provincial background of leftist politics and journalism, Mrs. Strong went to Moscow in 1921, got married, started the English language *Moscow Daily News.* (Michael Borodin, once the adviser of Mustapha Kemal in Turkey, and later the patron, on behalf of Moscow, of the Kuomintang-Communist merger of the Twenties that ended tragically after four years of reciprocal double-crossing, was editor of that paper for a good many years after his recall to the U.S.S.R. in 1927.) She was "greatly stirred by the building of the first socialist state in the world" and she wrote, during the "nearly thirty years" that she spent there, "hundreds of articles . . . and some fifteen books."

Throughout that period, she points out, she visited the U.S. yearly, lecturing and talking business with her publishers, and "stopping in other countries on the way." It appears that she visited Spain in 1937 and China for the first time during the 1925–27 Borodin period. In August, 1946, a widow, she took her fifth trip to China, Moscow bound, and went to Yenan. She spent the whole of the winter there, living in a cave. That was the turning point. In China letter number ten, she reflects: "Can I explain why I wanted to stay forever? There were no luxuries and few comforts. There were people with keen minds, deep thoughts and a world view. I felt my own mind developing. I wrote later: 'Never have I felt so close to the human power that builds the world as in that isolated, beleaguered Yenan.' " She had already had her famous interview with Mao about the paper tigers, which metaphor she described, showing scanty knowledge of Chinese traditional figures of speech, as "a poetic way of stating an elementary principle of Marxism."

It is not my intention to write a biography of Mrs. Strong, and those readers who are interested in her tribulations with the Soviet authorities should refer to her two volumes of letters (there may be a third out by now) published by the official Peking New World Press in 1963 and 1964. They are certainly worth reading, as are the works of her fellow-retainers, for they are all extremely revealing, if not quite in the way their authors intended.

To me, they are interesting in two respects. First, they give one a fair idea of the psychology of those Westerners who fell blindly in love with Red China because they had found fulfillment there. Second, they amount to a carefully kept record of the official Chinese Communist interpretation of international developments. At the moment, it is only the psychological, emotional aspect I am trying to underline—the gushing side. Alley as a poet I have already cited. Epstein, to the best of my knowledge, sticks to prose, another reason why he should stand high in my esteem. Mrs. Strong, when called upon, does not hesitate to contribute a few cantos to a communal poetic demonstration. There was, thus, in 1962 a "Support Cuba Poetry Evening" held in Peking which was broadcast over the national network, and, on that occasion, it would seem that Mrs. Strong really went to town. This we know from one of the contributors to her letter number five, already mentioned, a Mrs. Hinton, who says that she first heard Mrs. Strong's verses over the radio, "sitting in the steam-heated guest house at Yenan," presumably taking a holiday from her steady pasteurizing of milk at a farm near Sian. And, in turn, to make this reference intelligible, Mrs. Strong obligingly proceeds to quote herself as follows:

> Yesterday
> You were the chief
> of a small, green island,
> Leader of not quite
> Seven million people.
> Today for you
> The millions march in China
> and in a hundred tongues
> they hail your name.
> Today you are the Voice
> of the Three Continents,
> The Thunder of History
> Down the Ages,
> The fighting SHOUT
> Of men against Aggressors,
> In all times and lands,
> For the RIGHTS,
> Inalienable,
> Of MAN!

This is one typical example of the mutual admiration spirit that prevails among that small group of initiates. This admiration is genuine and essential. If it did not exist, they could not face one another. They could not look at themselves in the mirror. Perhaps, they could not stand the sight of Mao, which, anyway, they seldom behold.

I must however go back to the same letter number five and quote yet another of its several contributors, Sidney Rittenberg. This particular letter was written at a time when Peking was using the Cuban crisis for everything it was worth in the way of propaganda.

Rittenberg's piece thus bears the title " 'Cuba Time' in Peking," and here are bits of it:

Yes, "every day in every way, things get better and better." Though, strange to say, that isn't what you hear most talked about—it's Cuba. The whole country is in the midst of a ten-day celebration, in which seven hundred million Asians take their collective hat off to seven million Americans (in the broad and original sense of the word), who have looked the Paper Tiger of Wall Street straight in his nuclear teeth, and by their magnificent courage and unity saved their country from invasion.

I remember one November afternoon when Yü-Lin and I, hurrying across town to a friend's house, ran into column after column of Peking people moving out onto the streets. "Listen," said Yü-Lin. "Slogans in Spanish." And she was right— "Cuba Sí, Yankee No," shouted the marching young people, workers and women's groups. . . .

And back in our apartment, not long ago, the following little drama was enacted. I call it, "Out of the Mouths of Babes . . ."

Scene: Our home. Myself and 5-year-old daughter, "Little Pusher," just home from kindergarten, sitting cross-legged on a Ming table (dating from Columbus-was-a-pup days), looking at the full spread portrait of Fidel Castro on the cover of her mother's *Youth of China* magazine.

Me: "Do you know who that is?"

LP: (*Loftily*) "Who doesn't know who that is!"

Me: "Well, who is it?"

LP: "It's Ca-ss-te-lo."

Me: "And who is he?"

LP: (*Patiently*) "He's the Chairman Mao of Cuba."

Me: "And what is Cuba?"

LP: "It's a little country of brave people. . . ."

Me: "Where?"

LP: ". . . ."

Me: "Don't you know where Cuba is?"

LP: (*Humiliated silence*)

Me: "Cuba's right next to the United States, don't you know that?" (*A nod in response.*) "It's an island, darling—the whole country is just one island. Do you know what an island is?" (*Vigorous head-shake, business of raising head and placing turned-up nose in position to receive new knowledge.*) "Well, an island is . . ."

And that's *how our child found out about islands.*

I have met Rittenberg a few times, and I could have met him oftener. He was comparatively easy to get hold of and was a personal friend of my predecessor in Peking, himself a China enthusiast. But one grows very tired of hearing the same unmistakably predictable litanies, for they add nothing to what the local press has already forcibly brought to one's notice, and the simple fact that they are being recited by foreigners, and in perfect good faith, makes their constant repetition even harder to bear. It is always difficult for an agnostic to discuss God with a priest, yet with most priests there remain many other subjects of conversation and they are often remarkably cultivated and broad-minded people. But with the Peking Janissaries, everything either comes back to Chinese infallibility or is interpreted and commented upon in the light of Mao's thinking. I have never found Mao's thinking particularly luminous and therefore not particularly enlightening. And their unquestioning belief in the local fairy tales is irksome. Here is another instance, still culled from Mrs. Strong's invaluable *Letters.* It is still about Cuba, no longer about Castro, but about the hurricane that hit that country in October, 1963.

As the heroic Cubans plunged fiercely into the fight to rebuild the ruin left by the Oct. 4th–8th hurricane, help began to come from lands around the world. China surprised everyone by the speed with which her first 9,059 tons of rice reached Santiago port on the 19th, indicating some magic or good foreign contacts for ships cannot make Cuba from China in two weeks.*

It is of course quite true that ships cannot make the China-to-Cuba run in a fortnight. The rice China sent to Havana was not home-grown and had never been anywhere near the Chinese shores. Moreover, China, still only recovering from her three years of natural calamities, was not in a position to export grain, whether rice or wheat. Still, according to an announcement made by Chou En-lai on October 16 of that year, Chinese grain relief to Cuba finally came to a total of fifty thousand tons. There was much speculation as to whence the wheat came. Some said South Africa (which Peking denied); others mentioned other and more acceptable sources. I have reasons to believe that it was in fact Algerian grain, rebought from France.

Mrs. Strong further mentions that Chinese help to Cuba, on that one particular occasion, was "estimated at 30 million U.S. dollars by foreigners here." Reluctant Peking assistance to the "revisionist" Yugoslavs after the Skoplje earthquake, according to Red Cross figures, was twenty-five thousand yuans (roughly $5,000). The Vaiont dam catastrophe, which occurred in the same month as the Cuba hurricane, was not mentioned in the Chinese press and it seems that the Italian victims of that catastrophe, workers and peasants all, did not deserve a word of condolence from China. There might have been a different story to tell had Togliatti, the leader of the Italian Communist Party, toed the Peking line.

The political importance—and, indeed, value—of the Old Retainers' writings is not something I want to go into now. What I am trying to clarify is the attitude and the mental reactions of the writers. In another piece, Mrs. Strong mentions a letter from Sid Rittenberg who was "travelling south by fast express—only half a dozen stops from Peking to Wuhan." The rail journey between these two points covers some six hundred and fifty miles in about twenty-four hours. The train does a little over 26 m.p.h., counting the rather long stops. That is the author's "fast express." And I am in my heart convinced that if she happened to be traveling in the U.S.A., for instance, on a train with an equivalent rate of speed, she would describe it as slow; to her, nowhere in the world do trains run as fast as they do in China. "See no evil, hear no

* *Ibid.*, Vol. II, p. 24.

evil, speak no evil" seems to be the Old Retainers' motto. But only, of course, in reference to the country of their worship.

When some African country expells Chinese agitators and denounces Peking subversion, they shake with indignation at such "high-handedness." When the Prague government chooses to close down the Hsinhua Agency bureau and so cut Peking's European propaganda pipeline to Cuba,* they are up in arms again, and Anna Louise Strong is moved to an even more frequent penning of words in CAPITALS only. Chinese genocide in Tibet, of which they are bound to know, none of them will mention, let alone condemn. They are not mere idealists, lovers of social and political justice, lovers of mankind, haters of oppression. They are essentially sinomaniacs.

* Until the Hsinhua bureau in Prague was shut by the Czechoslovakian authorities, it enjoyed direct and private wire communications with the Agency's Havana bureau. It stands to reason that these were not used for the transmission of press messages only. There was also, of course, an equally private line between Peking and Prague which made the latter capital and that of Havana the two relays for Chinese propaganda and subversion in Latin America.

19

FISHFACE AND THE DRAGON

BROADCASTING HOUSE I had not been permitted to visit. Even the
premises of the *People's Daily* I could not enter. That, coming on
top of a good number of other "no-can-do's," had put me in a
filthy temper that day. For some time past, and rather out of
sheer exasperation, I had been toying with the idea of writing a
book. It was not going to be one of those magistral volumes
which can only be done by those who pass through. It had occurred to me that, travel being out, interviews being unthinkable,
and only snatches of information available here and there and
very occasionally, a good title might be "Peacock Feathers," with
implied reference to the ancient Mandarin's badge of office, a
feather off a peacock's tail. Also to be subtly suggested was the
picture of someone running after an elusive bird, if a rather
pedestrian one, and never able to get hold of more than a bit of
fundamental plumage. Fishface altered that slightly.

There was an official banquet that night in the honor, I believe,
of that faithful client, Norodom Sihanouk, and no sooner had I
entered the Great Hall of the People than Fishface disentangled
himself from the group of which he was the life and soul, and
sped toward me, maotai propelled, and began pouring the oil he
unfailingly lavished upon my troubled waters whenever required.
He would never mention my difficulties, but there was no doubt
that he always knew of them.

"Mr. Marcuse, are you happy?"

That was his invariable gambit.

"Not altogether," I said.

"If there is anything that you want to do or to see, all you have
to do is let us know," said Fishface mendaciously.

"I am beginning to wonder," I said.

"We are entirely at your disposal," said Fishface. "Now tell me if there is anything you want to see in particular."

"I," I said, "want to see a dragon."

"A dragon?"

"Certainly. China is famous for her dragons. The whole world speaks of Chinese dragons. They have been famous for centuries. The best dragons come from China. In point of fact, all dragons come from China. But I have never seen one."

Fishface bristled all over. He made horrified gestures. His hair tried to stand on end but brilliantine stood firm. Could I but have set his maotai breath aflame, he would have been spouting fire and my wish to see a dragon would have been gratified. But my box of matches, as Chinese matchboxes will, had fallen apart in my pocket, and it is doubtful whether I should have been able to draw a spark from its contents in any case.

Fishface spoke with great firmness. "You cannot see a dragon," he stated.

"But you just said I only had to ask."

"You can see everything that exists. Dragons do not exist."

"Does Broadcasting House exist?"

"Certainly."

"Does the *People's Daily* exist?"

"Certainly."

"I have not been permitted to see either."

"You would have found no dragon there," said Fishface, neatly sidestepping the issue.

He shook his head sadly and proceeded: "It hurts us to have to disappoint our foreign friends. Perhaps you would like to visit the 'Evergreen' People's Commune. That could be arranged quite easily. They breed fine horses there. I hear you are a horseman yourself."

"Could I ride one?" I asked with sudden hope.

"I shall make inquiries. But I think that foreigners are no longer permitted to ride horses in Peking. The time is past when the imperialists could ride roughshod all over the Chinese people."

"Let us forget about riding, then. Could I have a swim in the magnificent pool in the People's Stadium? I understand that the commercial attaché of the Swiss embassy, Mr. Wild, who suffers from a slipped disk, has been advised by his doctor to swim as much as possible and that he has been refused permission."

"I am not surprised," said Fishface severely. "The time is past when the imperalists could swim roughshod over the Chinese people."

"Very well, then," I said, "but still, may I see a dragon? I promise not to try to ride it, or swim it, not even smooth-shod."

"It causes us great sorrow," Fishface said sadly, "to see our foreign friends still imbued with superstitions which the Chinese Communist Party, under the luminous guidance of Chairman Mao, successfully exploded in this country quite a long time ago already. I must quite honestly tell you that there are no dragons."

"Extinct?"

"I must inform you, in my official capacity," Fishface said, "that there are no dragons and that dragons never existed. People once believed in them and there were, they thought, all kinds of dragons, including the bobtailed dragon on which typhoons were blamed."

"But," I said, "the dragon has traditionally been known as the symbol of Imperial Power in China."

"That is so," retorted Fishface, "but only the five-clawed dragon. The people's dragons had but four claws. It just goes to show that the power of those past oppressors of the masses was based on both popular superstition and social injustice. The tidal wave of the People's Revolution has swept it all away. Besides, an interview with Chairman Mao is very difficult to arrange."

"But dragons," I insisted, "what about dragons? I want to see a dragon. I am not particular about the claws."

"There have never been any dragons," Fishface said sternly. "The belief in such supernatural creatures was encouraged in feudal days in order to keep the toiling workers and peasants of China under the thumb of their exploiters. Dragons, let me assure you, never existed. The emperors encouraged the unenlightened proletariat to believe in the existence of such creatures of fancy and to fear them. It was very cunning. If the people could be made to think that the all-powerful dragon was on the side of the reactionary authorities, then of course it became much easier to keep them subdued. And cheaper, too. One dragon took the place of a thousand soldiers. And, mind you, no pay, no uniforms, no rice rations, no expensive weapons, no upkeep whatever. A useful fallacy, as you may gather."

"So," I said, "no dragons?"

"No dragons, no dragons. Never. Merely a popular superstition with ulterior motives."

"Well," I said, "that is a great blow to me."

"Why?" asked Fishface.

"Because," I lied, "I was thinking of writing a book on China and I had intended to call it 'Dragon Feathers.' "

"You must not do that!" said Fishface aghast.

"Why not?"

"Because no educated man will take it seriously," said Fishface.

"Why not?"

"Because everybody knows," said Fishface, "that dragons have no feathers."

"Are you still determined," asked Fishface a few weeks later, "to call your book 'Dragon Feathers'? I am more than ever convinced that it is not a good title.* I told you why before. Do not tell me that, since we discussed it last, you have met a dragon."

"I cannot say I have."

"Then you are bound to realize that there are no dragons."

"If I assumed that whatever or whomsoever I have not been able to see or meet in China is nonexistent, I should have to look upon your country as thoroughly barren and underpopulated."

"You cannot say that, for you have noticed yourself that the climate of Peking has changed, that the old 'yellow wind,' as it used to be called, no longer blows from the Gobi desert in the spring, and I remember your putting this down to the extensive protective tree belt which we have planted on our northwestern border. You went so far as to write that it was only in the fields of afforestation and agriculture generally that our Great Leap Forward had been successful."

"I went further than that," I replied. "I said that, had you concentrated on agriculture, instead of wasting your time on premature industrial ventures, China would be prosperous today. Moreover, I happen to know now that the first trees were planted by the Russians *inside* the Mongolian border. I understand that you

* Later, much to my regret, my publishers fully agreed with Fishface.

have reinforced the protective belt on your own side but I am hardly in a position to vouch for it personally since foreign journalists are not allowed there, except to cross it, traveling on the Chinese branch of the Trans-Siberian railway."

Fishface ignored this. "You do not think that China is prosperous today?" he asked.

"No."

"If you will forgive me, that is not a polite thing to say."

"Is it not true?"

"How can it be true if it is not polite?"

20

LIMITED LITERACY

❧❧❧

MUCH is made of the regime's efforts to teach the common people how to read and write and of the great success achieved in the field of public education. Seventy percent of the population are now supposed to be literate and all children to go to school. If that is still an exaggeration, it may no longer be one in a few years, after more schools are built and more teachers trained. Meanwhile, it would be interesting to know how many characters, and precisely *what* characters, the Chinese schoolteacher knows.

At the turn of the century, the Chinese script was made up of a total of 23,863 characters. At least, that figure was the official and traditional one and nobody questioned it, even though not even such an exemplary scholar as Dr. Hu Shih, now in the United States, claimed to be able to understand them all. Now, of course, many new terms, political and technical, have been added. They are combinations of existing ideograms, not original creations.

As to the number of characters a student is supposed to have mastered before he can pass his literacy test, figures vary and official texts of the present day often conflict. One may safely assume that it is somewhere between 1,500 and 1,800, and the requirements may still not be the same in the towns and the countryside. They learn enough, at any rate, to write letters and read the newspaper. The question is: what newspaper?

Fifteen hundred characters is more than one needs to go through the columns of the Peking *Workers' Daily*, which uses only twelve hundred, and, of course, the *Youth Daily* and the *Youth Weekly*, which are written in even simpler language. It certainly is not sufficient to assimilate the elaborate editorials of the *People's Daily*, which is actually the organ of the aristocracy (in the etymological sense), of the best people, of the more politically mature, whose vocabulary, if very specialized, is infinitely richer than that of the common man.

It is certainly not good enough to read Mao Tse-tung's prose (even though everyone without exception is urged to study it as the source of all wisdom) and quite useless when one comes to his poems, as they are for the most part so cryptic and so full of classical allusions as to be almost unintelligible. They often baffle the official staff of learned clerks appointed to translate them.

Early in 1964, a slim new volume of Mao's stanzas was released in Peking in the Chinese original. Its appearance at the very height of the Sino-Soviet controversy was not thought by anyone to be fortuitous. There must be a political significance.

Reading between the lines of Chinese prose had been the chief occupation of foreign observers, not only because it proved easier than reading the actual lines when one lacked the necessary linguistic knowledge, but also because the official versions in foreign languages, as distributed by the Department of Information, did not always tally with those produced by privately employed translators. The stenciled English and French texts, for instance, seldom tallied. Those sinologists whose mother tongue was French or English described them as inaccurate. East European nationals said the Russian version was deliberately tendentious. My own view is that discrepancies were entirely due to language difficulties.

So far, however, we had been concerned only with prose. Reading between lines of poetry was quite another thing.

There was no translation available in any language. The book was reported to be an immediate best-seller. It included twenty-seven poems which had already appeared in previous years in one periodical or another and ten unpublished ones. Even these were not really new. The first, chronologically, had been inspired by the fall of Nanking and was dated April, 1949, and the most recent, January, 1963. All ten took up a full page of the *People's Daily*. There was not one word of comment. Literary critics do not touch Mao, not even to praise him. Perhaps they do not know all the characters.

It was in the columns of the Hong Kong Communist daily

Wen Hui Pao that the controversy arose over the hidden meaning of some of the Leader's images. It is to be noted that Chinese Communist journalists enjoy much greater freedom of expression in Hong Kong than on what the Americans call "the mainland" (to keep Chiang Kai-shek happy), and that they make occasional use of it, not to criticize, but to display that sort of individual zeal which would not be tolerated in Peking. As it was, writing to the *Wen Hui Pao,* one distinguished mandarin claimed that American imperialism was being pilloried. Another, two days later, called him an ignoramus. To him, it was plain that Mao's most scathing metaphors were aimed at modern revisionists and, very particularly, at Mr. Khrushchev. Then we Peking foreigners got busy. Rather, we put our translators to work. They did not like the job, and nobody could blame them for not liking it. They were not quite sure that it came within their legitimate attribution to interpret Mao or that they would not be reprimanded if they did. Nor did they want to turn it down flat and prove uncooperative and perhaps be criticized for that also by the Service Bureau and for having shown suspicious reluctance. Then there was a question of face. Could they confess that Mao's verse was beyond them?

Each one of Mao's ten new poems may have had a symbolic meaning for all I know and extolled in lyrical, if esoteric, terms the victory of the Revolution over all those who had stood in its way or failed to recognize its great purpose. Mr. Ma assured me that it would take him at least a week to produce even a rough rendering of the lot. So I asked him to translate only the last in the series because it had been composed only fourteen months before publication and was therefore the only one perhaps in which a reference to the Russians might successfully be looked for. It took him the best part of a day, and I watched him occasionally from across our office. It was an awe-inspiring sight. He grew increasingly redder in the face and the folds at the back of his neck seemed to swell with the exertion. He looked like a man possessed, like a Chinese Faust trying to conjure up the Devil as he went through his dictionary at tremendous speed, occasionally muttering over its pages as if it were some cabala, or nimbly fingering his ever-present abacus from which he seemed to draw inspiration. The comparatively intelligible parts of the final version read thus:

On this small earth, tiny flies are breaking their heads against a wall, uttering mournful cries and bitter sobs. . . . Ants, climbing an acacia, boast of the importance of their realm. . . . It is hard for a lobster to shake a tree . . . withal, the four seas are stormy and the waters voice their anger. The five continents tremble, the winds howl and the heavens thunder. All insect pests must be exterminated! Not one enemy must stay alive!

This, Mr. Ma assured me, was a word-for-word, character-by-character translation, fully supported by the dictionary. The literal meaning of the poem, he said, he was unable to convey, let alone the hidden one. But was there a hidden meaning? There must be, of course. Of that, he was sure, even though he could not actually detect it, and would commit himself no further, leaving me to fend for myself in a strange world where lobster would uproot trees and flies cried and sobbed instead of going buzzbuzzbuzz like everyone else in Peking.

Those members of the diplomatic corps known as "Chinese secretaries," not that they are Chinese themselves but because of their knowledge of the Chinese language and classical literature (if not of the country itself, with which only a very few of them have previous experience), were much more positive and considered Mao's poem absolutely limpid, much as they disagreed among themselves as to its pellucid meaning. They could not translate it to me, but were of one mind about the last line. The reference to "insect pests," they pronounced, had nothing to do with gardening or even agriculture and was not to be taken as an encouragement to the rural communes to use more DDT, but held an ominous warning, unmistakable to all who could see it at all. They were unanimous that *they* could. It was as plain, they said, as the mole on the side of Mao's chin. It was obscure only to the Chinese, who couldn't even read their own language any more.

It is being claimed that, at Liberation, over sixty percent of the population was illiterate. I wonder how true that is.

In prewar Shanghai, Chinese newspapers used to sell like hotcakes and the press, at least in the foreign-run part of that city, had a much larger circulation than it has today. It also, of course, reflected a much wider range of opinion. I remember ragged coolies, sitting on the curb between the shafts of their idle rickshaws, eagerly reading the last edition of the local *Ta Kung Pao* or the *Sin Wan Pao*, which, like several other papers, printed ten times more foreign news than appears now in the pages of the *People's Daily*. I do not know how many characters they knew, but they certainly seemed to have no trouble reading not just the printed script, but also the cursive script known as "grass writing." You could hand them a piece of paper on which an address had been scribbled, and they would take you to your destination without a moment's hesitation. Try it now with any of Peking's female taxi drivers, and she will stop at every police booth, which means practically at every street corner, and produce her written instructions until she finds one where it will not be misread and she misdirected.

In those days, the standard of literacy seemed quite as high in other big towns. I saw common people display the same interest in the daily paper in Canton, Hankow, and Peking, and later even in faraway Chungking when the press was strictly controlled and censored by the Kuomintang government, but it made no less interesting reading because it was full of glowing accounts of, at first, not altogether authentic victories over Japan. Things were of course different in the countryside where newspapers did not penetrate, but, in the unoccupied provinces of central China through which I traveled extensively during the war years, I seldom saw a village that could not boast of a school. You could not possibly miss the schools, because the pupils were all reciting their lessons in unison, their small but piercing voices sounding like one, and the din was terrific.

The primer that was used to teach the children how to read and write was still the old *San Tzu Ching*, dating back to the thirteenth century and containing some five hundred characters arranged in rhyming lines of three. The first two lines ran: "Men at their birth are good by nature." I believe the Communists have discarded it.

It may well be that total illiteracy prevailed in remoter parts of the interior. Yet Father Evariste Huc, who spent fourteen years of his life traveling through the length and breadth of "Tartary, Tibet and China" and who was a remarkably good reporter in his way, wrote *circa* 1850 that China was "undoubtedly the country in the whole world where primary education is the most widespread," adding "there is scarcely one small village, not even a hamlet of a few farm-houses, where a school-teacher is not to be met. . . . With a few exceptions, all Chinese know how to read and write, sufficiently well, at least, for the needs of everyday life. Thus, workers and even peasants are able to jot down their daily business on little note-books, to write their own letters, to read the almanac, the notices and proclamations put up by the mandarins and often the productions of current literature. Primary education penetrates even those floating homes which cover, in their thousands, the rivers, lakes and canals of the Celestial Empire. On these little boats, one is always sure to find an ink-stand, brushes, an abacus, an almanac and some books with which these poor bargemen amuse themselves in their moments of leisure."

I see no reason to doubt Huc's good faith. He was very critical of the Chinese in other respects and would hardly have departed from the truth in order to praise them in a book that was not likely ever to fall into their hands. It is also improbable that the present regime will have his works translated into Chinese for the enlightenment of the masses. The Chinese schoolchild of today is convinced, as he should be, that his ancestors never knew one character from another and that the benefit of literacy is bestowed upon the nation for the first time in its history as the result of an unprecedented initiative of the Party and its great leader. In feudal days, as I was told, it was the privilege of the ruling class and so a means of oppressing the people. How this form of oppression worked was not explained.

In the West, literacy is all of one piece. We have an alphabet. Once, as children, we have mastered it, there may be words we cannot understand, but none that we cannot decipher, none that remains *soundless*. Faced with an unknown symbol, composed as it may be of two or more simpler and vocally intelligible ones, and whose separate meanings are clear, a Chinese may remain speechless. This is an asset to a system under which freedom of utterance is not encouraged. Controlled literacy curtails possibilities of written expression and, in the long run, of spoken expression also, and of thought. You cannot criticize (to put things in an extreme form) when you only know words of praise. There are, of course, words of contempt and abuse, and one must be able to read them, for they apply to the enemy. They belong to the vast thesaurus of slogans to which the Party adds and subtracts as the political need arises, and they are not to be used outside of their approved context. Officially, you may be called a "running dog of the imperialists" to your face. You must not take offense, for it is just a phrase. It indicates displeasure at your attitude, and will be used by authorized persons only. Nobody would ever dream of calling you simply a dog, or be permitted to, for that would be impolite and, what is worse, personal.

The more involved slogans which are to be shouted forth by the people in the course of mass demonstrations are all carefully rehearsed. They are taught strictly orally to those who will use them (and then only when called upon to do so in unison, at a word of command from their leaders) and only shown them in writing after their *sounds* have been fully mastered, and they can then be recognized rather than read when they appear in the form of huge posters (usually in shining gilt or white characters upon a red background) put up all over the city. I once went around Peking with my driver, a bright young lad who spent most of his time in my kitchen studying the writings of Mao Tse-tung, widely circulated in booklet form and in a much simplified text *ad usum populi*, at the time of the Panamanian crisis. We stopped in front of a large streamer inscribed with some ten characters that hung before the Peking headquarters of the Communist Party, across the street from the International Club. The following dialogue took place:

"What does it say?" I asked.

Without hesitation, he replied: "American Colonialists, get out of Panama!"

Then I pointed to the fifth character from the left and asked what that one meant, taken by itself.

He said: "American Colonialists, get out of Panama!"

"No," I pointed out. "That is the whole sentence. What I am asking you to tell me is the meaning of that particular character."

"American Colonialists, get out of Panama!"

"What about the last character, the one that has about ten strokes?"

"American Colonialists, get out of Panama!"

That happened to be a character I had good reason to know well. In its own right, it means "horse." It can also, like other characters, be used strictly phonetically as, incidentally, in the word "Panama." It is pronounced "ma," in the third tone. It is the first character of my name, in Chinese. It is also the first of the name of the prophet Mahomet, and most Chinese Moslems are therefore called "Ma." My own translator, the one who took such pains over Mao Tse-tung's poem, was a Mussulman and his name was Ma. Moreover, despite its nine strokes, it is a simple character which everyone can read and write. I tried again.

"Do you know my name?"

"You are Mr. Ma."

"Would you mind writing it down?"

He did so, just to humor me, after I had produced notebook and pencil.

"And our Mr. Ma in the office?"

"His name is the same as yours."

"Same character?"

"Same."

"How do you say 'a horse' in Chinese?"

"*I ko ma.*"

"How do you write this 'ma'?"

"Same character again."

"Now isn't that the very character you see at the end of the slogan?"

"It is."

"What does it mean?"

"American Colonialists, get out of Panama."

This war of nerves was getting the better of me. I made one last attempt.

"Well, if all the characters in that one single sentence mean the same thing, why are there so many of them?"

"You read it yourself."

"It says: 'American Colonialists, get out of Panama!'" I announced unguardedly, my well-washed subconscious taking over.

"You know Chinese very well," he remarked, driving off.

But later, he told the cook, for whom he was peeling potatoes, that I thought all slogans in Peking were about me and I must be suffering from delusions of grandeur.

It is easy to see where literacy begins. Now as before, it begins with the simpler characters, and so, of course, it must. What is difficult is to know where it ends, where, in that tremendously rich universe of the Chinese written word, the "No Trespassing" line is drawn.

It stands to reason that a man who has been taught fifteen hundred characters can only read a text written in the same number of characters and not just in any selection of fifteen hundred characters but strictly in those which he has learned. The same applies, of course, to him who has the command of two, or three, or four thousand characters. More words can be acquired by means of a dictionary, one simple "key" word leading to many, more complicated derivatives (which cannot, however, be spoken by the untutored for their actual *sounds* remain perforce a mystery until questions are put to the more advanced, and one does not like to display curiosity, not even in the apparently harmless field of philology), and by discreet research. The new dictionaries, however, are few and not overinformative, except for the numerous technical ones that deal each with one given branch of modern science and are made up almost entirely of neologisms and improvised Chinese equivalents of foreign terms. Also, the old characters have been "simplified" and it is only in this modernized form that they are now being taught. They will not help the coming generation to read the classics, nor are they meant to, or to make use of the ancient dictionaries, once models of lexicography, which are becoming less and less intelligible to the common man. There are still, of course, many true scholars in China, and more are being trained, but their work, like all other forms of research, is strictly directed, controlled, and supervised by the state and made entirely utilitarian. It is not designed to broaden the mind, but to perfect the word tools by means of which the mind can be better kept within its appointed channels.

The simple literature put in the hands of the masses is composed almost exclusively of set phrases, formulas, and slogans, repeated *ad nauseam* until they become so familiar that they no longer have to be read. They are clichés in the original sense of the expression, graphic entities that are to be recognized at one glance, not deciphered character by character. When adopted as official watchwords, they are usually numbered to make them even easier to memorize. They teach you what to do and what not to do, what to love and what to hate. In 1952, for instance, three years after Liberation, the Party launched the "Three

Anti" campaign against corruption, wastefulness, and bureaucracy (the latter "anti" seems to have remained dead letter to this very day), and soon afterwards came the "Five Anti" movement, and both swept the country. There have been sets of "principles," also neatly provided with numbers. In recent years, much praise was lavished on the "Good Four" Company of Nanking Road, a military unit stationed in Shanghai which specialized in the practice of four virtues, including a remarkable invulnerability to what was described as "sugar-coated bullets," meaning the temptations of the flesh, as they patrolled an area supposedly vice-ridden, but which, in fact, had already been thoroughly pasteurized by Madame Chiang's "New Life Movement" years before the Communist takeover. The "Good Four" slogans became part of the national catechism. Everyone in schools, universities, factories, offices, and people's communes had to learn them by heart, and they were displayed in writing everywhere. Even I, who cannot read Chinese, could spot them with absolute certainty wherever I saw them on posters and banners.

Didactic literature is couched in the plainest possible words and moves from one point to the next with incontrovertible elementary logic. The most typical sample of this style is perhaps to be found in the opening three sentences of Mao Tse-tung's "Problems of Strategy in China's Revolutionary War," a series of lectures he made before the Red Army College in Yenan in 1936, now available in booklet form. They read:

> The laws of war are a problem which anyone directing a war must study and solve.
> The laws of revolutionary war are a problem which anyone directing a revolutionary war must study and solve.
> The laws of China's revolutionary war are a problem which anyone directing China's revolutionary war must study and solve.*
> Which nobody can deny.

The higher one rises in the Party hierarchy, the more versed one becomes in the written language and, as one gets more proficient in the technique of dialectics, the larger one's vocabu-

---

* This quotation is from the official English version, published in Peking by the Foreign Languages Publishing Organization, 1962.

lary grows. Discussion, in spite of what is claimed, is not every-body's right, but the privilege of a carefully trained and dis-ciplined few. Now, just as under the old emperors, there are degrees in literacy, and one keeps graduating on as the mandarins did, even though peacock or raven feathers are no longer worn as badges of rank and office, any more than buttons of different colors on top of the official hat. They would look odd on the blue denim proletarian cap. But the pattern is there and the tradition, and, I venture to say, the unchanging spirit. The system—much more typically Chinese, to my mind, than typically Marxist—is still basically what it was centuries ago when literacy and moral training went side by side. J. Dyer Ball, in his *Things Chinese*, written about 1860, quotes without naming him another foreign author as expressing the opinion that, while the system has "considerable educative value," it yet "limits the mental and moral vision to the horizon which confined the mind of Con-fucius twenty-four centuries ago, cramps the intellect, stunts the growth of moral feeling, and bends the will to an antagonism to everything non-Chinese." Dyer Ball himself writes it represented "a marvellous training of the memory" and encouraged an "ex-traordinary development of the imitative faculty," but left "no originality, no scope for individuality." Elsewhere, he points out that a Chinese student after studying "for four or five years" the *names* of many Chinese characters still sees the great majority of them as "meaningless signs."

Plus ça change, plus c'est la même chose, as a Frenchman said, who had never seen China.

21

MINOR KEY

Iᴛ was expected that the Industrial Fair would be a success. After the first week—and it was to go on for two more—it was estimated that a daily average of ten thousand people had visited it. Not just any ten thousand. There was no question of the man in the street walking in on the spur of the moment. But students and workers would be taken to view it by their respective college and factory authorities. Foreign experts gave lectures to a hand picked Chinese audience of scientists on more than twenty highly technical subjects. It was one of several Western exhibitions held in Peking during 1964 and it featured precision instruments. Most of them did. The Chinese seemed to have an unquenchable thirst for intricate scientific knowledge and to be as keenly interested in precision instruments as in chemical fertilizer plants, several of which were already being built for them by various experts from the capitalistic, imperialistic West and from "American-dominated" Japan.

"They are very eager to buy," the director of the exhibition told me in his room at the Hsin Chiao Hotel, "but they are very suspicious."

"What of?"

"Of our good faith in all things. Of course, they always think that we are overcharging them and they try to beat us down to their figure. They will haggle for hours. They say that our prices are not competitive and that they could buy the same equipment much cheaper from the Japs. The only answer to that is: 'Why don't you?' It usually clinches the matter.

"Also, they are obsessed with the suspicion that we are forever attempting to pawn off obsolete stuff on them. Which we do not.

They always want the very latest, and it is very hard to convince them that we are offering them precisely that. I suppose that, if the parts were reversed, *they* would not."

"Perhaps they have been told about those happy-go-lucky days after World War I when the Powers were selling China airplanes that wouldn't fly and guns that wouldn't shoot," I suggested.

"That was before my time," the director pointed out virtuously, "but, of course, it may be that. Of course, in a way they are quite absurd. We *do* sell them the very latest we have but, have no illusions about that, what they are buying is, to them, prototypes. By the time they have succeeded in copying the original article and put it in use, it *will* have become outdated.

"There is another difficulty," he went on. "Since they will seldom tell us what they want the machinery for, and ask for advice nevertheless, one does not really know how to go about it. They may give one a vague idea, but if one begins asking precise questions, they shut up like so many clams and make us feel that we are a bunch of spies. But they certainly have a fixation about precision instruments. My personal feeling is that if one of these chaps wanted to buy himself a suit-length of cloth, he would never measure it with a three-bob yardstick; he would try to do it with the last word in electronic precision measuring apparatus designed, naturally, for quite another purpose, down to a millionth of an inch, regardless of cost."

I thought this over and asked one last question: "Tell me. About all these various precision instruments which you and others from the West are equipping China with. Are they not a help to her in, for instance, nuclear research and, incidentally, in manufacturing atom bombs bigger and better than the one which is supposed to be exploded any day now?"

"A help?" said the director, looking as if I had accused him of selling peanuts. "A help? My dear fellow, they are *essential*."

22

THE ANALECTS OF FISHFACE II

᠁

"I AM deeply worried, Mr. Marcuse," said Fishface, trying hard to look deeply worried. "I understand that you are not happy in Peking."

I was not prepared to discuss my professional problems with Fishface. The Information Department knew all about them and was not doing anything to find a solution. Mrs. Chen had just made it clear that it was very wrong of me to have problems. In fact, she had said, I had no problems. And by merely suggesting that I might have any, I had been insulting the Information Department, which meant the Waichiaopu, of which it was a branch, and therefore the Foreign Minister, Marshal Chen Yi, who was very fond of me, and through him the Chinese government, and through the Chinese government, the Party, which was above it, and so Chairman Mao himself, the beloved leader and guide of the Chinese people, and by way of consequence, the Chinese people as a whole.

I had pointed out that the exchange of press correspondents between China and France was supposed to be a matter of strict reciprocity and that, surely, the Hsinhua correspondents in Paris were enjoying freedoms and privileges that were denied me in Peking, where I was cooped up, whereas my Chinese opposite numbers were at liberty to travel all over France. Mrs. Chen had coolly replied that French regulations were governing the activities of Chinese correspondents there just as Chinese regulations were governing mine here and that, therefore, reciprocity was complete. She had, as a parting shot, repeated (for she was, by training, nature, and inclination, essentially repetitive) that I had been insulting six hundred and fifty million Chinese. The sudden notion that Fishface might be included in that number appalled me. I would not have insulted Fishface for the world.

"When I say I," Fishface went on, "I should say we."

"We?"

"We," he said. "We, the Chinese people."

This new thought was even more appalling. It conjured up visions of peasant, workers, and intellectuals, of frontier guards in Ladakh, watching out for Indian imperialist infiltrations, of others, on the border of Sinkiang, keeping the Soviet revisionists at bay, of patrolmen in faraway Lhassa, with their submachine guns at the ready lest the Tibetans should decide to un-liberate themselves, all being distracted from their duties and leaving the fields untilled, the blast furnaces to themselves, Party literature unwritten, and China open to foreign aggression and reactionary rebellion, just because I was unhappy in Peking. At the same time it was nice to know that I was the object of such nationwide solicitude.

"We like you," Fishface went on, "and we know that you are our friend. Is anything wrong? I understand your kitchen stove is not drawing properly. Is that true?"

"It has been true for the past six months."

"It will be attended to."

"It has been attended to constantly for the past six months."

"You see?" beamed Fishface. "Wonderful service!"

The place was, of course, the Banqueting Hall, and the time was just before the banquet. Fishface took my arm and led me to a table surrounded by generals of the People's Liberation Army, who had made short work of the available small chow and were thirsting for more maotai. Some was produced by a female comrade in pigtails.

"Are you still unhappy?" asked Fishface.

"Not when I see you," I said truthfully, for Fishface was my sunshine.

"Be frank with me," said Fishface. "You know we love you."

"Well," I said bitterly, "I wish your love could be less platonic."

"We are very strict about sex," Fishface blurted out, actually blushing. "No doubt, Mrs. Marcuse will be better soon."

"My wife is in perfect health, thank you. I was speaking professionally."

"Surely," said Fishface, "you get all the newspapers. Your translator, I hope, does his job well. If not, tell us."

"He is an excellent man."

"I am glad to hear it. And, of course, you have the Hsinhua teletype in your own office. And you get all the handouts."

"But nothing else."

"What more do you want?"

"Contacts. If only official ones. Briefings. Press conferences. Even exclusive interviews, if I may suggest it."

"But," said Fishface, "you would get no more out of interviews with, let us say, Chou or Chen Yi than you get from the *People's Daily*. That is what you fail to see. The *People's Daily* is saving you a lot of trouble. You are actually in a better position than your Chinese colleagues in France, where there is no official newspaper and they have to see Cabinet Ministers personally, which is a waste of time to all concerned."

"There is the *Journal Officiel*."

"What is that?" asked Fishface, absolutely agog.

"Well, nobody actually reads it, you know."

"Ah," he said, "something like the *People's Daily!*"

"I thought everyone read the *People's Daily*."

"Of course," he said. "Through the radio."

"It isn't the same thing at all. The *Journal Officiel* does not carry general news, domestic or foreign, but, as the name implies, only *official* news."

"Ah, like the *People's Daily!*"

"No, no!"

"Or the *Ta Kung Pao?*"

"Of course not!"

"Like the *Kuang Ming Jih Pao?*"

"Nothing of the sort."

"You don't mean like the *Workers' Daily?*" he said in disgust.

"By no means. It only carries the text of new laws and of decrees promoting civil servants."

"It must be a nice paper," said Fishface. "Are you also," he added as an afterthought, "the correspondent of the *Joornahle Offeeceele?*"

"It has no correspondents anywhere," I assured him.

"Like the *People's Daily*," he said.

"Honestly," Fishface resumed, "I hear from a very good source that you are not happy."

"What source, if I may ask?"

"As a journalist, you will understand that I am not at liberty to tell."

"Am I to assume that you are yourself a member of the Information Department?"

"Mr. Marcuse, please do not try to tell me that you do not know what I do! Next, I suppose, you will say you do not even know my name."

"It must be the maotai," I said, feeling that at long last here was my chance, "but even your name escapes me at the moment."

"You are making fun of me. You are taking advantage of my advanced state of inebriation. Coming from anyone else, I should think it unkind," said Fishface in a perfectly sober voice.

"Now, as a friend, please, I beseech you, tell me if you are not happy," said Fishface.

"I am getting hungry," I said, trying to change the subject. "When is Liu [for the President of the Republic was host] coming in?"

"It is not polite," said Fishface, "even for the Chairman to rise before his guest of honor has finished talking to him. And you know . . . these Africans! . . . But why, if I may ask you again, are you not happy?"

"Well, as you said yourself before, our information comes from official texts only."

"Good!" said Fishface.

"Not to me. Not to my agency. It is all so impersonal. And these constant repetitions! So monotonous!"

"There is only one way to speak the truth," said Fishface sententiously.

"But all those clichés! All those slogans! The reader becomes tired of 'running dogs of American Imperialism,' of capitalists 'and their lackeys' trying to undo you 'by hook or by crook,' of Khrushchev revisionists 'working hand-in-glove with neo-colonialism.' Don't you see? Can't we have a little variety?"

"We have to use these phrases because the people know them. They do not actually *read* them. It is very cleverly arranged.

They are taught to look only at the first characters. They know what follows. It is simple. We must not upset them."

More maotai came over. Fishface grabbed two glasses before the generals had a chance.

"Strategy," he said.

We toasted each other with great formality, then automatically turned away from the table, pretending to drain our glasses and slyly putting them down again, barely touched, behind our respective backs.

"You are familiar with Chinese customs," said Fishface, shamelessly. "But," he went on, "what about the Western slogans?"

"What Western slogans?"

"For instance: 'The Iron Curtain.' "

"Churchill, I think."

"Yes, yes. I suppose it makes sense. As an image. But, after China's Liberation, somebody invented the 'Bamboo Curtain.' Now, does *that* make sense? A bamboo curtain is something you can walk through at will. Things are not so in China."

"You're telling me!"

"And, I suppose," said Fishface, "if Italy becomes a People's Republic before you do, then you will start a 'Noodle Curtain.' No?"

There was a brief silence and Fishface said: "I am glad to see that you are happy again."

23

ON VARIOUS FREEDOMS

THE 1954 Constitution and the few texts of law that exist—there is no real civil or penal code—seem to guarantee the individual a certain amount of freedom. Since it is the *written word* that counts, it cannot be said that these freedoms do not exist. They exist on paper, where they belong. In actual practice, they do not, which is not even surprising and not in the least bit illogical, for, in the Marxist state, rights and therefore personal liberties are forever subordinated to the superior interests of the community. These interests may change with the times and can neither be assessed nor determined by individual members of the community. That is for its guardian, the Chinese Communist Party, to do and to take whatever action circumstances may demand.

It must be made clear that whatever decision the Party takes which seems to run counter to the letter of the law does not in the least violate it. Nor does it violate its spirit, for basically legislation is enacted to protect the *community* through the individual. Nor does a Party decision alter the law. It simply has nothing whatever to do with the law. Not only is the Party above the law (just as it stands above the government), but it was actually the Party that laid it down (no matter through what agency) and with the good of the people in view, which makes it doubly sacred. One may merely suppose that its enforcement has been temporarily suspended, that contingencies are such as to have warranted the assumption of special powers by the highest authority. That these were so from the very first does not astonish anyone. It is even somehow traditionally reassuring. Laws are one thing. Legal rights are another.

There being very little hard-and-fast codified law, there are few lawyers. The profession does not pay. In a totally political state, the tribunals are political and the prisoner in the dock becomes automatically a political offender. He is therefore undefendable (for were he not guilty he would not have been charged, a miscarriage of police being unthinkable), unless a plea of insanity be submitted . . . but even that seems farfetched, for, were the defendant insane, his madness would have been detected before the trial and he would not be facing his judges now. He is therefore a reactionary, to say the least, and, of course, a self-confessed one. How can counsel dare defend an avowed enemy of the people, known to be responsible for his actions? Also, it must be mentioned that, even given the chance, no one would dream of pleading not guilty. Apart from everything else, it would not be polite.

All offenses and crimes are perforce political, but not all are so named. Officially, or at least semi-officially, there are four classes of criminals, listed here in descending order of importance:

1. Proper political criminals
2. Former landowners, capitalists, and other ex-exploiters of the people
3. Black market dealers
4. Murderers, thieves, and other such small fry.

Evidently, one can be born a criminal. This makes matters worse because, when throwing oneself on the mercy of the court, one can hardly claim to have been led astray. One was begotten astray. Being a hereditary criminal is not an extenuating circumstance that is likely to land you in the idle comfort of the padded cell, away from the rustic cesspool, but rather an aggravating one, since it is class origin that counts.

The People's Courts seldom meet. The only comparatively busy ones are the first instance courts (and this is not their technical name), for there could not be any question, no matter what words have been set on paper, of any sort of appeal to a higher court. That, too, would be impolite and therefore unthinkable. It would be even worse than that. It would imply doubt as to the wisdom of the original court that passed sentence. And such a thought would be an offense—a political one, of course, since no magistrate can hold office and no regular court sit unless they enjoy the confidence of the Party. They are thus infallible, and to doubt their infallibility would imply doubt of the Party's and so of its leadership and so of the Fuehrer and of His Thinking. One becomes worse than a lawbreaker: a *thought-breaker*. One would then graduate automatically to category one, to the rare but not envied status of official political offender. There is no escape. The mere fact that you have to appear in court as a witness (for the prosecution, as it stands to reason that nobody will be not only brave enough, or unconscious enough even, but brazen enough to speak up for a non-existing defense) is in itself awkward. It indicates that you know something about the culprit, that you have presumably known something about the culprit for a long time, and that, had you reported him before, he might not find himself where he is—indeed he might not be a culprit at all —but a reformed character. The witness will feel as guilty himself as the man accused for not affording proper succor to the victim of an accident. No one in the witness box can be entirely blameless. It works.

This will look very Marxist to the Western student of the Marxist world. It is actually very Chinese. And traditionally so. In olden days, would-be plaintiffs would think twice before they went to court, for they were subjected, as a preliminary routine, to a thorough beating, the idea being that if they considered their claim worthy of consideration and were sufficiently certain of winning their case, they would gladly put up with a spot of rough-handling (during which procedure no questions were asked, for the purpose of the mandarins was not to secure a confession but to convince themselves that they were not wasting their time—which was after all that of the Emperor!—and it is difficult to find in history a more moving example of devotion to duty). Of course, there was in those days no ideological or disciplinary motive brought in. But the result was the same, and it was this: people were reluctant to go to court, either as plaintiffs or witnesses (witnesses suffered similar treatment), because, no matter how sound one's case happened to be, there was an ordeal to go through. Most disputes were settled out of court. But here the simile ends.

There are no preliminary beatings any more. There is preliminary suspicion instead. Cases can only be settled out of court with some sort of official sanction. There is absolutely no question, in any private litigation, of a compromise being achieved by person-to-person agreement. The official tribunals delegate their functions to the various committees, whether of the Street or the Factory or the Corporation or the University or, of course, the People's Commune, to handle most cases. These arbitrary committees seem to wield extensive powers. I know of a good many cases that were handled by them and of people being actually "sentenced" to various stretches of hard labor. Again, there is no appeal: it is considered an administrative matter. No text of law is ever invoked. It is there, though, inviolate, and for everyone to read. It is essentially symbolic, a symbol of the freedom of the Chinese people. The Chinese people know better than ever to refer to it in times of legal trouble. The old saying still stands: "If you want to get out of your trouble, don't bring your trouble into court."

There are many freedoms. There is the freedom to praise Mao. If you criticize Mao, then you criticize, by way of implication, the laws that were enacted under his wise guidance and so turn yourself into an outlaw. You are free to do as you are told and to go where you are sent and to stay where you are put and to do the job you are appointed to do. If you deny yourself the benefit of these various freedoms, then, obviously, you do not deserve to enjoy them and can no longer claim their benefits. If you refuse to be liberated, then it stands to reason that you must be restrained lest the reactionary baccillus with which you are plainly infected should contaminate others. Like that of Koch, it is mostly transmitted by mouth. By word of mouth, perhaps. (Or by a kiss, but not in China.)

No Chinese is officially endowed with the power of speech, for all power belongs to the Party, which may delegate some of it as needed. A person may be lent *permission* to speak, for it makes life simpler, but it can always be withdrawn. The political offender who is serving the rare jail sentence meted out by an actual court is left alone for hours every day in a symbolically whitewashed room furnished only with a small table, a chair, and a large portrait of the Leader. He has no one to speak to and is not encouraged to speak to himself. There, just as in any other sanatorium, silence cures. By the time the prisoner has come to look upon speech as a strictly rationed commodity that must neither be hoarded nor wastefully spent nor, above all, selfishly used for personal purposes—apart from the unrationed, strictly utilitarian, household words—he also knows that he must never *express* himself, but only repeat or report.

Which accounts for the unpleasant feeling that the resident foreign observer soon experiences that every Chinese he speaks to is repeating a lesson. All answers are stereotyped, thought and speech alike appear to wear a uniform, but there are moments when one wonders whether the uniform turn of speech does not hide many turns of mind. Soon, the gauze mask looks like a gag. Not a gag ha-ha, but a gag choke-choke.

24

MORE FREEDOMS

ANY CITIZEN of China supposedly has the liberty to move about the territory of his own country and to seek his own means of livelihood. Nothing is said of his right to leave the country. Here is a case in point, a double-barreled true story, double-barreled because it also brings up another theoretical right: that to marry.*

"Comrade" Huai (male), in the late summer of 1964, called on the registrar of marriages of the "Hsien" where he lives in Peking's suburbia and informed that official of his intention to marry "Comrade" Yü (female). He was asked why. "Because we like each other very much," was the ludicrous answer. After being very carefully cross-examined about his background and that of his fiancée, he was told that they were both too young (respectively twenty-four and twenty-two) to contemplate matrimony, that "personal affinities" did not provide a good enough reason and were not a substitute for "political affinities," as it was tactfully put. Then came the insidious question: "Since you are bound to know that it is the policy of the government and of the Communist Party to discourage early marriages for reasons which have been carefully and repeatedly explained, are we to assume that your application is essentially intended to defy this policy and show your disapproval of it?" It was added, without a clear negative reply being given, "You had better think things over. If you don't change your mind, come and see us again." Comrade Huai beat a somewhat shameful retreat and of course never dreamt of coming again. The engagement was broken off by Comrade Yü, who had taken fright.

Heartbroken Huai then decided to leave China and to go to

* The legal age is eighteen years for boys and fifteen for girls.

Hong Kong where some of his relatives were living. He therefore applied to the proper authorities for the necessary exit permit. He was asked why he wanted to go and whether he was not happy in his own country. Was he by any chance a revisionist? Perhaps his political consciousness was not all it should be? If so, he should state it publicly and seek enlightenment, which would be gladly imparted. By the way, had he mentioned his plans to his Street Committee? No? Why not? Perhaps he had better think things over and eventually come again if he thought it wise to persist in his decision. There was no categorical "no." There hardly ever is. And a categorical "yes" is of course almost—but not altogether—unknown. Huai retired, very much cowed, to face the prospect of prolonged celibacy and a lifetime job in Peking to the tune of seventy yuans (roughly $25) monthly (unless the authorities decided to send him elsewhere and to put him to a different task, and to alter his income, for better or worse, at their discretion) and a steady and exclusive diet of propaganda with compulsory biweekly political meetings and a relaxation program of books, art, plays, and films all based on "Mao Tse-tung's thinking."

But even traveling within the land itself is not as easy as it sounds or rather as it reads. The true case of a man who wanted to marry and who later wanted to travel abroad has just been recorded. Here now is a hypothetical case. I say hypothetical because no Chinese in his right mind could possibly ignore the difficulties he would encounter should he attempt to migrate to another part of China from that where he is registered. The material for what follows has been provided to me by a reasonably large number of Chinese who wish to leave Peking because, as they said, Peking being the capital, police control was perhaps stricter there than elsewhere in China. But they would not attempt it and they told me why, and I thought their reasons absolutely irrefutable.

First of all, we must accept as valid the Chinese official claim that there is no unemployment. Everyone is properly employed in the great task of building socialism and of that equally vague one called "the reconstruction of China." * But the fact that everyone is employed implies that no one can travel freely on per-

* There is an official Chinese color picture magazine which appears in various foreign languages and whose title is *China Reconstructs* in English and *La Chine en Construction* in French.

sonal business, unless there are family reasons to be invoked, which are traditionally looked upon favorably if rather closely investigated, or other valid reasons, equally verifiable.

Let us assume that the hypothetical Comrade Chiang, employed as a clerk in one of the many government enterprises in Peking, should suddenly become fed up with his job and with Peking altogether, and having no family ties locally, decide to move on to, let us say, Wuhan. Immediately, two possibilities arise:

Either Comrade Chiang has handed in his resignation or he has not.

We may discard at once the first part of this alternative, because no one is permitted to resign. This is only logical. If there is no unemployment, it stands to reason that any post left vacant will be very hard to fill as it can only be filled by means of causing another post to become vacant.

One might suggest that Comrade Chiang could, by great cunning, inefficiency, and laziness, get himself simply thrown out. But he would not have been left on the pavement. He would have been taken in hand at once and sent away to the country where he would make himself useful. Therefore he does not wish to be dismissed.

Now we have already dealt with two impossibilities: that of resigning and that of being sacked. There remains the possibility that Comrade Chiang will simply sneak away without saying anything to anyone and buy himself a ticket to Wuhan.

A comparative large number of Comrades Chiang have firmly assured me that they would never dream of doing a thing so foolish. But for the sake of absurdity let us assume that one Comrade Chiang does so. And that he succeeds in buying a train ticket at Peking station without being asked any alarming questions. Carrying his cheap suitcase, Comrade Chiang moves on to the platform, has his ticket punched at the gate, and safely boards the train.

So far, so good. But so far is not very far.

The rail journey between Peking and Wuhan takes twenty-four hours. And the dining car, where you can get good and inexpensive food, serves it on almost a round-the-clock basis. There is a snag, however. You will of course want either rice or bread with your food. And you must produce ration tickets. The ration tickets which Comrade Chiang carries are only valid in Peking. If he does not happen to possess the proper ration tickets which are required by the dining car attendant, then questions will be asked, which Comrade Chiang will be unable to answer. So Comrade Chiang will stay in his compartment and eat his own food, out of his cheap suitcase. Since meals are so cheap in the dining car, this will attract attention and questions will be asked. Perhaps not immediately. But it will be observed that Comrade Chiang gets off the train at every station where peasants from the neighboring People's Communes (where they are permitted to cultivate their own tiny plots and sell whatever they reap quite cheaply) will provide him with the necessary bread, fruit, and even poultry. But for these he will pay more than he would have to pay for the equivalent in the dining car, and it stands to reason that suspicion will immediately be aroused. Comrade Chiang cannot do without food, even for twenty-four hours. If he did, one would assume that he is ill, and summon a doctor at the first stop and of course ask his name, and his destination, and other awkward questions. But moving from one absurdity to another, we assume that Comrade Chiang reaches the Hankow station, once upon a time the terminus of the British-owned railway linking Peking and Hankow, the "Pinghan."

The station itself has not changed much since the old days. The station building was strongly built some fifty years ago by foreign architects and engineers and has withstood the test of time extremely well. But for Comrade Chiang, who is totally unappreciative of the durable monstrosities of the compradoric style, the problems are where to go, where to eat, and what next to do.

Every one of these is in itself insoluble if we continue to assume that Comrade Chiang has left his Peking occupation and Peking itself without any form of official blessing.

But since we have taken it for granted that Comrade Chiang is so benighted as to be totally unaware of what goes on in his own country, we shall go on assuming that these questions do not worry him particularly and that he makes his way unhindered into the now dilapidated town of Hankow.

It is quite possible that Comrade Chiang has an uncle or a cousin living in Hankow.

Comrade Chiang, we know, has not invoked the nearly always

well-received family pretext for his trip. And so he has not informed his possible relations in Hankow of his arrival. He is not
naïve enough to trust the mail. Also it is plain that he would not
possibly think of staying with his next-of-kin in Hankow, even if
they could actually put him up, which is itself doubtful. Nevertheless, let us suppose that Comrade Chiang has some cousins
twice removed or thrice removed living in Hankow and that he
presents himself at the gate of the old-fashioned house where
they once used to live by themselves, but which is now occupied
by three or four families. Let us go on being absurd and assume
that he is taken in, indeed made welcome, offered a bed of sorts,
and even, for such is Chinese hospitality, asked to partake of the
scanty evening meal. It will not be mentioned, not even discreetly, that he is eating the family ration of grain, and that he
had better register on the morrow and get his own supply, which
is not indeed so very abundant. But there will be no happy re-
union. The neighbors are about. And if his cousins do not ask
him what his plans are, what job he has been given in Hankow,
they are still a little uneasy and they take it for granted he will
report to the police on the next morning since he has obviously
had no time to do so on the very day of his arrival. It is understood that things will be straightened out as they have to be in the
next twenty-four hours. If they are not, then the entire family
will suffer, for questions will be asked by the neighbors at the
next meeting of the Street Committee and such a meeting is never
far off.

And if Comrade Chiang has no relations in Hankow, then of
course he will have to go to a hotel. It is not at all certain that he
will be taken in. He will be asked to produce several papers, including his ration cards. He may be asked to wait. But he will not
be forced to wait. He is free to go wherever he likes. He may
even go to a restaurant to fortify himself for the inevitable ordeal. But in the restaurant, he will be asked whether he has a ration card, for rice or bread. And if, in order to avoid that, he asks
for neither rice nor bread, then things will become even more
difficult.

In any case, whether he is a guest of his own relations, if he has
any, or tries to book a room at a hotel or order a meal anywhere
or applies for work on the next day, assuming that he has gone
through his first night in Hankow without a hitch, the time will

come very soon when, not a large force of police in uniform, but just one single person in a blue denim suit, perhaps a woman, will say:

"Welcome, Comrade Chiang. We have been expecting you. We have a job for you and we are very glad that you decided to come here, to help in the task of national reconstruction. You are leaving for Sinkiang tomorrow."

That is the last thing Comrade Chiang wishes to hear, but then, as I mentioned before, the story is purely hypothetical. And that is why all the Comrades Chiang who suggested it to me are still in Peking. However, they all wished me to make it very clear to the Western reader that they were perfectly free to travel wherever they wanted to go.

25

LOVE'S YOUNG DREAM

THE NINTH Congress of the Communist Youth League was held in Peking in June, 1964, attended by over two thousand delegates from all over the country. Typically, nothing was known of the Congress while it was in session—not even that it had been convened—and reports on its activities were only published afterwards. "Upholding the Red Banner of Mao Tse-tung's thinking," it was then stated, "the Congress fully discussed the question of promoting the revolutionization of the youth of China and worked out the future tasks of the Communist Youth League." It also adopted a new constitution including "a clearcut provision that the League should take Marxism-Leninism and Mao Tse-tung's thinking as its guiding principle." This was, it was added, "of paramount significance" since it meant that "the League must unswervingly abide by the instructions of the Communist Party and Chairman Mao Tse-tung and closely combine the education of young people with mobilizing them to take part in the revolutionary movements of the entire people, thus enabling them to integrate themselves with the masses of workers and peasants in the actual struggle to transform the world." (Hsinhua, July 1.)

But in order to "transform the world," the Chinese youngsters must first learn to transform themselves into wholly dedicated sexless beings, as love seeks privacy and draws the individual away from communal life, thoughts, and pleasures. "When dealing with problems of love and marriage," stated the *Chinese Youth* fortnightly, one must "do away with all bourgeois ideas." This might be mistaken for an encouragement to free love, but it is just the opposite. Neither physical nor sentimental attraction is to play any part when mating is contemplated. What counts is "a shared political consciousness which can lead to greater joint efforts in building socialism and increasing production."

How to remain chaste though married and, failing that, how to remain childless (the question of being both unchaste and unmarried should never arise) seems to be the gist of sexual education in China, and practical advice in that respect is being freely given by word of mouth at youth meetings as well as in print in all the youth publications.

The same *Chinese Youth* magazine in its September 1, 1963, number points out in an edifying article that sometimes the young must model themselves after older people. The article is about a visit paid to an unnamed Northeast China industrial plant by a visiting North Korean delegation which can have been of no mean standing since it was shown around by Premier Chou En-lai and Foreign Minister Chen Yi.

"During this visit," the periodical says, "Premier Chou had informal conversations with the workers. Among other things, the Premier was urging everybody to arrange their personal life with proper regard to the interest of the state. He expressed the hope that young unmarried people would make it a point to marry late and that the married couples working at the plant would take care to apply strict birth control. The workers were deeply moved by the Prime Minister's words.

"In the crowd, Premier Chou saw a female comrade with a small boy in her arms. At once, he went up to her to shake her hand and then they began talking. The Premier asked whether the child was her own. The comrade, whose name is Li Ying, answered that he was her second child and aged four and that she also had a daughter of ten, now in primary school. Premier Chou then asked some questions as to her age and the date of her marriage. Li Ying said that she was thirty-two and had been married at twenty. So it is plain that Li Ying married rather early, but since she had had only two children in twelve years, one now ten and the other four, one could see that some time had elapsed between the two births. Premier Chou warmly expressed his approval of that point.

"Li Ying added: 'This is due to the fact that we always applied birth control in a planned manner. Two years ago my husband underwent sterilization.' Premier Chou then asked whether this operation had been carried out according to the wishes of hus-

band and wife and Li Ying answered: 'It was done entirely voluntarily.'

"Premier Chou looked extremely pleased and said they had
both done well, especially the husband. He further said: 'This is a
very good thing and one may say indeed that you are both setting everyone an example in the matter of birth control.'

"Then," the youth magazine continues, "the Prime Minister
summoned the father of the child, one Sun Yen-wen, a member
of the Communist Party. The latter told Premier Chou that he
was forty years of age, that he had enlisted in 1945 in the P.L.A.
in which he became an officer, and that he had been transferred
some years back to the industrial front together with his wife. He
added that they had been educated by the Party whose guidance
they faithfully followed and that they had thus practiced birth
control voluntarily in order to offer the maximum of their
strength to the Socialist Construction of China."

Sun Yen-wen, it was further elucidated, was assistant manager
of the plant where his wife worked in the accounting section, he
was an orphan, and they were all living together with his mother-
in-law, which meant a household of five people. His pay and that
of his wife combined came to a total of more than two hundred
yuans, so they had no financial problems and, if they had applied birth control, it was not because they had economic difficulties but so that they could devote all their strength to their work.
Sun further volunteered the information that the operation had
not affected his health and that it had "made everybody very
happy." Before leaving, Premier Chou repeated: "Old Sun, you
are indeed a paragon of birth control, especially as it was you
who took the initiative in the matter of family planning." Chou
urged everybody present to emulate the Sun family.

After the Korean visitors and the two Chinese statesmen had
left, the periodical further tells us, "people were still laughing." It
must be remembered that in China laughter does not exclusively
express merriment.

Not everybody, however, is like Sun and his wife. And not everybody is quite so public-spirited as old Sun. Even though, in
the waiting rooms of Peking's maternity wards, there are large
glass cases displaying a remarkable variety of contraceptive drugs
and devices for expectant daddies to gaze at, and even though
prolific fathers are urged—but never forced—to undergo sterili-

zation, I know of one, a father of four, who declined despite strong encouragement because, as he put it, although he would not have minded himself, and his wife was all for it, *his mother* would not *permit* it. Which shows that the spirit of old China is not quite dead.

Between these two extremes—the "neutralized" Sun and the old woman who refused to allow her married son to emulate him —there are many sensible prospective couples like male Comrade Ting San-yueh and female Comrade Kao Lin-ling from Tou Chun Chemical Factory in Kweichow who wrote jointly to the *Workers' Daily* as follows:

> In our factory, there are far too many young people who take advantage of their leisure hours to indulge in flirtation,* which very badly affects their work and their studies.
> We are two young technicians, both aged twenty-three. We have never made love to each other and have never considered the marriage question as we feel that our professional level is too low and that we must first acquire more knowledge and make use of our time off to study. We are contemplating falling in love in eight or nine years. . . .
> If young people barely aged twenty-five already start looking for someone to fall in love with or to marry, it is because their outlook is wrong and because they have acquired bad habits.

This letter appeared in February, 1962, which was early in the birth-control campaign and at the very beginning of the anti-love campaign which automatically followed. Had it been written a few months later, the necessity to put politics first, to emulate Lei Feng, and to be guided by Mao's thinking would have been mentioned as a compulsory matter of course.

In November, 1962, the *Workers' Daily*, already quoted, was telling its readers that "neither love nor marriage spells happiness for the young. Happiness is to be found only in a strong determination to devote one's life to the Revolution. . . . Thus does collective happiness lead to personal happiness . . . a lifemate must thus be sought within the revolutionary movement so

---

* The literal translation from which I am quoting says "love activities," but as I cannot imagine these activities being anything but platonic, the word "flirtation" seems more appropriate.

that socialist construction can be worked for by man and wife together." Even before that date, as early as July, 1962, Professor Yeh Kung-shao had made use of the *Youth Daily*'s columns to warn the students that, in the interest of their studies, it would be better if they refrained from "speaking about love." He advised them to marry late (I am harping on this again, but it is just as impossible to give a picture of Communist China without repeating oneself as it would be to impersonate a stutterer without stuttering, too) and not to have more than two children. As to ordinary love between man and woman, it was to be described in a booklet issued in 1963, much to be quoted and paraphrased by Party publications for the young as a "psychosomatic activity which consumes energy and wastes time."

It was further very sensibly pointed out that love of the masses, love of the Party, love of Chairman Mao took up no time at all and was in itself a powerful tonic. Try it, the advertisement said, and you will feel your spirits rise, together with your productivity, and your usefulness to the community will increase tenfold. Millions of testimonials. And all for free. Who would hesitate?

Apparently, some people do. Seventeen years after Liberation, reactionary and bourgeois ways of thought still persist, even though all reactionaries and all bourgeois have been called paper tigers by Mao. Do paper tigers, one then wonders, breed in captivity? It is sad to admit it, but they seem to, as shown by young Hsiang Yang's letter to the *Peking Daily*. This, and the editor's comments, were translated for me by an East European correspondent well versed in Chinese. His English I shall leave as it stands.

I am one organizational cadre and twenty years old. This last spring, I met the young girl and we have fell in first-sight love at one each other together. I want to be matrimonious immediate so as we be together soon. Too my mother she wants grandchild rapid. But when I say this to my fiancée, she is objectionable saying: "We are too much youthful and have only superior primary school education, so more better marry later and learn more culture before." My mother repeatingly is urging we join wedlock but my fiancée remains disagreeably. I am in most difficult position and what you have to say about this I receive with thanks.

The editor's retort follows:

Comrade Hsiang Yang!
   The view of your mother and your fiancée is so contrary that not only yourself but persons who want give you some suggestion feel difficult. But this matter being in existence, it is necessary solve it; thus I am putting forth my opinions as references to your consideration of the problem. People of ancient time say marriage is great incident of one's lifetime. . . . In old novel stories, about "young talented men and beautiful women," first-sight love is often to be seen visibly in the writing. This reflects that in feudal society there is no freedom for youthful men and women to have contact so that when they meet there is first-sight love and become engaged secretly. Looking at it today such matters is incredible. Of course when young boys and girl meet first time it is possible that impression reciprocously not bad but true love must be established on foundation of deep understanding as ideology must be unanimous. In your concrete situation you have known few months and have certain understanding. This is to be rejoiced, but when your fiancée says better wait long period to learn more knowledge and ideology she has correct attitude. Also, there was one poet saying "one unmarried person is like horse at liberty, marriage is to tie cart to horse," which means with marriage are children, which children must have to eat, be clothed, cry, get sick, so I advise take example certain comrades who marry under situation of mature thoughts and foundation in work and learning and rich in experience in life. So more better you accept your fiancée's opinion of marry years later and so you explain kindly to your mother so she will surely agree because good for you.

   The general trend is the same a year later, but the stress on the political factor is heavier and the tone of the mentor has become harsher. The letters to the various editors (they may or may not be genuine letters) offer more serious problems. Thus in November, 1963, one Cheng Shen-kun who had sought advice from the *Workers' Daily* is sternly told that:

   . . . a man, when he is about to select for himself a fiancée, must forever bear in mind her class origin, for indeed a person's social origin often exerts various influences on his or her political attitude and state of mind. If you choose a wife whose political outlook is different from your own and who thinks like a member of the exploiting classes, then you may yourself in your future married life fall victim to her bad influence. Therefore young workers who are still unmarried must never forget that class struggle still exists nowadays and that certain landlords, reactionaries, and capitalists sometimes try to make use of their womenfolk to corrupt the revolutionary youth so that they will participate in their intrigues for a bourgeois restoration. One must therefore remain constantly vigilant. . . . A proper revolutionary foundation is lacking where you and your friend are concerned. You might perhaps continue a satisfactory relationship with her if you were successful in helping her to build such a foundation. Should she, however, reject your assistance or that of other people and should she persist in her erroneous position, then you should break with her altogether. . . .

On the other hand, at your age of twenty-eight, you should be in no hurry to marry. Should you for your friend's sake give up your post as foreman, then you would be committing indeed a grave and dangerous mistake. A revolutionary young man must think first of the interests of the Revolution and should not barter his revolutionary principles for vulgar love.

The life of the Chinese adolescent is not as uniformly adolescent as a moralizing adolescent press would have us believe. A careless word is occasionally dropped and the grapevine has not gone completely dead. Rumor has it that the suicide rate is high among students and that the state is making great efforts to turn out enough psychiatrists to man the overflowing asylums. None of that is ever mentioned in the newspapers. Nor are cases of self-slaughter or insanity among the young. Still, one does hear of some, and here is one instance among several which I have selected because I can vouch for its authenticity:

In the autumn of 1964—that is well before the anti-love and anti-sex campaign had reached the dimensions it has now taken —a Nanking university student fell in love with a girl student and wrote to her to declare himself. The girl handed the letter over to the university committee with the result that the boy was severely lectured by the Party and, as is the custom, by his fellow-students. Quite undaunted, he wrote her another letter which again she turned over to the same inquisitors, and he was threatened with expulsion and with a spell of political re-education in a particularly smelly part of the countryside. This seems to have driven him out of his mind. Armed with a knife he ambushed his irresponsive sweetheart and repeatedly slashed her face before stabbing himself to death. *Both* their families were then called upon to make public confessions of their guilt in bringing up their children so carelessly and were afterwards subjected to "all sort of indignities," even though the girl herself, who was by then lying on a hospital bed with her face full of stitches, had never given the suicide the slightest encouragement and had done precisely what the Party expects of any girl who receives love letters.

This strange procedure will surprise the Western reader; it is nevertheless part of the common responsibility system under which chastisement is meted out not only to the culprit but to the victim as well and which accounts for the salutary fact that, as I may already have written somewhere else, everyone is constantly afraid without knowing exactly of what or why. That sort of thing, I was told, happened "all the time."

Public wooing was never a Chinese habit but still, in the old days, young couples could be seen holding hands or even holding each other by the waist in Peking's lovely Pei Hai park on a nice summer evening. This is unthinkable now; less than ever do young men practice the Great Leap Forward at the opposite sex. You may still see young couples walking slowly side by side, but they never touch, keeping, I suppose, to their respective sides of the General Line and communing only in lofty thoughts of a higher production quite foreign to that of babies and talking in quotations from Mao's *Selected Works*, scarcely to be mistaken for erotic literature. It can further be assumed that they do not woo in private for the simple reason that they have no privacy.

The sexual urge in the young is not just something that must be curbed. It is essentially something that must not be permitted to arise. In order to nip it in the bud, various means are used simultaneously. True leisure is almost entirely done away with. Hard physical and mental work is made compulsory and so is political sublimation. Love incentive is banned in literature, the arts, and from the stage and the screen. Finally, and that proceeds logically from the above, strict measures are taken to make either sex unattractive to the other and indeed to make the sexes scarcely distinguishable from each other. Women who dare use makeup do so at their own risk (even though lipstick and face-powder are sold at Peking's state department store and on state occasions, when a selected crowd is taken to the airport in special buses to welcome various "friends of China," even the children's cheeks are rouged), and austerity in dress and hairdressing is the strictly enforced rule. That is probably why the cotton ration has remained stingily static while food rationing was gradually being given up. Yet I heard of several young girls who had got themselves in serious Party trouble for wearing—and thereby economizing rare and precious material—tight-fitting trousers instead of the approved and very wasteful shapeless variety. In point of fact I know a number of Chinese women from overseas— Hong Kong or Malaya—who are frequent visitors to Peking and who have two wardrobes for use: one in proletarian China, and the other for south of the border, after the little iron bridge between Chinese Shumchum and British Lowu has been crossed.

To dance or not to dance is also a question. The new regime introduced itself to the people of the Yangtse valley and South China with a harvest folk dance from the northwest called the *yangko*. No procession or parade was complete without its gaily (if very chastely) dressed *yangko* dancers of both sexes I found to my surprise that it was no longer being performed in 1962. There were other country dances, mostly done by national minorities, but they were seen on the stage rather than in the streets. Ballroom dancing was not considered proper, but nevertheless schools and factories would, reluctantly it seemed and certainly "by popular request," hold an occasional dance, foreign style. Moreover, at the International Club (the former, essentially diplomatic, Peking Club, now run by the Waichiaopu) members could dance every Saturday night to the strenuous strains of an orchestra that apparently had not learned any new tunes since the Japanese invasion in 1937 and had turned those it knew— musical museumpieces like "The Isle of Capri," "The Last Roundup," and even "Sonny Boy"—into lullabies by means of which it rocked itself to sleep once a week from ten to eleven P.M. A few bored people from the Soviet-bloc embassies would drop in for half an hour, but the attendance was mostly Chinese. High officials from the Ministry of Foreign Affairs, male and female, and from other state or Party departments (I saw General Lo Jui-ching there fairly often) would take their minds off the Revolution for one evening and concentrate on revolving about the dance floor in arm's-length couples. Trousered women frequently danced together, but not men.

As to dances held by purely Chinese organizations, they were certainly frowned upon by the more puritan element, and there would be occasional protests in the press along the lines of the following, which appeared in the *Youth Daily* in January, 1963, a time when the average standard of living was only just beginning to improve after the Three Years of Natural Calamities (1959 to 1961) and a minimum of nonpolitical relaxation was still permitted as a compensation. Its author, Fang Yun, apparently took the trouble to write to a Peking newspaper from Kaifeng, in Honan, where he lived and worked. He is quite censorious.

Comrade Editor! [he writes] we have recently been discussing the problem of dancing in our factory. I personally do not like dancing. To be quite frank, I detest it. But I will tell you in the light of what is happening in our city of the reasons for my contempt for dancing.

Dances are being held frequently here. There was one only a few days ago which had been organized by our factory and a great many people of the town attended it together with many young people from the factory itself, and some people danced until very late at night. Some dancing fanatics had come in by dishonest means as they had not been able to obtain entry tickets beforehand. Some had truly the manner of hooligans. Since the girls were reluctant to dance with them, they took every opportunity to step painfully on their toes. And, while dancing, they were making impolite gestures.

I am strongly opposed to this kind of dancing. I consider that such evenings can become occasions for the lowly instincts of the bourgeois class to be disseminated and to flourish. Also, certain youngsters feel that they must dance all the same from the moment they know the steps. Their legs begin to move automatically once they hear dance music. I have met people who dance privately two or three times a week and some, who work with the night shift and go on duty at midnight, will dance until eleven P.M. so that, in the workshop, they still think of dancing and their legs are sore through too much dancing and this is bad for both their health and their work.

The editor's reply is exactly as the reader may by now imagine, and only these short bits deserve to be quoted:

... Young people are easily corrupted by bourgeois tastes. In the past, ballroom dancing was a form of bourgeois lewdness. Today, we must remain watchful and keep dancing healthy and clean. If hooligan elements offend our Communist morals, then we must act energetically. ... However, we must remember that dancing, before becoming an instrument of reactionary lechery, was invented by the working class as a means of harmless and rare communal diversion from a life of sorrow and oppression. It has, as such and when kept within its proper bounds, a cultural significance.*

It goes without saying that rock-and-roll and the twist were banned from Chinese dancing evenings, when everyone behaved with, as far as I have heard, complete decorum. But that was Peking. I still have to see the fleshpots of Kaifeng.

No amount of physical exertion or indoctrination will do away with the normal sexual impulse of young people, and so, in August, 1962, one Kiu Shui wrote to the editor of the *Youth Daily* to explain that he was twenty-three, and had been masturbating for two years, but, even now that he had given it up, he feared that "this vice may forever affect my marital life later and make me both impotent and sterile." He says he has no longer the will to live but still, weak and pessimistic as he feels, he would like to know whether he still has a chance to "contribute to socialist construction and agricultural development." The reply, published as usual together with the writer's letter, is reassuring in the extreme and makes light of Comrade Kiu's fears. It ominously adds that real sexual excesses of the kind that may affect one's work and political outlook are "not committed singly."

Homosexuality is taboo, and the Chinese press, otherwise re-

* I nearly choked once when I heard rumbas and tangos played during a state banquet at the Great Hall of the People. That was during what one of the Old Retainers described as "Cuba Time," and I was later informed that these dances were part of the Latin American folklore and therefore respectable. On the other hand, when Europeans danced modern dances in the privacy of their various embassies, the Chinese looked upon them, it transpired, as degenerates, but when the same steps were performed by Africans in *their* embassies, with an occasional but strictly nonparticipating Chinese guest present, they became healthily folkloric and cultural.

markably outspoken on questions of sex, never mentions the subject. About male homosexuality, I have heard nothing but vague and inconclusive allusions. Sapphism seems much more frequent. A young European woman, one of the drujbas, who worked as a translator for the Chinese government, had once occasion to complain to the hostel management about the attentions of one of her female Chinese colleagues, appointed, as she thought, to spy on her, but who nevertheless had become a little too personal and intimate. "She was actually pawing me," were her words. The culprit was "reprimanded." A woman correspondent on the usual V.I.P.P. tour also mentioned that several of the female interpreter-guides who accompanied her on the various stages of her journey had made to her "unmistakable advances."

It seems on the whole logical that under a system that prohibits free intercourse between the sexes and frowns upon early marriage, the young should feel encouraged to follow the safest course, even if it is not the natural one. After all, untimely children are also officially unwelcome.* Next to complete chastity, there is nothing like self-abuse and homosexuality to keep the birth rate down.

---

* In 1963 already, the fourth child, in a legitimate household, of course, was denied cotton-ration coupons, while people who married only after the age of thirty were granted an extra ration as a token of official approval. The wages of chastity were cotton. I have since seen in 1966 press reports from Hong Kong and quoting refugees from the mainland that after the third child, sterilization is being forced and that those who refuse lose their jobs, which also means losing their ration cards, and moreover that people who "marry secretly" will "face banishment to labor camps." All of this I am inclined to disbelieve, especially the last part of it, since it is absolutely impossible for anyone to marry secretly in Mao's China.

26

FISHFACE INCOGNITO

☙❧☙❧

WERE my eyes deceiving me? I had come to look upon Fishface as a sort of minor deity, a former homeless lar who had once stood beside Tien An Men Square, waiting for the Great Hall of the People to be built around him. I had never seen him outside that edifice. It had not occurred to me that he might materialize elsewhere. Yet there he was, attending a National Day reception at one of the major East European embassies.

The Ambassador was not available: he sat with his guests of honor, Foreign Minister Chen Yi, and Peking's Mayor, Peng Chen, in the usual improvised alcove, away from the crowd. But the Minister-Counselor was in the midst of the group of foreign correspondents, superfluously urging them to drink more of the embassy's excellent vodka and to clink glasses with him. I tanked up and drew him aside.

"Very fine reception," I said.

"Thank you."

"Fine Chinese attendance."

"Thank you, not so fine. Only Chen Yi and Mayor Peng. Long ago time, before China become Stalinist great-power-chauvinistic adventurist, every year we get Chou En-lai. Sometimes Liu Shao-chi also he come. Now, no more. Never mind. We drink."

"Have you," I asked, "the list of all your Chinese guests of today?"

"No list. No, not never, no list. We send out general invitation through Protocol. Not never know who will come. Before, always come Chou, sometime also Liu. And lots more peoples. Plenty faces. More faces we see, more face to us. Witticism," he explained.

He became suspicious. "Why you want list, eh? Do not answer me. I know. You want tell the world what poor reception this is. Only Chen Yi and horrible Comrade Peng. You want make us ridiculous with ulterior motives. Never mind, you are welcome guest. We drink."

"Look," I said, pointing discreetly, "what I am trying to find out, with no ulterior motive, is what that man over there calls himself."

"Never he call himself. Why must? He call others. Others call him."

"By what name?"

"By name Comrade."

"Comrade what?"

He scratched his head. "I know," he said, "but I've forgotten. . . . However, we, between ourselves, call him . . ." He said something in a language totally foreign to me.

"What does it mean?"

"It means someone who has face like fish. Excuse me, please."

He hurried away, bent on his hospitable duties. I steadied my nerves with another vodka. From across the room, Fishface was gliding toward me.

"Good afternoon," he said. "Fine reception."

"Thank you, not so fine," I replied. "Long before time ago, every year Chou he come. . . ."

I checked myself. There was no mistaking the ironic smile on the face of Fishface. Nor the look in his all-seeing small eyes. Fishface, the uncanny. Fishface, the mysterious. The man whose real name nobody knew. I wondered what they called him in the Secret Service. Probably Ling Ling Chi. That's Chinese for 007.

27

THE LITTLE SHANGHAI OF MR. LI

"I HOPE it is not your intention to go to Shanghai in a nostalgic frame of mind," said Mrs. Chen, looking fixedly at me through her rimless spectacles. The thick lenses magnified her eyes and the anticipated reproof in them as well. I had been in China over a year and had already had a few tiffs with the Information Department. *Persona non grata* I had not yet become, but I could have been *gratior* than I was. It was plain that Mrs. Chen suspected me of "ulterior motives."

Things were quiet in Peking at the time and I had suddenly decided to ask permission to visit Shanghai.

My secretary had rung up the Information Department and the Information Department had answered that I should write a letter. This I had done. Then I had been asked to come to the Information Department in person in order to explain in detail by word of mouth what my purpose was in wanting to go to Shanghai. An appointment had been arranged and here I was.

To her question I replied: "Why should you expect me to?"

"Because we know you have lived in Shanghai before Liberation."

Mrs. Chen said this triumphantly. She felt she had really got me there.

Of course, when I had applied for my Chinese visa in Berne, I had had to fill a very exhaustive form, in duplicate, giving details of my previous stays in China and the duration of them, and what I had been doing. This had been duly transmitted to the Chinese Foreign Office while I was quietly waiting for my green light from the Reds. Mrs. Chen was certainly conversant with my Chinese past, but she looked as if her own personal spies had only just ferreted it out and the shock of it should unseat me.

"The Shanghai you once knew," said Mrs. Chen, "no longer exists. And we hope you will not be looking for it."

This struck me as rather absurd because Mrs. Chen seemed to have forgotten that I had left China in August, 1950, and that Communist Shanghai was not altogether new to me. But she still seemed to think that I had said good-by to Shanghai in those happy days when there was dancing on the roof of the French Club, when one went through the streets in rickshaws, when one enjoyed extraterritorial rights throughout China and lived in foreign Concessions or Treaty Ports. Actually, all foreign privileges had been given up by China's allies during the war at small cost to them since, at the time, all the old Treaty Ports were in the hands of the common enemy, the Japanese. But that was one thing that had been constantly ignored in Peking, where you were made to feel that the Unequal Treaties had been abrogated by the Communist regime.

"How long did you live in Shanghai?" asked Mrs. Chen, who already knew.

"Oh, about seven or eight years, on and off," I replied.

"When did you first come to Shanghai?" asked Mrs. Chen.

"In February, 1932."

"And how did you find things there?"

"Wonderful," I replied unguardedly.

"Do you mean that things were better then than they are now?"

"Yes, in a way," I said.

Mrs. Chen promptly asked: "And may I ask in what way?"

"In that," I said, "I was over thirty years younger."

I had spoken in perfect candor but this set Mrs. Chen's mental processes into unfortunate motion along certain preselected channels.

"So you *do* regret those days?"

"Don't we all?"

"We do not," said Mrs. Chen indignantly, and it was amusing to think that thirty years ago she was attending primary school somewhere in California, the daughter of Chinese immigrants who had possibly made a fortune in chop suey, that her American English was then more fluent than her Cantonese, and that the odds were she did not know enough Mandarin to have asked her way in the streets of Peking.

Mrs. Chen thought it time to relapse into Chinese and her interpreter woke up with a start, with pad and pencil ready.

"Tell me," asked Mrs. Chen, "where you lived in Shanghai."

"In many places."

"Well, where did you stay in 1932?"

"When I arrived in Shanghai, I first stayed at Mr. Sheek's boardinghouse in Yuen Ming Yuen Road. Quite a respectable place."

"And how long did you stay there?"

"Not very long."

"And where did you move to then?"

"To Mr. Sheek's other boardinghouse, not far away, in Peking Road, practically around the corner. Or, perhaps, in Jinkee Road. Parallel to Peking Road, you know. Same thing. I can't remember exactly."

"Jinkee Road?" asked Mrs. Chen.

"Yes, you know, just behind Sassoon House."

"Behind what?"

"Sassoon House. Corner of the Bund and Nanking Road. Built by Sir Victor Sassoon. Office flats, and the Sassoon Arcade. Lots of smart shops. And of course the Cathay Hotel."

"And who was this Mr. Cathay?" asked Mrs. Chen, who perhaps really did not know China's ancient Western name.

"Sir Victor's partner, I presume," I said wearily.

She let that pass but was rather testy about the address of Mr. Sheek's second boardinghouse. We finally settled on Peking Road and Mrs. Chen went on: "And why did you move?"

"Because there was no modern sanitation in Yuen Ming Yuen Road."

"Well," said Mrs. Chen, "we have it all over China now. And where did you stay after that?"

"I had a flat in Temple Lane," I replied.

"Temple Lane? What is Temple Lane?"

"Well, that used to be off Hart Road."

"What was Hart Road?"

"Well, you know, it used to be off Bubbling Well Road, just before you got to St. George's."

"What was St. George's?" asked Mrs. Chen, frowning.

"Why, surely, Mrs. Chen," I exclaimed, "you must have heard of St. George's. It was once the best-known dance hall in Shanghai!"

"Well!" said Mrs. Chen, speaking English again.

"And where did you live after that?" said she, collecting herself.

"Why, I used to live in Weihaiwei Road."

"Ah yes, Weihaiwei Lu. And after that, where did you stay?"

"I moved to Frenchtown."

I gave her my various addresses, as far as I could remember them, and they were all written down by the interpreter on his pad. Of course I had to explain that Frenchtown was the French Concession. But far less questions were asked thereafter, as if the fact that I had moved from the British-dominated Foreign Settlement to another and equally foreign settlement, but run by a country now so friendly to China, was in itself an extenuating circumstance.

Mrs. Chen did not ask me where I had stayed in Shanghai after the war, when I had returned to China in 1947, and there were no more foreign privileges and the abrogation of the Unequal Treaties had been acknowledged by all. Again it seemed that, to her, the gap between the end of World War II and the Communist Liberation—a gap, after all, of four years—had never been. That China, after the capitulation of Japan, could have lived under the Kuomintang, and might even have prospered, had there been no civil war, was something to be ignored.

"Tell me about the Shanghai you knew," said Mrs. Chen.

I was on the mat. I had to do my self-criticism, voice strong personal disapproval of the semi-colonial life I had once known and indeed enjoyed, and it didn't really matter how hypocritical I became. It was just that the words had to be spoken.

I got out of it gracefully (as I thought) by saying: "No right-thinking Chinese today would approve of the Shanghai I knew then."

"Well," said Mrs. Chen, "you must be prepared to see a completely different Shanghai."

"That is precisely why I want to go there."

Mrs. Chen then began telling me all about Shanghai. I listened. After a while I began to wonder whether she had ever been there. All she said was that I should find it quite unrecognizable, with no more vice rampant or even, and especially, *couchant* (in the French, rather than the heraldic, meaning).

I thought it unnecessary to remind her that the Nationalist government had already done away with all that and with opium smoking, which was punishable by death, and that, by and large, in any country where a government enjoyed financial as well as political support from the U.S., it found it essential to assert its independence by taking the tarts off the streets, closing the brothels, the gambling joints, and the opium dens, much indeed to the annoyance of many male American residents. Then Mrs. Chen went on about the Four Good Company of Nanking Road, which had successfully demonstrated its immunity to the "sugar-coated bullets" constantly fired at them by imaginary prostitutes. Mrs. Chen told me that Shanghai had expanded tremendously and that which was particularly worth seeing was not to be found in the city itself but in its suburbs. Through all of this verbiage, Mrs. Chen was a little uneasy. Comparison is not welcome in China.

The Chinese Communists—I had already noticed that in Peking—were as proud of the Shanghai skyline as if they had built that essentially foreign city themselves. Pictures of the Bund I had seen in a great many Chinese magazines, taken, as I could easily spot, either from the top floor of Broadway Mansions, British-built in the early Thirties, or from the old French weather tower, at the other end of the Bund. Peking stationers sold them, much magnified, and sometimes even woven in silk, and they hung in the shops next to the portraits of China's leaders. It was easy to pick out familiar landmarks: the old Custom House, the *North China Daily News* Building, the dome of the Hong Kong and Shanghai Bank, Sassoon House, and many others including the Bank of China, the only structure to have been built with Chinese money, and Kuomintang money at that.

"This is the Bund," said Mr. Li. "Very fine, very impressive. A symbol of the growing industrial and economic importance of the city."

"Do you still call it the Bund?"

"It is not the official name, but we use it out of courtesy to our English-speaking friends because it is so easy to remember."

Mr. Li, of the China Travel Service, had met me at Lunghwa airport and had not taken happily to the news that I would be staying at the British consulate (never to be mentioned under that name) and that he could cancel the totally unasked-for booking his organization had made for me at the Peace Hotel.

"We think," he had said, "that if you really want to see Shanghai, you should stay at a Chinese hotel."

"Where is the Peace Hotel?" I had asked out of sheer curiosity.

"At the corner of the Bund and Nanking Road."

"Oh, the old Cathay Hotel!"

"Peace Hotel; not as you have just said."

I had explained that Douglas Spankie and his wife were expecting me and that the China Travel Service had not been requested to provide me with accommodation. I had obviously not been playing the game. It was plain that I had deliberately questioned the authority of the authorities and that nothing could be done about it. When you travel in China, you do not stop at the hotel of your choice. You just accept your billet. If I had asked for a room in a hotel other than the Cathay, I should have been told politely that, unfortunately, all hotels except for the Peace Hotel were full. But once I had firmly stated that friends were putting me up, it became difficult to object—as long as those friends were not Chinese. But then, the thought of a Chinese playing host to a foreigner is absurd.

It had been plain from the look on Mr. Li's face that he was trying hard to view my case in the light of Mao Tse-tung's thinking and wondering whether it would be safe to tell me that friends of the Spankies had unexpectedly arrived from London that very morning for a long weekend and were occupying all the spare rooms in the British chargé d'affaires' office in Shanghai (*not* the British consulate) or that the whole family had suddenly been stricken with a highly contagious disease.

Finally, he had said: "I must make a telephone call."

Afterwards, he had looked much relieved, having passed the onus of responsibility on to his superiors, and now we were rolling along the Bund at a cracking fifteen m.p.h. in an antiquated but very roomy American limousine and Mr. Li was telling me that this was the Bund, very impressive.

"I have been here before," I said. "In fact, I used to live here."

"On the Bund?"

"No. Nobody ever lived on the Bund. Here, in Shanghai, for many years."

"Before Liberation?"

"Before and even after."

"Then you *must* remember the Bund!" Mr. Li exclaimed almost angrily, as if I had been deliberately keeping that piece of intelligence from him and basely tricked him into showing me the Bund.

"You know, I believe I do."

"Then you will notice the change."

The change was there all right, not in the skyline, but in the Bund itself, and it was a change for the better. Trees and shrubs had been planted along the waterfront making it a long, continuous garden, not exactly luxuriant, but green and clean, if unpleasantly separated from the now much narrower roadway by a high wire fence of a kind not normally seen around public parks and squares. There was very little traffic, even less than in Peking, and it reminded me, not as nostalgically as Mrs. Chen would have thought, of the days when I was driving up and down that very Bund trying to find a parking space.

"Shanghai, since Liberation," said Mr. Li, "has become the busiest and most prosperous city in China."

We turned into the vast compound of what had once been the British consulate-general and was still officially acknowledged British property, and Mr. Li dropped me on the Spankies' doorstep, announcing that he would come and pick me up later in the day and take me to see the local Waichiaopu representative with whom I should discuss my program.

This official turned out to be a welcome improvement on those few of his colleagues, almost exclusively from the Information Department, whom I had been permitted to meet in the capital. He was in early middle age, I thought, and he had brisk and pleasant manners. I had to listen, as was inevitable, to the usual propaganda record, but he managed somehow to boil it down from the standard long-playing tirade to a nominal fast 78 r.p.m., for which I was thankful. He spoke much more freely than was customary in Peking. We even went so far as to discuss briefly the Sino-Soviet situation, which was only just beginning to deteriorate openly. He assured me that the Chinese interpretation of Marxism-Leninism was not, "as often believed by foreigners," merely *closer* to the true meaning than the Russian interpretation, but that it was "the only true one." As to my plans, I had only three days to spend in Shanghai, nothing very definite in mind but one minor thing or two, and I would be grateful for suggestions. These were immediately forthcoming, and they were the usual ones: a People's Commune, a brace of factories, a satellite town or two, the permanent industrial exhibition. If I thought of something else later, I merely had to tell Mr. Li, who would make the necessary arrangements.

(Which did not turn out to be true, for, on the next day, having heard that an anti-colonialist exhibition was being held and that no foreigners were permitted to visit it, I asked Mr. Li about it, but he proved remarkably uncooperative. He had never heard of such an exhibition. After I became very insistent, he went off to ring up his principals and came back with the information that indeed no such exhibition had taken place in Shanghai. Perhaps I was thinking of another city? No? And why should foreigners not be allowed in? Could I tell him? I could not. So, you see, there was no exhibition. Later, I was in a position to inform Mr. Li that the Shanghai anti-colonialist exhibition was a reality, and he, sighing, made his way to the telephone again and, returning, reported that, indeed, it had been held but had closed on the day before my arrival.

"Was it your office you just rang up?" I asked.

"Yes."

"And was it your office you rang up yesterday?"

"Yes."

"And your office told you yesterday that there had been no exhibition at all and today that it had just ended?"

"Yes."

"Do you expect me to believe that the Shanghai branch of the China Travel Service only learns about exhibitions in Shanghai after they have shut their doors?"

Mr. Li went positively green with the loss of face.

"But I never told you," he stammered, "that there had been no exhibition, only that . . ."

I cut him short. "Mr. Li, I suspect you are lying through your teeth."

Mr. Li's complexion went from green to red like a traffic light without bothering to go through amber, even though amber was its natural color. He looked about to lose his self-control and his voice shook when he said: "I am a member of the Chinese Communist Youth League."

By which I assumed he meant that by accusing him of untruth-

fulness I had been slandering that juvenile body of promising ancestors *in toto*. However, he magnanimously suggested that we
should not quarrel, and no more was said on the subject until the
morning of my departure, when I went to the airport in the old
limousine with the driver driving in front and Mr. Li driving me
crazy in the back reciting his favorite piece about the imperialists, bureaucrat-capitalists, feudal landlords, exploiters and para-
sites who had once lorded it over the toiling masses of Shanghai.

"By the way," I said, "I happen to know for a fact that the anti-
colonialist exhibition is still running."

"I know," replied Mr. Li unblushingly, "I heard this very
morning. What a pity you can't stay longer! It would have been
a pleasure to take you there."

The Waichiaopu representative and I parted on the best of
terms. He had seemed to take it as quite natural that I should be
staying with the Spankies, only I must not refer to the British
consul as there was no British consulate at Shanghai. I felt like a
lazy schoolboy who makes the same mistake over and over again
through sheer inattentiveness and is being reprimanded time after
time by a kind and patient marm who knows he is hopeless and
cannot help wishing that sterner methods could be employed,
much as it would hurt her to have to resort to them.

The next morning at eight o'clock, Mr. Li turned up, punctual
to the minute, just as I was finishing a delicious English breakfast
over which, all things considered, I should have liked to linger.
He drove up in the old Buick with the same tough-looking driver
at the wheel, sent in word that he was there, and practically
bundled me into the waiting car.

"You will have," he said, "a bird's-eye view of Shanghai."

It occurred to me very foolishly that he might have chartered a
helicopter and I wondered how much it would cost my office,
but no. We merely crossed the Garden Bridge over the Soochow
Creek, which waterway is only separated from the British compound by the breadth of Soochow Road, and the car stopped on
the other bank, not in front but behind that tall yet squat ugly
building which had been known in my days as Broadway Mansions. We went in through the back entrance and it was only
when I found myself in the ground-floor lounge that I realized
why: the front door had been walled up. On the inside, no trace

remained of it, for a wide aquarium stretched across it and the goggle-eyed fish, busily darting hither and thither, seemed to be keeping watch over this local specimen of the Great Wall of China and to be ready to prosecute trespassers.

"This way, please," said Mr. Li.

We stepped into the elevator, and shot up to the sixteenth floor. The door opened. We stepped into a large apartment and, through it, onto a terraced roof.

Mr. Li spread his arms wide. "Now," he said, "you can see Shanghai."

There was nothing to be seen, even from that vantage coign. As often happens in late spring, a low sky hung over Shanghai, a thin drizzle was falling, and the famous skyline was shrouded in mist. I was reminded of one of Mr. Li's colleagues who had escorted me through Canton over a year before and who, on our way to the airport very early in the morning, had remarked that the dawn was the best time of day to appreciate the fragrance of the countryside. He was perfectly right, for we were in the process of overtaking a procession of honey-carts and the smell was overpowering. But not to him. He spoke the phrase he had to speak at that particular hour when seeing foreigners off. Likewise, even though visibility was practically zero, Mr. Li, with his eyes and his mind equally shut tight, had quite as naturally, quite as impersonally, to suggest that I take a good look at Shanghai, which I had done often, and from that very spot, at a time when he was still a mere twinkle in his father's spectacles.

"A very gorgeous sight," said Mr. Li, rubbing it in. "One that we do not like our foreign friends to miss."

"I must remind you again, Mr. Li, that I have *lived* in Shanghai. For years on end."

"Then you must notice the change," Mr. Li pointed out, speaking through a sort of slowly whirling fog, like the ghost of Hamlet's father in the film version.

It was apparently one of his stock phrases.

"Tell me," I asked, "what do you do with this building now?"

"All sorts of official offices."

"And this particular floor?"

"A workers' club."

"Many members?"

"Thousands."

"But there is no room for thousands of people."

"They turn up in turns."

"For drinks and relaxation?"

"For political discussion. Tea is served."

"Are you a member?"

"Occasionally. It is not for me to decide when I am or not."

"Are you a member today?"

"No. Not today."

"Then, what are we doing here?"

"Special permission for you."

"I am grateful."

"Thank you. This is a very fine building," Mr. Li added, tapping the tiled floor with the heel of his rubber overshoe as if he owned the place and was offering it for sale.

"Tell me," I asked as we walked back indoors, "who is now in occupancy of the penthouse above our heads?"

"Nobody. Another workers' club, perhaps. Why?"

"I was just wondering whether the tub that was cracked in one of the bathrooms had finally been replaced. I could never get it done."

"You?"

"Me. I once lived up there."

"You? In a Chinese workers' club? You are not being sincere with me!"

"But I am. Let me tell you the story of this building. It was British-owned at first, then sold to the Kuomintang government. The Japanese occupied it during the war, as enemy property. When China was liberated in 1945 . . ."

"China was liberated in 1949," Mr. Li corrected me sternly.

"I mean liberated from Japanese occupation."

"That was a great victory for the People's Liberation Army but that was not liberation. Liberation: 1949."

He spoke the figure as if it were his last price for, perhaps, Broadway Mansions.

"If that was not liberation, and if your Red Army wasn't here, then why the hell did the Japs clear out of Shanghai?"

"Because the People's Liberation Army had inflicted such severe defeats on them all over China that there was nothing for them to do but panic and withdraw for strategic reasons."

"Well, to continue, in 1945 the building went back to the Nationalist government, and it was leased to the American Forces, and the four top floors became the Foreign Correspondents Club of China, founded in Chungking during the war. That is how I happened to live here, graduating as time went on from a mediocre flat to a better one and finishing up in the penthouse. But I never succeeded in having the bathtub changed. It was quite beyond mending, you know. But then Liberation came—mind you, I was in Nanking at the time—and the foreign correspondents had to move out."

"Because the American Imperialists wanted the whole building?"

"No, because the People's Liberation Army was taking it over as enemy property."

"From the Japanese?"

"No, no, the Japanese, as I have just pointed out, had left in 1945. From the Kuomintang."

"But you said the Americans were living in it."

"Yes, but they, too, were on the way out."

"You mean that they were being driven out at the point of the bayonet by the People's Liberation Army."

"Not at all. It was all very genteel and formal, and there was no bloodshed whatever."

"I cannot believe it," said Mr. Li. "Look at South Vietnam now! The Imperialists never give up until they are forced out at the point of the bayonet by the Liberation Army of the People."

By this time, we had reached the landing and Mr. Li was pressing a button. Soon the elevator came up for us, and the door was held open by a female in pigtails and blue denim suit. We went in.

"This is the lift," Mr. Li said.

"We have already used it on our way up," I reminded him.

"But it is called a lift in English, isn't it? And the Americans call it an elevator, no?"

"So what? It means the same thing."

"Yes, it means going up. But now it is taking us down *under the same name*. This has already been pointed out to us as a piece of typical bourgeois capitalist nonsense. *You are going down in a machine that claims to be taking you up.*"

"Cheer up!" I said. "Apart from the fact that it is taking *you* down as well at this very moment, console yourself with the thought that in Chinese you call it 'lightning staircase'—*tien ti*, to be precise—which means nothing at all. And for the matter of

your being taken down when you are told that you are going
up . . ."

Very fortunately, we had reached ground level, and the clang-
ing open of the doors drowned the end of my sentence. Still, I
could now be certain of one thing which I had already suspected:
Mr. Li and I should never become bosom friends.

Mr. Li was as anxious to show me the new, suburban Shanghai
as he was to prevent me from having a close look at the old. I was
determined to see both, pressed for time as I was, and I found it
very difficult because Mr. Li was also aware of my deadline and
did his utmost to make me linger where I did not wish to stay and
so leave me little leisure. To him it was routine; for once, I got
the V.I.P.P. treatment: I was taken on a number of sight-seeing
jaunts that held little jollity but were still not without interest,
not only because of what I was shown, but chiefly because of my
interpreter's remarks. The simple fact that I had known the
Shanghai of former days, Mr. Li tried systematically to ignore,
not because he had chosen to, but because he had not been
briefed for such a contingency and was remaining very strictly
within the limits of his standing instructions. To him, I had to be
a newcomer with no past experience of China as a whole and especially not of Shanghai, and if I was possessed of such an experience, he had no choice but to overlook it since no provisions had
been made for him to deal with it. He would not and could not
take it into account. Also, his firm belief that, in the field of scientific and industrial inventiveness and progress, China was far
ahead of the West was not to be doubted. It was first made
blatant as we walked through the permanent industrial exhibition.

The exhibition was impressive, but in terms of time, not space.
China's achievements were undeniable, and in quite a number of
fields. There were tractors and motorized agricultural imple-
ments that had never been manufactured in the country before
Liberation, as well as many precision instruments. There was a
dentist's chair, complete with drill, also made in China, and a vast
range of chemical products, fertilizers, dyestuffs, and medicines.
There was unmistakable evidence of considerable progress, effort, ingenuity, and skill in copying. But the tractors and trucks
and engine-driven plows were, to the Western eye, rather obsolete. The electronic drill, known in Europe and America for over

a decade as part of any dentist's standard equipment, was still unknown, and Mr. Li, when I mentioned it, simply would not believe that it existed elsewhere. In 1936, I had been shown the
lights in the Ginza by a Japanese student who had asked me
whether we had them in France.

In Mr. Li's view, penicillin was a Chinese invention, just as to
him, in another context, Japanese imperialism had been liquidated
by the People's Liberation Army, "with some belated help from
the U.S.S.R.," and the Americans had played no significant part
in the war, suffering defeat after defeat until China's Red Army
had made it possible for them to stage a comeback by "pinning
down the bulk of the enemy forces." To Mr. Li, all this was
Gospel. China was leading the world in all respects. When I mentioned to him that Vice-Premier and Foreign Minister Marshal
Chen Yi himself had publicly stated on the eve of May Day, 1962,
that it would still take China "several decades" to become a
strong socialist power, he looked at me with undisguised suspicion as if I had just made up these brave and honest words and
was once more engaged in "slandering the Chinese people." Yet
they had been printed by the *People's Daily* and other newspapers. Perhaps he did not read them and the Marshal's speech had
not been quoted quite as fully in the broadcast version of his
speech. That sort of thing often happened.

The Shanghai Machine Tool Works to which Mr. Li took me
next had been owned and operated before Liberation "by U.S.
and Kuomintang capitalists." It was then called the China Farm
Implement Works, employing twelve hundred workers, out of
which total only four hundred were drawing a full-time salary as
against five thousand full-time workers now. In those days, the
factory, its director told me, Mr. Li interpreting, was engaged
solely in "assembling parts from the U.S.A." and otherwise producing simple spades and hoes. Samples of these were on view in
a glass case, lest one forgot. But, also on view, not in a glass case
but still in operation, was a very large machine, electrically pow-
ered, "made in U.S.A." for everyone to read who could, and
which obviously had not been designed for the manufacture of
simple farming tools. It was readily admitted that it had been part
of the pre-Liberation equipment of the works, but when I asked
whether it had been used to manufacture shovels, my question

was not translated. I tried again. Mr. Li's eardrums had obviously stopped vibrating, and so had his vocal chords. The director was looking benignly at both of us. After a while, he broke the silence, but it was to talk about something else.

The factory, he said, had evolved its own set of "good" principles. They were five in number and went as follows:

1. Study the works of Mao, emulate Lei Feng and the Four Good Company of Nanking Road (the one that was sugar-bullet-proof)

2. Increase and improve production

3. Attend free-time schools regularly in order to develop the revolutionary spirit of the workers

4. Rejoice in selflessness

5. Submit to discipline and abide by the regulations and the leadership of the Party and the state.

All workers were now literate. Their "cultural level," I was told, was at a par with that of junior middle-school pupils. Before Liberation, forty percent of the workers could not read. The works ran its own schools, including the political evening schools. Class consciousness among the workers had made considerable progress, keeping pace with production, and the "shining beacon" in both fields was "the Three Red Banners." Meals were taken in common in vast, drab, but very clean refectories. "Some families" had quarters of their own, a few miles from the factory, and a shuttle bus brought them to work every morning and took them back in the evening. Did the workers ever go to the city itself, quite a few miles distant? Yes, sometimes they did, in groups. Not severally; why should they? Most workers slept in dormitories, including, I was told, married men and women. What? Mixed dormitories? Of course not. Were men and wives separated? Yes, but I must not think that couples employed by the factory were; they were the ones who enjoyed the relative privacy of a home. Only those married men and women whose respective spouses worked in other parts of the country slept in dormitories. Did the spouses live far away? Sometimes not so far, sometimes quite far.

Later, I learned that many people had been sent to quite distant places such as Sian in Shensi province and even further west into Chinghai and even Sinkiang. The women mostly worked in Sian factories. They came to Shanghai once a year and spent a fortnight with their husbands before returning to work. The train fare was paid by the state. Children? Not encouraged. Those that were born were looked after in nurseries and kindergartens and taught to sing: "Mao is my father, the Party is my mother." Who said that the regime had destroyed family life?

At the Shanghai works, I was given, not figures, but percentages of production. These can be found elsewhere, for they are given to everyone. I am not an economist and I will not quote them. They showed a yearly improvement. Such an improvement exists in practically every industry all over the industrial world, and I do not see why it should be particularly noteworthy or praiseworthy in China where, moreover, it cannot be verified. I took greater interest in the slogan-bearing banners hung all over the place and in the bulletin boards where the names and photographs of those workers who had excelled themselves were on display. From the questions I asked and the answers I received, it would appear that professional proficiency could not be achieved without political proficiency and that one could not learn to use a shovel properly unless one was fully conversant with Mao Tsetung's way of thought. Which, for once, made sense.

Much against my better judgment, I find myself doing what the V.I.P.P.'s do, just because on that exceptional occasion I was being treated like one. On the strength of the material achievements to which (excluding all else) my attention was forcibly and smilingly drawn, I was at times tempted to forget my own past experience of China, recent and otherwise, to wax enthusiastic over things which I knew full well to be at least partly phoney and overmendacious claims which I knew full well to be cold-blooded, systematized, inhuman distortions of the most evident truth.

In Shanghai the beautiful simplicity of the system struck me with even greater force: you do not allow visitors to see anything but that which you want them to see. You do so with the utmost good grace, and you imply that if they cannot see more it is because (a) they cannot stay longer in the country, and (b) China is still in the stage of "reconstruction" and in many towns the local inns are not good enough for distinguished foreign guests. This, the visitor puts down to Chinese tact and an exaggerated (but all the more touching) tradition of hospitality. You produce a performing capitalist and a performing priest, just to show how liberal the much-maligned regime really is. You throw in a couple of banquets. Goodwill and maotai flow like water, and, as the mood mellows, you have someone, all smiles again, do a bit of well-rehearsed extemporizing on world peace, coexistence, and the little suspected affinities that have existed from time immemorial between the country of your guest and China. From the very first, you take it for granted that he knows all about the black record of the Imperialists in China and suffers from a serious guilt complex and you then undertake to console him. After all, he had nothing to do with it. Had he but known China as she was under the heel of the Colonialists, Reactionary Capitalists, Warlords, and the Chiang Kai-shek gangsters, he would have wept tears of blood and never stood for it. At least, you take that for granted and you are sure that your confidence is not misplaced. He shall be "judged by his deeds"—that, of course, is not uttered but implied. You drop a hint about those correspondents who come to China with preconceived ideas and who leave it with more of the same. You show him all those sights which are generally taboo to the resident correspondent: the primary and secondary schools, Peking University, the School of Fine Arts, the Museum of the Revolution, the People's Stadium, a jail, a sprinkling of People's Communes and factories. He has already been shepherded through the Great Hall of the People (a place of admiration which even foreign residents are permitted to visit), built in nine months "without blueprints" by volunteers from all over the country and so a tribute to the ingenuity and resourcefulness of the masses. Then you take him to Shanghai, hoist him onto the top of Broadway Mansions, and show him the Bund and its wonderful skyline.

The night before, I had been dining with French friends from Peking in the old Cathay (now Peace) Hotel, on the seventh floor, Chinese fashion, in the Dragon Room. It was a coincidence, but Mr. Li had already suggested that I should have a look at the Dragon Room and had undertaken to get permission for me to enter the hotel, which I could not do freely, since I did not happen to stay there. He had told me that this dining room was a masterpiece of the modern Chinese art of interior decoration. I had by then grown weary of the game and had not bothered to tell him that I had known the Dragon Room many years before,

before Liberation, before the war, and that it had been decorated by an Austrian refugee named Fisch.

I found the decoration much as it had been when last seen almost fifteen years ago, and the Chinese food (which had not been served in my day) was excellent. The band was no longer there, of course, and the tables had glass tops so that the immaculate white linen underneath could be used forever without washing. In the lounge, outside, the old comfortable armchairs were still there, but they stood in impeccable stiff rows against the walls as if the floor had been cleared for dancing, which was not the case. They bore those white cotton covers which already disgraced Chinese establishments before the Communist takeover and which the Reds had inherited together with many other things, including the Japanese sanitary gauze gag, from the days of imperalism and feudalism.

And now I was saying to Mr. Li: "Let us walk up Nanking Road."

"It would be more comfortable to take the car," Mr. Li said.

We were standing at the corner of the Bund, with the Whangpoo behind us. To our right stood Sassoon House and the Cathay Hotel with the front entrance through the arcade safely barred. To our left stood what seemed to be the empty shell of the erstwhile Palace Hotel, with boards replacing the former panes on the ground-floor windows, its door also boarded up. Before us stretched the vista of Nanking Road up to the corner of Honan Road where there is a slight curve.

"Why not take the car?" Mr. Li insisted. "You are paying for it."

"And for the driver's services and your own, which I do not at the moment require. Why don't you both have a cup of tea while I navigate Nanking Road without a pilot?"

"I shall go with you," Mr. Li sighed, "and the car will follow us."

And so we set forth on our journey with Mr. Li suddenly changing from his usual sluggish pace to a brisk trot and talking nineteen to the dozen in an effort to focus my attention on himself.

"This," he said, "is Nanking Road. Before Liberation, the sidewalks were crowded with prostitutes selling their bodies for money to the lustful Imperialists, feudal landlords, Kuomintang

bourgeois capitalists, and other reactionaries and modern revisionists."

"Nonsense. No streetwalker ever showed her face in the lower
part of Nanking Road. You had to go much further up, to the
corner of Chekiang Road in fact, where the Sincere and Wing
On department stores were, before you could catch sight of one.
They stood about in clusters with their amahs. That is before the
city had been made as wholly virtuous, on the outside at least, by
the Chiang Kai-shek government as the Liberation has kept it
since, if not quite so clean."

"Beggars," Mr. Li went on, "poor people, defenseless women
and children, were being constantly jostled and pushed into the
gutter by arrogant foreigners. . . ."

"Not constantly, Mr. Li. And not by *all* foreigners, for they
were not all arrogant. The majority were not. In the days of the
Unequal Treaties, that is before the war, there were indeed a
large number of people—British, American, French, to say nothing of the Japanese—who were stupid and callous by birth and so
arrogant, and their attitude to the Chinese, let me tell you, was
not resented by the Chinese alone. They were largely to be found
among the minor officials of the International Settlement and the
French Concession. The police were brutal to a degree, and not
to the Chinese only, but to anyone they thought they had no
cause to fear. I remember stopping in the middle of Garden
Bridge once, when I was still new to Shanghai, to ask two British
policemen for some trifling information. They were standing on
the pavement, idly discussing, if my memory serves, the bed-
worthiness of some tart or other. They would not condescend to
turn their silly heads or speak to me until I got quite angry and
said I would report them for their discourtesy. They then turned
on me and threatened to take me to the police station unless I
took myself off at once. I replied that the first thing I would do
there would be to ring up my consul. They then became most
urbane and apologetic and said that they had mistaken me for a
White Russian. Paper tigers, as you might say. The wives of such
people were often even worse than their husbands. Some of these
wives, incidentally, were White Russians who had married for
the sake of a passport. The White Russians, as you perhaps know,
Mr. Li, were stateless and enjoyed none of the foreign privileges
except the *de facto* protection of a flag which was not the flag

of their former country, and that only as long as they did not cross into Chinese-administered territory. They hated the Chinese whose legal status they shared in the foreign city, which humiliated them no end. They were contemptuous, and the Chinese returned their contempt with a vengeance. Forgive my lecturing you, Mr. Li. I shall charge you twelve yuans for it at the end of the day and we shall be quits."

I was not really trying to lecture Mr. Li, but to drown his voice and possibly to disconcert and shock him into silence. But he was carefully *not* listening; his words came tumbling out faster and faster, jostling each other as it were; his tone rose higher and shriller. I realized with interest that he was not merely reciting his usual piece, playing his worn record, but that he *must* not hear me, that he had no permission to and was afraid to, and that he was literally shutting his ears lest I poured venom into them, Shakespearean fashion, and so achieved the dreadful purpose of all foreign guest-devils he came in contact with (of which he had been duly warned), which was to poison his mind with ulterior motives. He chattered away in fear of corruption, and I believe that if he had chattered himself hoarse, his teeth would have taken over.

This cheered me up greatly and I went on soliloquizing.

"To go back to my policemen," I said, "by far the most objectionable were the Sikhs in the Settlement and the Annamites (they're known as Vietnamese now) imported respectively by the British and the French from their colonial empires. They loved to lord it over the Chinese, Mr. Li. Perhaps it is nice for people who are oppressed at home to be able to oppress others abroad. Running dogs of the Imperialists, no doubt, slaves content with their fate, the worst enemies of the Revolution, as Marx said."

Mr. Li had stopped in his stride and we both stood stockstill in the damp air, jabbering at each other, or rather going on with our simultaneous monologues. Mr. Li's voice was no longer so high-pitched or so loud. He was certainly not trying to indoctrinate me; he was mumbling some Chinese *vade retro Satanas*, some exorcism, some mumbo-jumbo in which the magic words: "Three Red Banners . . . East Wind prevails over West Wind . . . all enemies of the people are surely doomed . . . Chairman Mao's thinking . . ." kept recurring, spoken with true fervor.

"But not all foreigners were like those," I continued happily.

"You must not forget that most of them, and certainly the more important of them, were merchants. They were the people whose fathers had built Shanghai and made it prosperous, not only for themselves, but for the Chinese also, up to a point. And if the Chinese fared so badly in Shanghai, why did they flock to it, not just from the countryside but from such nearby towns as, for instance, Wusih, Soochow, and Ningpo-More-Far? The pay was bad, working hours quite inhuman, living conditions very hard generally. Why did the Chinese workers stay? Why didn't they go back whence they had come or move elsewhere? They could have gone, Mr. Li, and nobody would have stopped them for, in those days, the Chinese were free to move as they pleased," I added, driving the point home.

Mr. Li muttered on: ". . . Socialist construction . . . Great Leap Forward . . . Four Good Company . . ."

But I was not to be checked. "Are you aware, Mr. Li," I asked, "that it was in the French Concession that the Chinese Communist Party was founded in 1921?"

That brought Mr. Li down to earth. "In Shanghai, yes, I know. But not in the French Concession. That is American propaganda."

"American propaganda," I pointed out, "would have made it the International Settlement."

Mr. Li resumed his incantations, and I went on to explain that these Shanghai merchants were certainly complacent but not arrogant, that their customers were Chinese and that no businessman can afford to be arrogant with the customer. On the other hand, they had brought to the country many commodities that were unknown before. " 'Oil for the lamps of China,' " I quoted. Indeed, some of these *taipans* had a great admiration for China, and they had remained friends of China to the present day.

This must have registered, for Mr. Li stopped in the middle of a recital of what Mao had said at the Yenan Anti-Japanese Military Academy, which, I assumed, was particularly efficacious against the evil eye, and said again that this was "American propaganda."

"Are you aware," I said sternly, "that there existed on the China coast what we called Merchant Dynasties? Of these, the leading two, both British, were the houses of Butterfield and Swire and of Jardine, Matheson, and Co. The head of Jardine's now is Mr. John Keswick and he lives in London, but ever since

Liberation, he has come to China at least twice a year and he is always received in Peking (where I saw him a fortnight ago) as a welcome and honored guest. There used to be a Keswick Road in Shanghai. It was, to be precise, one of the extra-Settlement roads."

But Mr. Li was no longer to be moved. He had gone into another vocal trance and was dead to the world. In the end it was I who became silent and Mr. Li soon followed suit with obvious relief. Still he kept walking at a tremendous pace for his short stature, and I, not sharing his hurry, lagged behind. Occasionally, he would stop, turn around, and wait for me to catch up. The car, driving close to the curb, brought up a slow rear, and Mr. Li need not have worried, for the driver was keeping a constant eye on me. He seemed to be a much more important and, indeed, efficient person than my interpreter.

So this was Nanking Road, as Mr. Li had said. It bore a vague family resemblance to a street I once knew intimately, but it certainly was another street altogether, very different even from the Nanking Road I had last seen in the summer of 1950 after eighteen months of Communist rule, when there were still foreign shops and foreign customers and the street, despite this, looked much more truly Chinese than it did now because it was full of tiny stalls (which had not been the case in the days of the International Settlement) and the pall of rigid discipline had not yet fully descended upon the crowd and there was still considerable individual diversity in dress, manner, and gait. Even the once familiar façades were hard to recognize, and not only because they were mostly in a state of sad disrepair. After so many years, one expected to see changes and signs of age. Their structure—I was about to say their *bone* structure, for they were to me faces rather than façades—had not changed. The outlines, the contours, were the same. Of course, all the foreign signs and names had gone. But it was not that. It was like looking upon the countenance of an old friend and seeing on it an expression so totally alien to its character as to distort it almost beyond human recognition and make one question one's own feelings. There was something uninviting, almost furtive about Nanking Road, somehow implying that it had something to hide. It reminded me of Mrs. Chen, who was so ashamed of her Western background and yet, deep down, secretly smug about it, and who was perpetually oozing the sour sweat of inhibition. The same skeleton that disgraced Mrs. Chen's cupboard was now leering at me from every shop window in Nanking Road and performing for my benefit a discreet *danse macabre*. A thin gray drizzle was falling from the leaden skies.

"Shoes," said Mr. Li. "Plenty of shoes. All made in Shanghai."

The shop had once had two large plate-glass windows. Now there was only one. The other was covered with boarding. A yellow patch over an eye. Another eye full of shoes, all made in Shanghai.

"I used to buy books here," I said. "Perhaps you were right, Mr. Li, and we had better take the car."

Seen from the car, Nanking Road was less spooky: one was no longer part of it, one was looking at it, and only at its ground floor, and its upper stories of broken windowpanes were mercifully hidden. There were indeed many shops, quite undistinguishable now from those of Peking's Wangfuching, offering the same plentiful vegetables and fruit, fresh or tinned foods, the same consumer goods, and they were by no means empty of customers. And we had now reached that part of the street where the shops had always been Chinese. On the way, the conversation between Mr. Li and myself had run on the following lines:

"Government offices," from Mr. Li.

"Used to be Whiteaway's Department Store."

"Furniture."

"Macbeth and Gray, the tailors and haberdashers, you know."

"Drugstore. All medicines made in Shanghai."

"Formerly Marcel's Restaurant."

"Public Library."

"Shanghai Municipal Library before the war. The Japs took it over. Nobody knows what happened to the books."

"Plenty of books now. Chinese books. Would you like me to ask permission for you to visit it?"

"Isn't it a public place?"

"You still need permission. Foreigners are not allowed in without permission, not in any public place in China. Only the shops."

"Aren't they public places, too?"

"They are places of business."

As we crossed Szechuan Road, I had noticed that the entrance into Central Arcade was forbidden to one and all. A heavy iron grating, securely padlocked, made that very plain.

"We shall now drive to the People's Park," said Mr. Li.

We reached it and drove through it. Mr. Li exclaimed in a triumphant voice: "You cannot tell me that you have seen *that!*"

"Indeed, I cannot. In my days, it was the Shanghai Race Course."

"What is a race course?" asked Mr. Li unexpectedly.

"You know: horses . . . races."

"Races . . . ah, races!"

The penny dropped. And, fully automatically, Mr. Li's private little Wurlitzer changed the record.

"Some foreign correspondents," Mr. Li said sternly, "have been slandering the Chinese People's Government by accusing it of pursuing a racist policy. . . ."

I let the disc play itself out.

That little book I had seen for sale in Peking, *How Not To Be Afraid of Ghosts,* why was I constantly reminded of its existence, here, in Shanghai?

I had an hour to myself, away from Mr. Li, and I was walking in the streets of ex-French Town, through which we had driven on the previous day on our way to some suburban factory. But we had not stopped anywhere, and I had not suggested that we should, for I was utterly tired of Mr. Li's running commentary, of his pushbutton phrases, of playing mug to that small beer.

I had visited two of the forty-odd "new workers' villages" reportedly erected on Shanghai's outskirts since Liberation, that of Tsao Yang and the more modern Minghan workers' settlement, which is a minor satellite town, the Hungjao People's Commune, and a kindergarten where well-fed, rosy-cheeked, and adequately clothed children had greeted me like a long-lost uncle and had sung for me three songs, "Chairman Mao," "We Are Good Children of Chairman Mao," and "I Have a Good Mother," which mother, I was told, was the Chinese Communist Party. A great effort was certainly being made to develop the surrounding areas, but the core of the city, downtown Shanghai and the old French Concession, remained in a condition of neglect. New suburbs flourished together with new factories and communes on the periphery, while the city itself decayed and crumbled to dust. Broken windows, boarded-up windows, locked doors. There was, of course, the public garden, along the Bund, and there was that other public garden where the race course once had been, and there was the Sino-Soviet Friendship Palace, built by the Russians in the huge former compound of the Hardoon family, a frightful eyesore, a fine and typical example of the flamboyant Bolshevik meringue-and-barley-sugar style that irresistibly suggests to the beholder that Russian architects must be recruited from the pastry-cook profession. There was otherwise very little new.

It was true, nevertheless, that in French Town squalid structures, already looking old and ramshackle, had been erected in the vast grounds of the *Cercle Sportif* where the many tennis courts used to be. They seemed uninhabited and the club itself was shut, its doors heavy with chains and padlocks.* In Avenue Joffre, the pavement was broken and the uncared-for road surface full of potholes. The housing terraces which had had several entrances now only had one each, the others being walled up. So were either the front or the back doors of most houses, turning them into traps: once in, you could only leave the same way you had entered.

The shops, as I've said, were not badly stocked or by any means empty of customers. But here again one must keep one's sense of proportions. In the old days—not only those of the Unequal Treaties, but those of Kuomintang rule as well—there had been more shops, they had been still better stocked and had had more Chinese customers up to the last years when inflation had set in and the money was no longer worth the paper it was printed on. Compared to the Shanghai of two years back, the Shanghai of 1963 was perhaps flourishing. Compared to the Shanghai of 1937 (on the eve of the Japanese aggression) or even to that of the first postwar years before Liberation, it was not. After all, with the Chinese population estimated at five million and the foreign population under twenty thousand—250 Chinese to every foreigner (including the not very affluent White Russians and the German and Austrian refugees)—it is plain that Western ingenuity, to which the credit for Shanghai's prosperity is generally given, would have gone bankrupt without the purchasing power of the Chinese. Actually, up to 1937, when hundreds of thousands of peasants from the countryside, fleeing before the Japanese, sought sanctuary in the foreign areas, there

* I understand that the club, now, has been given a lick of paint and is to be used by the "intellectuals."

were far less starving Chinese in the city—and there were far more today—than official propaganda would have had us believe. If there were no more beggars on the streets, it was not because everyone had enough to eat (as will be seen later) but because it was forbidden to beg.

But again, it was hard to understand why so much trouble was taken to build outside Shanghai and why what already existed, including the readily available facilities inherited from the Foreign Devils, was being visibly shunned. There was a dead Shanghai, and the crowds that moved through its streets and patronized its shops did no more to bring it back to life than the sight-seer does to resurrect Pompeii when he buys postcards there. The difference was that Pompeii was a well-preserved ruin, and Shanghai was allowed to disintegrate. The municipal authorities fought shy of it, as if it were accursed. I was overwhelmed by the absurd sentiment that they would have liked, while preserving as a screen the Bund skyline in which they took some mysterious pride, to raze everything behind it: *Carthago delenda* . . . and that they did not quite dare; that Mr. Li, for instance, would not have liked to walk through it at night, lest, on the stroke of twelve, the specters of humiliation would suddenly materialize, wearing expensive shrouds and rattling gold watchchains. This, of course, put an entirely new complexion on the gallantry of the Good Four Company of Nanking Road. Sugar-coated bullets, my foot!

The title of the book, mind you, was exactly as I have said: *How Not To Be Afraid of Ghosts*, not *How Not to Believe in Ghosts*. As I sauntered past walled-up doors and, sometimes, windows, and barred gates in French Town, the distinction appeared significant.

I mentioned this to Mr. Li when I saw him—discreetly, so as not to put him on his guard.

"Mr. Li," I asked, "do you know a book published in Peking called *How Not To Be Afraid of Ghosts?*"

"Certainly," said Mr. Li eagerly. "There is an English translation under that title. Do you wish to buy a copy?"

"I have read it. But I am puzzled. I have been told many times that since Liberation, enlightened as they had become by Mao Tse-tung's thinking, the people had stopped believing in dragons, spirits, and ghosts. Why then is it necessary to tell them how not to be afraid of what they no longer believe in?"

Mr. Li thought this over and gave me for once a candid and sensible answer: "People," he said, "no longer believe in ghosts. But some people are still afraid of them."

"Do you," I insisted, "believe in ghosts, Mr. Li?"

"I am," said Mr. Li with dignity, "a member of the Chinese Communist Youth League."

As has already been gathered, Mr. Li, when in a tight conversational corner, would proclaim himself a member of the Communist Youth League. A member of the League, it was implied, could not lie or indulge in nonpolitical pleasures or be superstitious. A member of the League, above all else, was *different*. The Party as a whole began to look like a sort of freemasonry in which the red-scarfed Pioneer was an apprentice, the League member a fellowcraft, and the regular Party member a master mason. Mr. Li had definitely been initiated and was now of the second degree, with the degree of master Communist still outstanding. But what was most important was of course the initiation. It set one apart from the rabble, one's social status changed, one belonged to a privileged class—dedicated, no doubt, but privileged as well, like the clergy of olden days. Also (which was both clerical and masonic) one was entrusted with more and more Secrets as one rose in the hierarchy, one drew closer and closer to Mao's Grand Orient, the fountainhead of all light and knowledge and wisdom. The masses, in whose name everything had to be done, for whose welfare and political awareness one toiled incessantly, were interesting only as an entity, almost as a mere symbol. Individually, the uninitiated were negligible, drawing as they did the right to exist from the fact that they belonged to, and therefore represented, the worshipful and anonymous Masses.

It was after our visit to the Hungjao People's Commune that Mr. Li lost face.

I had enjoyed the commune, which was well run and prosperous. It has been described by others, for it is a must on every conducted tour of Shanghai, and I shall not attempt to describe it too. I had been shown the green, well-tilled land, the private plots of the peasants (seven percent of the total cultivated area), the irrigation system, the living quarters of the workers, schools, and the health center. The cheerful young manager who had taken me around had been brisk and matter-of-fact and had kept his explanations almost completely free from propaganda. He had not once spoken the name of Mao Tse-tung. Mr. Li had inserted it, of his own initiative in his English rendering, as a sort of free gift from the China Travel Service.* The commune in itself, an obvious showpiece though it was, represented a fantastic improvement over pre-Liberation days in the field of agriculture, and in working and living conditions in that area.

The Hungjao country, I knew well. I once used to ride over it, crossing the narrow, rail-less bridges of stone or timber over the many creeks on spirited but immensely surefooted Mongolian ponies. Early in 1942, I had "operated" there in a mild way as a member of a Chinese guerrilla unit. We would shift our ground every night, with the Japanese patrols always twenty-four hours behind us. Much of this clandestine travel was done in sampans, for the creeks were too numerous for the Japanese to keep constant watch on them all. The Chinese policemen of the puppet Wang Ching-wei regime, whom we occasionally encountered, were friendly enough and no more kindly disposed toward the invaders than we were ourselves. This maze of creeks was thus invaluable to the Chinese resistance fighters. Now, being escorted through the length and breadth of the very extensive commune, I noticed that while some creeks had been considerably widened, others had altogether disappeared. I cannot say whether or not these had been filled merely in order to increase the arable acreage, but I was again reminded of the blind walls and the walled doors in the city. One thing I am sure of is that, today, no unauthorized craft could possibly navigate the east Kiangsu waterways with impunity.

We had left the Hungjao commune after much handshaking, smiles, expressions of goodwill, and, finally, waving, as our car moved away.

"Very impressive commune," I said and was loud in my praise, and Mr. Li applied himself to the unwonted task of beaming.

---

* A young Chinese who managed to smuggle himself out of the country told me recently in Europe that, when foreigners were taken for a visit to the communes, the people they spoke to were not real members of the staff but, as he put it, "actors" especially brought in. This I am inclined to disbelieve despite the indisputable precedent of the show put up at the Peking railway station for the benefit of Felix Greene.

"There are over seventy thousand such communes in China," he said.

"*Such* communes or just communes?"

"They are all doing well under the leadership of the Communist Party and in the light of Chairman Mao's thinking. Some biased correspondents have maliciously reported that the communes were a failure. Now you know it isn't true."

" 'As the singsong girl said to the bishop,' " I quoted.

"You must put out of your mind this belief that singsong girls still exist in China," Mr. Li remonstrated. "All former prostitutes have been sent to the countryside for the purpose of re-education."

"And so has the clergy, I believe."

"Yes, indeed," said Mr. Li, once more pacified.

Things had gone well so far. Mr. Li was now taking me to the old Chinese town just to show me how clean it had become. But we had branched off to the left into Great Western Road, along which we had come three hours previously. It had been one of the extra-Settlement roads, by which expression was meant a road stretching beyond the Settlement boundaries but still under foreign jurisdiction. Since Liberation, much had been done by the Chinese to improve its surface, and trees and shrubs had been planted on either side. But it was taking us in the wrong direction.

"Look here," I said to Mr. Li, "this is a very roundabout way to go to the old city. We should continue down Hungjao Road."

"This is much nicer," said Mr. Li.

"But I have already seen it. Besides, I'm paying for this bus by the mile and I don't see why I should waste time and money on unnecessary detours."

"Much nicer," said Mr. Li, suddenly looking uneasy.

"I don't care how nice it is. Please, tell the driver to take the next right turn."

Mr. Li pretended not to hear.

"Mr. Li, I definitely want to drive along Hungjao Road. In fact, I want to have a look at that part of Hungjao Road which you are anxious I shouldn't see. Tell the driver so."

In hesitant and almost apologetic tones, Mr. Li spoke to the driver, obviously a much more important personage than his own humble self. It was the driver's turn to be affected with deafness.

"Stop the car!" I said as we came to a crossing. "Send the car away. I shall not require it any more. I am going to walk, and I shall report you both."

But it was only when I opened the door and threatened to jump out (which I had no intention of doing) that we came to a standstill.

"It is quite all right," sighed Mr. Li after a brisk exchange with the driver. And so, finally, to Hungjao we drove, and through the most nightmarish slum area I had ever seen anywhere in China, at any time.

The great claim of the regime that there was now employment and food for all, I already knew to be a lie. In Peking, at night, I had seen old people—and children as well—looking for food among the refuse heaps of the *hutungs*. The Swiss writer and photographer Fernand Gigon had made the Information Department livid (and greatly embarrassed his own embassy) by taking and later publishing a flash picture of a woman so engaged. But such squalor as Hungjao Road presented I could not have imagined: the abominable wooden shacks made of old planks, neither rain- nor wind-proof; the emaciated children; the people of all ages in their pitiful rags sitting on their doorsteps (if such a word can be used) or standing idly by, ankle-deep in mud. And, of course, the rubbish piled high and the people going through the filth with the concentration and thoroughness of gold diggers. One wondered how such destitute creatures still happened to have anything to throw away and what fantastic hope made them go back doglike to their own refuse. The stench was pestilential.

There was about two miles of this and I had the greatest difficulty in keeping the driver on his course. At every road intersection, he would try to turn left, away from this obviously taboo sight, and I had to insist that I would walk if I was not driven where I wanted. This thought—that I might thus see even more of what I had not been supposed to see at all and that he would be blamed for it, as I carefully pointed out—made him finally amenable and we drove straight on, but at a much faster rate than before, until we reached the old Haig Road.

"How do these people live?" I asked Mr. Li.

But Mr. Li had once more been stunned into speechlessness and even when I deliberately wounded his Party pride by suggesting that perhaps we had been passing through another satellite town, he remained sulkily silent, his face a sickly green.

"We still have plenty of time," said Mr. Li. "Perhaps you would enjoy a drive into the country."

We had already driven through the country and the prospect of another such jaunt in a downpour did not appeal to me.

"What I want to see," I replied, "is a bottle of beer. Kindly take me to a bar."

"Certainly," agreed Mr. Li, but he looked doubtful.

We drove to the big department store in Nanking Road, where, indeed, they sold beer on the fourth floor. I pointed out that this was not a bar, and Mr. Li very judiciously observed that I had only asked to *see* a bottle of beer.

"However," he added after a few words with the pigtailed female behind the counter, "you can drink it here. Only you must also buy a bottle opener. Hardware department, first floor."

"What about a glass?"

"If you must have a glass, you can buy one. Crockery, second floor."

"Let us," I said firmly, "go to a *bar*."

Mr. Li excused himself and asked where the telephone was.

"There are no bars in Shanghai," he explained after his return. "In the old days of the Imperialists and feudal Capitalists, when vice was rampant, there were more bars than riceshops, and the people went starving as their oppressors drank themselves into a stupor on sweat from the workers' brows. And," he added as an afterthought, "from the peasants' brows."

I suggested a hotel, and Mr. Li reminded me that one was not allowed to enter a hotel unless one lived there or knew someone who did, in which latter case, one should give one's name at the reception desk downstairs, and if one's friend was in and willing to see one, then one could go up in the elevator.

"But," said Mr. Li, suddenly brightening up, "you have been given permission to visit our Seamen's Club. You can get a beer there."

The Seamen's Club was the old Shanghai Club. Its beautiful teak bar had once been internationally famous because it was reputed to be the longest in the world. At one time, the news had come that a longer bar had been built somewhere in the United

States, at Las Vegas I think it was, but a member away on leave saw it and promptly sent word to the effect that this bar was indeed longer than ours, but that it wasn't *straight*. "*L'honneur est sauf*," a member of the committee had exclaimed, voicing his relief in French.

"Have they still got a bar?" I asked.

"They have the biggest bar in the world. We are very proud of it."

I already knew that the Chinese had hypnotized themselves into the belief that they had built the club and that they occasionally said so quite convincingly. The young skipper of a Danish freighter whom I had met in Hong Kong during my last breather there had told me that, while one had no sympathy for the Reds, one must admit that "they haf build a fonderful clob for the sailors in Shanghai." But I had not thought that they would be proud of something as despicable as a bar. Surprisingly enough, as it transpired later, Mr. Li knew the origin of the club and its former name. He described it as "a former meeting place of Imperialists and Colonialists." There, he said, did these unworthies foregather to hatch new plots for the exploitation of the toiling masses of China and also to revel in sinful orgies with prostitutes from Nanking Road. "There were rooms upstairs," he added darkly.

"But," I objected, "women were not allowed in the Shanghai Club."

This, he would not believe. Perhaps legitimately wedded wives weren't, but that was only in order that members could bring in tarts. He was quite positive and said so two or three times, implying that I was too naïve, or perhaps (which I thought even more offensive) too virtuous in my youth to be aware of certain goings-on that were perpetrated under my very nose. I asked him to stop, lest Queen Victoria should turn in her grave. Who was she? I explained. He said she could do no such thing, being dead. I said it was not a European custom to bury people alive. He said that lavish funerals were a thing of the past in China, but that it was gratifying to know that the world's longest bar was to be found at Shanghai.

And so our conversation went on along the set and logical lines of historical materialism. It was now understood between us (as a concession from Mr. Li) that the foreigners had taken a rather important part in the past development of Shanghai. But what mattered was not who had actually built a busy, prosperous, and very much alive city-port on the mud flats of the Whangpoo next door to an ancient but vegetative and insignificant Chinese borough, but who had redeemed it from sin and damnation, and only he, who had done that, had a right to pride and a right of ownership. By the time we reached the Bund, the discussion had become so personal that, to the driver, if he understood English (which I am convinced he did), it must have looked as if I had once personally held Shanghai in bondage and Mr. Li had freed it from its shackles and my yoke.

In the process, it became clear that a Chinese had, by force of duty, to be proud of everything that existed in China, of everything, rather, which the honored guest was permitted to view, for fear that the guest himself would show pride in past foreign achievements. Any knowledge of history which the guest might display about China, the East, the West, or, for that matter, his own country, had to be pooh-poohed as well. Not having been acquired in the light of Mao's thinking, such knowledge was not only false but also evil. Mr. Li had in his mind a very clear picture of the world at large and kept watching it with a complacent eye fixed on the dummy windows painted by the Party on China's Great Wall.

We had now climbed the front steps to the Shanghai Club and we were stopped at the entrance by an official in blue denim. Mr. Li explained that we had permission to enter, but we were not allowed in until after this had been confirmed by telephone. As I showed signs of impatience, Mr. Li acidly reminded me that I was no longer a member.

The long bar was still there, but a thin brass rail had been added to it for drunken sailors to hang on to and thirty-three bar stools (I made a point of counting them) firmly screwed to the floor and set much too low for anyone to sit comfortably and lean on the bar at the same time. There were also a number of square, glass-topped tables, of the type found in all Chinese hotel dining rooms. At one of them sat two men in working clothes, sipping Chinese vodka and fiercely shouting at each other in Spanish.

"Polish sailors," volunteered Mr. Li with aplomb. "They are engaged in a friendly discussion."

"Beer," I said.

There was only one boy behind the endless bar, and he made his unhurried way toward us. When he saw me, he gaped, but quickly controlled himself. It was only after Mr. Li had briefly departed (for even a member of the Chinese Communist Youth League has a bladder) that he grinned in recognition and whispered without looking at me the traditional "long time no see."

Mr. Li, having returned, declined to join me in a drink. The beer that was brought to me was, he explained, brewed in Shanghai in a Chinese brewery. It tasted exactly like the popular "U.B." beer of my youth, a product of foreign Shanghai. Mr. Li said Shanghai was proud of its beer. It was, according to him, in great demand throughout the world, almost as much as Tsingtao beer. (The latter also had a prewar taste and came from a once German brewery.)

Behind the bar were three hugely enlarged photographs with titles in Chinese, Russian, and English. They showed "Old Miners Playing Chess Games in a House for the Aged," "Workers Sunbathing," and "The New Face of an Old City," *viz.* the main street of a workers' village. On the opposite wall hung three equally large oil paintings featuring groups of workers and peasants in various ecstatic states against backgrounds suitable to the captions, which were: "Long Live the People's Communes," "Long Live the General Line," and "Long live the Great Leap Forward!" From the high ceiling the fifteen old-fashioned fans still hung, their blades motionless. The two Spanish-shouting Poles looked as if they might soon come to blows.

"They are arguing about a girl," I told Mr. Li.

"Do you speak Polish?" Mr. Li asked with some anxiety.

"I know a few words," I lied, adding, just to watch the effect: "They are arguing about a Chinese girl."

"That is not possible."

"A Chinese girl they both know in Hong Kong."

"Hong Kong," said Mr. Li, "is part and parcel of the territory of China. But it has not been liberated yet. There, vice flourishes and destitute Chinese refugee girls have to sell their bodies."

"Refugees from where?"

"From Taiwan," said Mr. Li, not batting an eyelid.

The sailors at the table had paused for breath and were now gesticulating for more vodka. I forebore asking Mr. Li why these refugees stopped in Hong Kong instead of coming to the main-

land. I suggested instead that we visit more of the club, but, as I
was told, I had only been authorized to see the bar.

"There is nothing else to see, anyway," said Mr. Li.

"What about the library?"

There was no library. I wondered what had become of the
books. There had been thousands of them, some very old and
quite invaluable, a mine of information on China and the early
history of Shanghai, most of them now out of print.

"Not very many people here," I said, changing the subject.

"The foreign sailors only come here late in the afternoon, after
work is finished, for a bit of nightlife."

"How late does the club stay open?"

"Ten o'clock, then nightlife stops."

"How many ships in the harbor now?"

"Fifteen . . . eighteen . . . perhaps twenty. If you want to
know exactly, I can telephone. No? Good. Shanghai, now that it
has been freed from the iron heel of Imperialism, has become the
largest trading port in China."

I did not tell Mr. Li that Shanghai had once been the largest
trading port in the Far East, that there had been times when fifty
ships in the harbor would have been considered an alarmingly
low figure and that, today, the docks seemed, by comparison, almost idle and deserted. Mr. Li, however, had embarked upon another diatribe and was informing me all over again that the
Shanghai Club had been a den of iniquity.

"The Kuomintang clique had tolerated such things, but the
People's Liberation Army took over the club at once."

"Nonsense. They did nothing of the sort. Shanghai was liberated in the spring of 1949, and when I left in the late summer of
the next year, the Shanghai Club was still open and functioning
normally, as were most of the other foreign clubs, including the
French Club. As far as I know, only the American Club had
closed its doors, not because it had been ordered to, but because
practically the whole of the American community had been
evacuated home."

This, Mr. Li again refused to credit and I was, much against
my wishes, drawn into another argument. Mr. Li's "Polish" sea-
farers had forgotten to resume theirs and were rising unsteadily
to their feet. The boy rushed forward with the bill. They paid
and left.

"The foreigners," Mr. Li was saying, "never did anything to

improve the livelihood of the people. Sanitary conditions were frightful. You remember the Siccawei Creek? It was a filthy, stinking, mosquito-breeding creek. Did the foreigners fill it? No. But our municipality did. It has now become a fine avenue bordered with trees, shrubs, and flowers. You cannot say that it isn't so. You have seen it. I took you there myself."

"Very true, but what about the Yangkingpang?"

"The *what?*"

"The Yangkingpang. It was also a very filthy creek, and much broader, and it ran between the Foreign Settlement and the French Concession down to the Whangpoo many years ago. The foreigners filled it and it became Avenue Edward VII. The Kuomintang changed the name to Chung Cheng Road. I do not know what you call it now."

"Possibly," Mr. Li grudgingly admitted, "but if the foreigners did it, it was for their own convenience, not for the welfare of the masses. Nowadays everything is done with the welfare of the masses in view."

"I must confess," I said, "that you are making the best possible use of the old Shanghai Club premises. I trust the Chinese sailors enjoy it as much as the foreigners."

Mr. Li looked positively shocked. "This," he said, "is a club for foreign seamen."

"Surely this is where they meet their Chinese colleagues?"

As I uttered that sentence, its profound absurdity struck me. Since when did foreign visitors and the Chinese meet freely, unchecked, on equal terms?

"No Chinese seaman," said Mr. Li, "is permitted to enter the club. Chinese seamen have their own club."

I digested this. There was a moment of silence, and it was broken by the old Custom House clock striking the hour. I listened, and I could not believe my ears. The good old Big Ben chimes, still. *They* hadn't touched *that.* And the Shanghai Club did not accept Chinese. It was fantastic. Mr. Li was studying his feet and paying no attention to me. The boy behind the bar smiled again and, apparently reading my thoughts or the expression on my face, discreetly motioned across the bar in the direction of the nearby Custom House.

No Chinese members. And the Custom House clock still ringing out the Big Ben chimes! Shanghai was still Shanghai.

Part Three

THE FORBIDDING CITY

28

TO THE PURE ALL IS PURE

COMING EVENTS cast no shadows before in Peking because there is something definitely surgical about the lighting, but the arrival of honored state guests is nevertheless heralded by the putting up of temporary public latrines for the use of the cheering crowds who will line the way from the eastern airport to the official guest-house, which is on the other side of the capital. There will be tarpaulins strung between iron stanchions and adequate shallow holes dug in the ground on both sides of the road, and, in the city itself, into the unpaved pavement. After the parade, everything will be speedily and carefully removed. And when I say every-thing, I mean everything: the screens and the stanchions, the offerings, the communal *ex voto*.

For many years, I thought that the word scatology applied in English, as it does in French, to a specific kind of earthy pleas-antry. The Oxford Dictionary however says that it means "the study of coprolites." In China, it has nothing to do with fossils. Nor is there anything jocular about it. The well-trained Chinese does not relieve himself: he performs a national duty. This has been carefully explained to him and he is acutely conscious of it, which robs him of his last possible moments of privacy, for he feels that Big Brother is watching even then.

Constipation is reactionary. It is a form of hoarding, of petty bourgeois capitalism. One finds it hard to believe that it is not in-tentional, that it does not reflect a critical attitude toward the re-gime and the General Line. Agriculture comes first—more food must be grown and the fields, therefore, properly fertilized. Ev-eryone is expected to help. Costiveness and sabotage are almost synonymous.

There seems to be no satisfactory equivalent in the English language for the French word *vidangeur*. Harrap's suggests "nightman," meaning one whose business it is to remove night soil, but I do not like it because it holds, to my mind at least, a derogatory connotation. It suggests something shameful and perhaps even illegal. It conjures up the picture of thunder-box crackers breaking into the homes of unsuspecting citizens under cover of darkness. For the same reason, I also do not like the puritan word "night soil," with its sly hint of a genteel self-inflicted dawn-to-dusk intestinal frustration that would make one long for the comfort of the winter months, when days are short. The present Chinese word for *vidangeur* I confess I forgot to learn when I had the chance. The old equivalent of scavenger, *ting tao fu*, is certainly no longer in use, because the last of its three characters indicates that the profession was entirely in the hands of the ladies. It smacks of feudalism, and reminds one of the dark ages before Liberation when there was no equality between the sexes. Discrimination of that sort has been done away with, and nowadays, in all walks of life, you will see men and women working side by side at the same job and for the same pay, and, for instance, shifting manure in the light of Mao Tse-tung's Thinking.

In that highly specialized branch of scavenging, all honors go, however, to one man. He has outdistanced all competitors in what the newspapers call his "productivity."

His name is Shih Chuan-hsiang, and he has been given a medal by the Chairman of the Chinese People's Republic, Comrade Liu Shao-chi, who shook him by the hand and congratulated him personally and officially dubbed him "Shock Nightman" and "Hero of the People." That happy scene was abundantly photographed and filmed, and pictures of it can still be seen in Peking. This is all very proper and very logical, and only the Barbarian will smile. When there are seven hundred million people to feed, agriculture comes first. 1959, 1960, and 1961 were for China years of natural calamities. There were floods in some parts of the country and drought in others. The country was on the verge of starvation and the wicked diplomats in Peking said that the only Chinese who could still feed himself was Mao because he, at least, had his words to eat.

Afterwards, the food situation improved rapidly, largely due to the efforts and devotion to duty of men like Shih Chuan-hsiang.

Recently, thanks to technical assistance bought from capitalist countries, China has built several important chemical fertilizer plants. Artificial fertilizers were unavailable until recently, and the natural varieties, animal and human, were the essential and invaluable commodity on which the future of the nation and the success of socialist construction depended. Not an ounce of it was to be wasted. A sort of cult came into being.

Actually, it had always been so, and I remember the days when the stuff was sold at village marketplaces and fetched different prices according to quality. This was determined, missionaries told me, by actual *tasters,* whom I never made any attempt to see at work for fear of being called upon to settle an eventual argument between experts. This ancient custom is now forgotten, but Shih Chuan-hsiang has quite a following and was reported to be busy training what he himself has called "a new generation of manure shifters." He has received considerable praise and encouragement from an enthusiastic press.

The *Peking Evening Daily* was the first to announce, on April 3, 1964, that his young disciples had been awarded, in February of the same year, the name of "Vanguard Collectivity of the Night-soil Shifter Brigade of the Chungwenchü District," and they were rightly proud of it.

My repeated requests for an interview with Shih Chuan-hsiang met with no success. I don't think that even those special correspondents on a brief visit to China, who were being given the V.I.P.P. treatment and were certainly in good odor, ever got within sniffing distance of him. They were perhaps received by Foreign Minister Chen Yi, and even by the Prime Minister himself. But not by Shih Chuan-hsiang. He could not spare the time, one was told. He seemed to be working harder than anyone else in China, and his hands, like those of the innocent, were always full.

Not everyone could join Comrade Shih's brigade. Nor was he an easy taskmaster. The *Peking Evening Daily* told us that of the many "learners," who had worked with him over a period of one year or even two, he retained only seven, the others being dismissed as unworthy. "Now" (the early spring of 1964) "on top of the seven workers already accepted, two young men have joined Shih's team," the paper adds. "One had previously graduated from middle school and the other only enjoyed the benefit of primary education. Political commissars in the Chungwenchü District carefully analyzed the work of these young people and now unhesitatingly bear witness to their ardor (*sic*). Still the commissars are not uncritical and they point out that these apprentices are still laboring under the handicap of three prejudices. First, they fear that they will be laughed at by other people. Second, they fear that the work itself will prove too arduous. Third, they feel that the work is not absolutely clean."

Faced with this treble problem, Shih sought advice from the "Directorate of the local Party branch," and after the matter had been given due consideration, he was told that it was better to practice than to preach. Thereafter putting himself between the shafts of what was known, in my Shanghai days, as a "honey-cart," Shih would take each one of his most inhibited young men through that very district where he lived and show him in his own neighborhood how to empty cesspools efficiently and carry their contents in wooden hods to the waiting cart in the *hutung* without, as he himself proudly pointed out later, ever spilling a drop. At first, the newspaper recounts, one of these young men, Ch'i Chen-kang, "took great pains not to be recognized by his neighbors. He would pull his peaked cap low over his eyebrows and avert his face when he met people he knew. Whenever he spoke before them he disguised his voice lest it betrayed his identity. But Shih put him to shame by being himself cheerful and showing considerable enthusiasm, joking with the children of the district who affectionately called him 'Uncle Shih,' and displaying especial gratification when some old lady of his acquaintance said to him: 'Old Shih, please make sure that our cesspool is properly emptied.' Shih would then answer in a sonorous and genial voice: 'I shall not only empty your cesspool properly but I shall also sweep around it.' Very soon, the young man lost all timidity and acquired pride in his work."

There is the edifying episode, in the same article, about old Shih, obviously tired by his exertions, being asked by a worker from an artificial flowers factory (where he had just been emptying apparently well-filled latrines) whether he would care to sit down for a short rest. Shih contemptuously replied that he never sat down when on duty and never rested before the day was done. I cannot help thinking that artificial flowers—a traditional industry of China—were smelled down upon by Shih for the two obvious reasons that they give forth no fragrance and that they blossom dungless—which latter consideration may account for the factory's cesspools being so well filled and perhaps—but he would never say so—for Shih's not being quite his usual urbane self.

It is further recounted that, at first, the apprentices had much trouble carrying the hods on their backs because the straps wore their shoulders raw. But, through persistent labor, their skin got thicker and thicker, and they developed calluses and so the load became much less painful to carry.

Another prejudice, which Shih's pupils had to overcome under his guidance, was that of the conventional bad smell and the unsavoriness of their activities. "Shih explained to the youths working under him what the words 'bad smell' and 'uncleanliness' really meant, and to do so, he had to tell them about his own past."

Before Liberation, Shih had worked as a night-soil shifter for twenty-one years. He once lived in what he described as a pigsty and fed on rotting vegetables. He was constantly humiliated. On one hot summer day, when he had just emptied the cesspool of a rich family of lawyers, he asked one of the household servants for some water, as he was thirsty. He was about to drink from the water ladle when the lawyer rushed forward and snatched it from him, giving him instead a chipped and filthy bowl where dead flies and decaying fish heads were floating on the foul water. Shih, always a fastidious man, would not touch it. He returned to the night-soil shifters' headquarters with tears in his eyes and asked his foreman for permission to leave. But the incensed foreman told the police and they beat Shih up until his face was covered with blood.

Such was the old social order, Shih says, when night-soil shifters were treated not like men but like unclean animals. "Now, encouraged by the Party and the authorities, and having achieved their proper place in society, fertilizer workers can pursue their political and cultural studies after working hours and even watch television in the evening."

Once the queasy Ch'i Chen-kang had seen the light he said: "Certain products of the chemical industry are much more smelly than excrements, and factory workers are sometimes covered with grease, but they are not ashamed either of the bad smell or of dirt. Night-soil scavenging also plays an important part in socialist reconstruction. Therefore, we no longer object to either so-called stench or dirt. Now, under Shih Chuan-hsiang's guidance, we are all full of zeal. And so it came to pass that, last month, we exceeded our target by twenty-eight tons." Ch'i was soon to tell his own story to the press in much greater detail, as will be seen.

There is no doubt that the little-read Peking evening paper, much smaller in size than the morning papers, had a scoop there, but not a chance one, for there is no such a thing in the Chinese press. Still, the *Jen Min Jih Pao* took twenty-one days—three weeks—to take it up. But when it did so, it was with a vengeance. One of its better-known commentators, Shan Pan, after lavishly praising Shih, who was still going strong, bitterly denounced the old bourgeois misconceptions and prejudices which were still rampant and must be forever removed. Shih's work, he pointed out, was not just manual. It had a "deep intellectual and ideological significance," for "it is not enough to show the younger generation how to do manual work properly and proudly. They must also be shown how to get rid of the evil influences of the past and to look with proper pride upon the work to which they have devoted their lives." . . .

"Learning the tricks of the trade is comparatively easy. The technique of a profession such as that of Shih Chuan-hsiang is not hard to master. But just to be satisfied with oneself because one has acquired a certain manual skill is not sufficient. It is a superficial attitude. One must become impregnated with the socialist significance of one's work. And that is why cesspool scavengers must work in depth." Thus wrote Shan Pan in the *People's Daily*.

The article in the Party organ had actually given the official stamp of final approval to the press campaign after a sort of preliminary test period. Soon it became one with the "Love-and-emulate Lei Feng" campaign to which Mao Tse-tung himself had lent his personal support. It was, like all such campaigns, extremely repetitive, and culminated in a long article supposedly written by Ch'i Chen-kang himself. It emphasized the profession's "ideological importance," demonstrated that it had reached the top rung of the social ladder, and bore witness to the fact that it had received its letters patent from the Party.

"I am twenty-three," Ch'i writes, "and I left middle school

after only one year. I joined the model team of scavengers of Chungwenchü district in the summer of 1962. I come of an ancient line of nightmen.

"I had had, of course, a good socialist education in the new society. Nevertheless, for a long time, I found it very difficult to rid myself of ancient ideas and prejudices. I went through a severe mental crisis. I did not really enjoy the work. I thought it was dirty and evil-smelling and also I thought there was no future in it. There was a time when I was put out of countenance whenever I happened to run across one of my old friends with my daily load upon my back.

"Even in the heat of the summer I would pull the peak of my cap down over my eyes and wore the largest sanitary gauze mask I could find to cover my features for fear of being recognized. When I walked into peoples' homes in order to perform there my repugnant function, I felt ashamed and spoke to no one. I practically sneaked in and then sneaked out again. When I met old school acquaintances and they asked me what my job was, I was ashamed to tell them the truth and merely said that I was engaged in highly confidential work."

He does not spare himself in his self-criticism. He confesses that he was dispirited for a long time and had grown negligent. Whenever dissatisfied customers complained about his work, he felt he was being personally and deliberately provoked. He remembers saying once in an angry voice to an old woman: "I come to empty your chamberpot, not to clean it." When I read these words, I felt there was a Shakespearean ring to them.

This attitude caused considerable sorrow to his old father, a nightman, it seems, of no mean standing, with a puritan turn of mind and greatly attached to family traditions, but not by any means an old stick-in-the-mud. He was, despite his age, a believer in progress and in socialist construction. Perhaps he only thought it convenient to be modern. But we must let Ch'i go on with his own story:

One day, I said to my father: "Papa, my heart is torn by conflicting thoughts and emotions. I always feel that nightmen are inferior to other people." My father became very angry and replied: "Child, when I was your age, I was doing the work you are doing now, but I was working for the landlords

and I had nothing to eat, no clothes to put on my back and I
dared not complain." He added: "You are unaware of your
own luck and happiness. You must purge your heart of doubt
and bourgeois prejudices and put it all in your work. The time
will come when you also will have to train younger men."

However, I paid little heed to my father's words.

Fortunately, about that time, the political leaders of the
scavengers' organization became duly alarmed at the "mental
instability" of some of its younger members. Evening classes
were then started to provide enlightenment and ideological
training. Reports submitted by the leaders themselves and by
the old master Shih Chuan-hsiang were publicly read and
analyzed and discussed.

"Thus," Ch'i points out, "we were given a very thorough class
education. It was explained to us that in the old days scavengers
lived like beasts of burden." The old Shih story with the fish
heads was repeated again and again and it was pointed out that
this was merely a trifling example of how the workers were
treated by the reactionaries. Under the Kuomintang, Ch'i was
told, "employers would sack their ailing workers or those who
were too old to work. Many poor people thus died of hunger or
sickness. Some also were buried before they were quite dead.
Now, the government and the Party always look after the nightmen well. They see to it that they get proper medical care,
should they fall ill, and they are entitled to old-age pensions as a
matter of course." The fact that old Shih had been elected to
represent his profession at the National Conference of Heroes of
the Working Class and had been received in audience by Chairman Liu was also constantly mentioned as conclusive proof that
"all trades and professions are now dedicated to the service of the
people, every kind of productive work is revolutionary work,
and there is neither difference nor superiority nor inferiority between one calling and another."

Ch'i then goes back to his own case. "Then I understood," he
wrote, "that the Party and the state were holding our profession
in high esteem and that we were enjoying the respect of the people as well. How could we then ourselves despise the work we
were doing?

"Before Liberation, my family led a miserable life. My father
was a nightman, like myself, and my mother a washerwoman. But

with their combined earnings, which were extremely meager, they could hardly feed themselves and their children. My elder sister had to live with a man with whom she was not even married. One of my brothers and my younger sister died of illness because no medical attention could be provided. As for myself, a few months after my birth, I fell on my head and it has never been straight since.

"On the eve of Liberation," Ch'i further recounts, "the entire family had nothing but an old blanket to sleep under in the cold months. My father was overworked, but there was no money for drugs or better food. Fortunately, Peking was soon liberated and the Party saved the whole family. The state spent over one thousand yuans in bringing my father back to health. Now, he is retired and pensioned off. Should he fall ill again, he would still be looked after at the expense of the state. One of my brothers is now in middle school. How could we all live happily without Liberation? When I had fully understood that, then the words of my father, which I had once treated so lightly, came back to my mind. And I realized how thoughtless and wrong I had been."

After concluding his self-examination, Ch'i went straight to the leaders and to old Shih himself and opened his heart. Then, Shih often asked him to come to see him for "intimate talks during which my class-consciousness was stimulated." At this time, the Lei Feng movement was sweeping the country and Ch'i began to look at himself in the light of Lei Feng's thinking. He saw how right the Party had been throughout. "Our leaders often tell us how glorious our job as cesspool scavengers is in the new society. If we work assiduously, then, on the one hand, the City of Peking will become much cleaner, flies being no longer able to breed, and the health of the population will improve. On the other hand, more manure will be made available for agriculture. Peking is the capital of our country and we have many foreign friends here. Therefore, the cleanliness of the city and the health of its inhabitants will, as they improve, bear witness to the spiritual and public-minded aspect of our calling. And then, as Chairman Mao has said: 'Agriculture is the basis of our national economy and in order to make agriculture prosperous, we must have tremendous quantities of fertilizer.' We are, therefore, pioneers in the fertilizer movement, we are the front-line soldiers of agriculture. For the past two years," he concludes, "under the educational leadership of the Party and of the old workers, and with the warm solicitude of the masses, I have achieved considerable progress in my profession and in my way of thinking, and I have joined the Communist Youth League. I love my work and I am determined to remain a nightman as long as I live."

Now, having carefully read and studied the various articles which I have just quoted and many others on the same theme, I felt it was quite wrong of me to laugh at what, to my degenerate Western mind, merely read like Party propaganda written by a Chinese Rabelais, but that I should see the good in it, the genuine effort to do away with old prejudices and promote national construction. I thought there was much goodwill and devotion to duty expressed in it. Shih and Ch'i might not be great luminaries, but their hearts were certainly as strong as their stomachs and they must be very brave men to do so cheerfully day after day and indeed night after night a job which I, sitting comfortably in my office as I was, would never have resigned myself to do, except at the point of a bayonet. So I went to discuss it with one of those Chinese who are in the employ of the embassies and who can, occasionally, and if they know you well enough, be quite forthcoming. He, too, had read the whole series and he was furious.

"All this," he shouted, "is a pack of lies. The scavengers are not held in high esteem by the population. In fact, even though they have to be called *tung chih* [comrade], like everyone else, I can't think of any self-respecting Chinese wishing to shake them by the hand. I myself would certainly hesitate to shake hands even with a waiter. And I would not be seen with one in the street, or I should be laughed at by my neighbors. And the Party knows these things full well. This represents nothing more than a recruiting campaign because now, as it happens, agriculture comes first again. But should they go mad once more and start another Great Leap, giving precedence to industry, then all these scavengers would be rounded up and driven off to the factories as peasants were in '58 and then they would be told that they must give up this disgusting work which they are doing; that they will now become engaged in real productive activities, which will be much more edifying and uplifting and useful to the Revolution and bring them closer to a true understanding of Mao Tse-tung's Thinking.

"Also," he went on, "how dare they pretend that scavenging is a noble and glorious calling when, at the same time, we are all being threatened with a forced trip to the countryside, there to do precisely that, should we become guilty of the slightest political offense? This is known as a severe and humiliating form of punishment. The sentence is usually three to five years. We call it 'being sent to the s——t-mines.' "

That was, of course, perfectly true. I went away feeling that Shih and Ch'i and their colleagues were in a position of exceptional impunity. They could practically cock their sensitive noses at the law. A stretch of penal servitude of the usual pattern in the rural areas would be no more to them than a nightman's holiday.

At long last I had found what I knew must exist: China's privileged class.

29

LEUCOPHOBIA

⊱⟨⟩⟨⟩⊰

IN CHINESE schools, children are taught that Japanese Imperialism was defeated by the Chinese People's Liberation Army with some belated assistance from the U.S.S.R. If you mention to a Chinese of the younger generation (as I did, for instance, to my interpreter in Shanghai) that the Americans were not altogether foreign to the ultimate defeat of Japan in World War II, he may not, out of sheer politeness, accuse you of lying outright, but he will make it clear that you have been misinformed and have fallen victim to bourgeois propaganda. If you tell him that you once saw a bit of fighting yourself on the American side, then you will arouse his worst suspicions and cause him to work overtime on his report on your speech and behavior. I was once told bluntly that "the Americans, the Kuomintang, and the Japanese were all on the same side," but a Chinese journalist whom I met on that yearly occasion when the Peking press receives foreign correspondents at a very lavish buffet dinner was aware that the U.S.A. had fought the Japanese. "However," he added, "everyone knows that the Americans would have been beaten without the help of the People's Liberation Army."

"So there *was* a time," I said, "when the Liberation Army and the Americans were fighting side by side?"

"Not side by side. On different fronts. Ours was a much larger one. The Americans were always on the defensive, anyway."

I was tempted to ask whether the Chinese Liberation Navy (there never was one) happened to be present at the battle of the Java Sea when the Japanese were first made to taste defeat, and whether the P.L.A. marines (there were none) had landed in the Philippines and perhaps at Okinawa, but I forbore, knowing full well that no action fought anywhere but in China was of any historical importance, unless, as in Korea, China herself rushed to the rescue of a fraternal country, the victim of colonialist aggression, and her heroic forces inflicted crushing blow after crushing blow on the Imperialists, thus winning decisive victories (plural), later to be mentioned in Chinese history books exclusively.

"What about Hiroshima and Nagasaki?" I said instead.

"The American atom bombs were used against Japanese women and children at a time when the Japanese Imperialist forces had already been crushed by us."

He was, no doubt, quite sincere. Truth has nothing to do with the facts; it consists rather in what the Party calls their correct interpretation, which often means distortion. If the facts don't fit the truth, then the facts are wrong. Marxist concepts such as "historical materialism" and "dialectical materialism" cease to be empty formulas in a crabbed Party jargon and suddenly acquire to the Western bystander a very concrete significance when he sees them applied to mass indoctrination with the deliberate purpose of eradicating objectivity and of doing away with individual thought through a strictly controlled and rationed brain-diet.

It is particularly striking, I suppose, in China where, under the camouflage of "orthodox" Marxism-Leninism,* the real trend is toward traditional, imperial omnipotence, and materialism in its purest form is being enforced as if by divine right. China, of course, has always been *par excellence* a country of conjurers and jugglers, but never before have these been allowed to rule the land, nor has there existed such confusion between truth and make-believe.

History, to us a solid and finished product, is plastic, malleable stuff to the craftsmen of the Forbidden City. Ancient and modern history alike. Chinese history and world history. Not clay that will harden once given shape, but soft wax that can be molded and remolded and still molded again. And if you point out that it is being made to change shape all the time, you will meet with a strong denial, stubbornly maintained in the teeth of all evidence. Still, the true, unspoken, but clearly implied answer will be: "The shape doesn't matter; it is still the same wax."

All aliens are by definition contemptible and evil, with the exception of the Albanians and the members of pro-China splinter

* Now officially "Maoism," or even "Maotsetungism."

groups of foreign Communist parties—but then they all are *ipso facto* ideological vassals. The Japanese, China disposes of with a shrug: everybody knows that their civilization came from the mainland. India is feudal, caste-ridden, and inefficient. The Africans, no matter how much interested flattery China showers upon them, she despises, which is very soon driven home to every African student in Chinese universities. But when it comes to the white man in general, contempt verges on hatred, blind and furious, if often contained, irrespective of social systems or political persuasions (with the above exception concerning her white liegemen), and everything that comes from him, material or spiritual, is bad, stupid, and harmful. I am convinced that even Marx and Engels will soon be considered mere providers of a raw material, the nature and possibilities of which had never been fully understood, let alone exploited. Even Lenin and Stalin, who certainly made efforts in the right direction, failed to "stabilize" it, as atomic scientists would say, and to give it that never-changing, ever-lasting quality which only the Chinese Fuehrer's genius could impart.

In China, Marxism-Leninism is beginning to look like somebody else's Galatea to whom Mao played Pygmalion. China will not rest until the Fathers of Socialism have become posthumous naturalized Chinese citizens and their dead faces have been painted yellow. Everything and everyone white is an eyesore and objectionable in the extreme. White, I was once reminded, used to be the color of mourning in China. In that respect and in others, the Chinese attitude is pathological: it shows the symptoms of a new disease: *leucophobia*.

How much China has learned and is still learning from the West (whether the Communist or the bourgeois West doesn't matter) is given little publicity. Western and Japanese industrial fairs are periodically held at Peking, but the general public may not visit them. It took a man of Chen Yi's caliber to state publicly that China was "still an underdeveloped country" and that she would only become a great socialist power "after many more years of hard struggle." But he said that early in 1962 and it has not been repeated by anyone. If China may in some respects lag behind the "developed" countries, as is occasionally acknowledged, then it is entirely due to the fact that she was "exploited" for centuries by Colonialism and Imperialism, Feudal Landlords

and the Comprador Class. Also, we are told, China is the mother
of all inventions, including the airplane, evolved from the paper
kite, and the moon rocket, a development of the fireworks flare.
Years ago, during the reign of Stalin, everything was said to have
been invented by a mythical Russian named Popov. I now suspect
that he was of Chinese origin and that his real name was Po Po-
fu.

As to the foreigners who lived and worked in China, they were
by definition enemies of the Chinese people and members of inferior races. Their very presence was a humiliation (true enough,
or the treaties could not have been termed unequal) and they
were without exception ruthless and inhuman exploiters (which
is not strictly true, for they brought considerable wealth to the
country, if only because they built railways, ports, and cities, to
which the Chinese proletariat flocked to seek better—if still
scandalously poor—working conditions than they could expect
from native employers and concerns). They built and ran hospitals and schools and even universities, and that cannot as yet be
denied, because there are still old and middle-aged Chinese with a
memory in good working order, but they did not do so to help
China, but to hoodwink the people. They never did anything for
China's economic, social, or cultural development or the welfare
of the masses. That is constantly rubbed in.

A slip is sometimes made, though, as happened in 1964, when
foreign correspondents were given their yearly briefing—with no
statistics or figures mentioned, only percentages—on the eve of
the National Day parade. Referring to the large but still vague
number of hospitals built during the past year, the spokesman revealed that, before Liberation, the only hospital of more than two
hundred beds existing in Peking was the Union Hospital. In those
days, it was known as the P.U.M.C. (Peking Union Medical College) and was an American foundation.

No mystery is made of this, but since the Americans are never
up to any good, the hospital was a pretext to turn poor Chinese
patients into human guinea pigs and to gratify the U.S. doctors'
sadistic instincts. In proof of this, and lest it should be forgotten,
heart-rending articles appear periodically in the Peking press.

Thus did the *Peking Daily* in its issue of May 22, 1964, publish
"documents" allegedly discovered in the archives of the old

P.U.M.C. The headline in bold large print read: "Crimes Committed toward Children by American Doctors."

The literal translation of the choicest bits follows:

Amongst the P.U.M.C. archives of forty-three years ago there is a dossier which reads as follows:

"En Pao-shan, aged ten, was taken in on August 22, 1921. He was chosen as a fit subject for experiments on the treatment of trachoma."

The doctor in charge of the ophthalmological ward was one Howard. In the dossier, it is stated that En Pao-shan was not suffering from trachoma, but after he was admitted to the hospital, the American physician introduced trachoma virus into his eyes so that he should be afflicted with that disease in its most acute form. This caused En to suffer agony and severely affected his eyesight. This experiment was the more cruel in that antibodies were unknown in those days and trachoma was very difficult to cure and in that Howard left En Pao-shan without medical care after he had contaminated him with the disease. The Chinese were not looked upon as human beings by the Imperialists, and En Pao-shan even less so than most, since he was an orphan.

The American physicians at the P.U.M.C. were particularly interested in orphan patients who were quite without protection.

The Public Health Service of the hospital had long made it a practice to choose orphaned children to study the effects of typhoid fever and scarlet fever. Boxes containing fleas were attached to the children and the changes among the fleas (*sic*) were observed.

The doctors did not even hesitate to experiment on pregnant women. The head of the obstetric section, for instance, conducted an experiment on one pregnant woman, thus ruining her health and adversely affecting the formation of her unborn child. . . .

The archives of the P.U.M.C. further contain a file on the death of Tung Liao-yung, also a victim of the American physicians.

He was a young peasant of Feng T'ai, who at the age of fifteen had done the work of an adult. He was honest, frank, and reserved. At the age of twenty-two, as he worried very much because of his material situation, he suffered from disorders of nervous origin. He was sent to the P.U.M.C. for treatment.

On July 2, 1935, in order to study the effects of radiations on the brain, a Dr. Raymond, head of the psychiatric section, submitted Tung's head to X-ray irradiation on six different spots. This had no connection with the treatment of his illness and could only cause his death.

These are the notes recorded in his file:

"On July 2, at the beginning of irradiation, the patient does not answer questions put to him; he does not eat and vomits a liquid analogous to blood. On July 3, he has fever resulting from the irradiation. On July 7, the patient tries to tear all the burnt skin of his head. On July 17, he scratches himself and one has to pare his nails. On July 31, the head of the patient begins to putrefy. On August 6, the scalp is entirely putrefied. . . . Later in August, the patient regains consciousness but his only words are: 'I am going to die.' "

So, Tung Liao-yung, who had previously suffered at the hands of the landowner class, was also a victim of the atrocities of American imperialism before his death. On December 18, 1936, the abominable American imperialists robbed Tung of his life. He then weighed only 60 lbs. After his death, his body was dissected at the hospital. The photographs then taken show that his scalp was completely rotten, and the skull visible; one could see the damage to the brain and the decay of brain cells through a microscope.

At the same time as Tung Liao-yung, another man called Wu Ch'iu-hswan also died from a similar cruel experience. Dr. Raymond drew thence this only conclusion: irradiation of the human brain by X rays give the same results as the same experiment conducted on the head of a dog. . . .

Raymond, this tormentor whose hands were covered with Chinese blood, had thus committed a series of crimes. About 1936, under the pretense that the use of a certain drug made it possible to distinguish between real epilepsy and a disease outwardly similar, he tested this theory on forty-nine patients. Soon after the injection of the drug, the patients had convulsions. In this state, they risked at any moment to break their bones, injure themselves in various ways such as biting their tongues, etc. When they did, Raymond filmed them with a camera. . . .

Such inhuman experiments were also carried out by other doctors in various wards of the American hospital. . . . In order to have plenty of human material for their tests, in addition to the patients taken from the third-class wards, the hospital had organized a "dispensary" where the poor and homeless could come to serve as subjects for experiments. In a monthly scientific review, a P.U.M.C. doctor once published an article on the rounding up of twenty thousand hunger-stricken Chinese for experimental purposes. He wrote: "They are more numerous than rats."

This is enough [the article ends]. One cannot go on reading these records of the inhuman atrocities committed by American imperialism in this "charitable" institution. These documents constitute accusations against criminal atrocities.

Nevertheless, for good measure the same issue of the *Peking Daily* prints a corroborative version of the En Pao-shan story told in En's own words.

His childhood, he says, had been fully of misery. When he himself was one year old, his brother died "from vomiting blood because he worked too hard earning the family's living." When he was four, his mother also died. She had four children. Aged eight, En entered a Christian orphanage "which was supposed to be a charitable institution but where small children were treated like coolies. . . . They slept on the bare ground, despite the cold in winter and the heat in summer, and were bitten by flies and mosquitoes." They were ill fed and ill treated and "weeping was forbidden." In the summer of 1921, four foreign doctors "including the American, Howard," came to take four sick children away for treatment at the P.U.M.C. En wondered why the children they selected, himself being one of them, were among the strongest "rather than others who were weaker." En was not aware that he was ill, but thought that "life in the hospital would be better than at the orphanage."

The very next day, at the P.U.M.C., Howard came to visit him "accompanied by several people dressed in white." There and then, En relates, "they pulled one of my arms and stuck a needle into it. I understood they were taking blood from me." After this was done, they "lifted my eyelids and touched the inside of my eyes with a stick. A few days later, my eyes swelled like rotten peaches. . . . These people came back, talking and laughing. . . . I fought and turned over on the ground, but I was only ten years old and I was held down by two strong men."

However, a coolie whose function it was to sweep the corridor told him that he had better make a quick getaway for "those who come to this hospital for tests are ill-fated."

The same kindhearted sweeper took a message to En's sister, who promptly turned up and "threatened to commit suicide" unless En was discharged at once. The answer was that he would be released in a few days, when the cure would have been completed. Indeed, very soon he became a free man again, but whether this was the result of successful medical care or of his sister's formidable presence remains a moot point. According to the patient's own testimony, his eyesight "has never been very good since those days" and his health is "now getting very bad." Whether or not his present ailments, occurring forty-three years after his brief stay at the P.U.M.C., can be traced back to it is another moot point. He himself is quite positive, however, as he ends his narrative with the words: "All this is the result of the atrocities committed by American imperialism and my hatred of the Americans will stay with me to the end of my days."

Needless to say, the foreign religious institutions in China, and especially the missionary schools, fared even worse in the Chinese press than the foreign lay hospitals. At irregular intervals the Peking newspapers published horrifying accounts of atrocities committed in the past by priests and nuns. No foreign correspondent ever quoted them for fear of involving the one remaining convent school, the Peking Sacred Heart convent, which was still being tolerated by the authorities. They told stories of Chinese children being mercilessly beaten and even maimed by the foreign sisters and there invariably followed the easy comparison between the abominable bourgeois and imperialist past and the happy socialist present. I shall not bother to quote the absurdities of the Chinese press on that subject, but I may recount a story which I got firsthand.

When my father and mother left Shanghai early in 1951, they traveled by rail to Tientsin, in North China, there to board a ship. They put up at the old Catholic convent school in the former French Concession. The nuns who ran it were at that precise moment in a very parlous position because a strong local campaign had been launched against them by certain Chinese elements—mostly students from Peking. They had been accused in the local papers, not only of maltreating their Chinese pupils, but actually of killing and *eating* them. As evidence, the guts of newly killed chickens, whose innards had been thrown out onto the street dungheap, as was the general custom, were produced and publicly described as the intestines of Chinese babies who had allegedly been roasted, Peking duck fashion, and made a feast of by the nuns.*

Western art, literature, music, and philosophy—foreign culture in general—are not only contemptible but also dangerous. Of the English writers, Dickens alone proves acceptable. But then, not all Dickens. Only *Oliver Twist*. And not all of *Oliver Twist*, but only a few selected passages which students of English are made to read in order that they should know of the squalor, brutality, and meanness of England *today*. This piece of information I obtained from a foreigner who taught in 1965 in one of the Peking universities. Great care was taken, she added, not to make the student realize that Dickens wrote in the last century but to convey the impression that he was a successful living author.

Shakespeare, the *Kwangming Jih Pao* declared in May, 1966, must be taken with more than a grain of Marxist-Leninist salt, for "he preaches harmony between the various social classes and expresses objections to the principle of class struggle," and so "his writings, unless they are read with a critical mind based on the thinking of Mao Tse-tung, may have a destructive effect on our revolutionary attitude."

Foreign novelists also have been harshly denounced at various times and in various Party publications. They include Defoe, Jane Austen, Thomas Hardy, Balzac, Maupassant, and—of all people!—Zola.

The graphic arts of foreign countries are to be rejected *en bloc* if only because of the nudes.

The official Chinese approach to the literary and artistic West was clearly defined in a long article on Debussy which appeared in the intellectual periodical *Wen Hui Pao* on March 2, 1964. It read in part:

As Chairman Mao has already indicated, since the Opium War in 1840 foreign imperialism, while indulging in military, political, and economic aggression, also carried out cultural aggression with a view to paralyzing the minds of the Chinese

* That sort of nonsense was to be brought up again fifteen years later by Mao's Red Guards.

people. The Imperialists went in for religious proselytism, and the building of hospitals and schools, and the publication of newspapers, and at the same time they were urging Chinese students to go abroad to pursue their studies. All these things were part and parcel of a policy of aggression whose purpose it was to produce cultivated Chinese cadres which would be docile to their Occidental masters and would so help ensnare the Chinese masses.

The article—over four thousand words in the literal translation I possess—is devoted to a very critical analysis of the works of the French composer Debussy. But Debussy is only a pretext and the author, one Fang Hsing, could have written in the same vein and practically the same words about any other foreign composer, writer, painter, or sculptor, for Debussy is certainly not a composer with whose works the Chinese public is familiar.

Nevertheless the author takes considerable pains to explain that Debussy (unknown presumably to most of the readers) must not be mistaken for a great man of the past. His music "must be studied and scientifically analyzed in order to do away with that form of superstition known as the worship of alleged foreign geniuses. In our Chinese musical circles, Debussy's works must be discussed in the light of Marxism-Leninism and of Mao Tse-tung's thinking."

The author goes on ruthlessly:

According to some people, Debussy was at the turn of the century a composer with progressive ideas and, in his own field, a revolutionary. He was said to be a realist, a democrat, and a patriot. Thus was he made to look like a musical giant, a notion that has now been proved completely groundless. . . . What Debussy actually represented within the framework of music, letters, and arts was the decadence of Western Europe at a time when capitalism developed into imperialism and when the bourgeois society was beginning to crumble. His musical activities were meant as a camouflage for the decaying capitalist society and as a means of giving the bourgeoisie a new lease on life and to consolidate its reactionary domination. They were meant to undermine the soul and thwart the fighting spirit of the people, for they had no link with real life and were in the final analysis just opium mixed with honey. . . . To-

ward the miserable toiling masses he showed nothing but contempt and repugnance. . . . It has been said that in Debussy's
music there is a certain amount of "oriental color" but in this
we see nothing but an imperialist attempt to influence us. . . .
This becomes very clear if we study Debussy in the light of
Marxism-Leninism. . . . Debussy and other foreign composers
were nothing but reactionaries in spite of what some people
still say. Chairman Mao has written that "in regard to literary
and artistic works of the past it is first of all important to
determine their approach to the broad masses of the people."
According to that principle it is easy to say that the ideological
character of Debussy's compositions is of a dangerous nature.
We must therefore remain doubly vigilant when dealing with
foreign artistic productions.

There are about twenty pages of this, of a strongly jingoist
nature.

It so happened that shortly after this long article appeared in
print the French pianist Samson François arrived in Peking where
he was to give a number of recitals before giving two more in
Shanghai. When the French Ambassador, M. Lucien Paye, told
me of his impending arrival, I expressed the hope that he would
not play Debussy. M. Paye told me that his first concert was to
be devoted essentially to that composer's music.

"But didn't you read," I asked somewhat aghast, "the *Wen Hui
Pao*'s recent story about Debussy?"

He hadn't and I sent it to him. His comment was: "For
heaven's sake, don't breathe a word to Samson François about
this."

Whereupon the virtuoso arrived and played Debussy with his
usual considerable talent before a house packed with selected
Chinese officials who, one may assume, had all read Comrade
Fang Hsing's withering piece but who still enthusiastically
cheered M. François and clapped their hands callous because, as
Mao Tse-tung has said, "politics come first" and, in China, politeness also, and this happened at the height of the Franco-Chinese
euphoria that followed the recognition of Peking by France and
the establishment of formal relations in which "cultural exchanges" were to play such an important role.

"I was delighted to find in a Chinese audience so deep an appreciation of French music," Samson François told me.

30

LEI FENG

THE NOTION that you should let Mao do your thinking for you
and that, if you still must think, it would be wise to think like
him is not new. It was first propagated at the very time of Liberation, but mildly and discreetly, like something one is sure to
accept as a matter both of course and of elementary gratitude. A
hint only so far, and a veiled one, but those who failed to take it
found themselves among the victims of the Red terror of 1951,
the first purge in the history of the young People's Republic, the
first trample from the iron foot in the velvet slipper of the new
mandarin class. Still, it did not really become a "must" until after
the second (and seemingly bloodless) purge of 1957, an inevitable
sequel to the failure of the Hundred Flowers movements. As to
the real deification campaign, which to this day has not reached
its climax, it was only launched in the early weeks of 1963. It was
aimed at the rising generation, Mao's official great hope for the
future of China and also his private concern and fear.

Indoctrination, of course, had been going on all along in the
nurseries, the primary and middle schools, and the universities,
and among the Pioneers (the regime's Boy Scouts and Girl
Scouts) and the Communist Youth League. But it had always
come from above and from older people. The doctrine of the
perpetual revolution was, despite its name, something out of the
past—almost an ideological fossil. Mao's disciples, Mao's apostles,
were his own contemporaries, and it is not inconceivable that, to
people in their teens, they may have sounded simply like old
bores. The Old Guard was badly in need of new blood, young
blood, or, to put it less metaphorically, of a youthful zealot who
would preach the old Gospel through lips that were not
withered, in a voice that would be, not cracked, but strong and

235

vibrant and full of life, and who would wield, not the calligraphic brush of the unapproachable and dated masters, but a reassuring pencil stub.

And so, very early in 1963, the highly improbable character of Lei Feng materialized out of nothing.

Literally out of nothing: when he made his unexpected appearance and became famous overnight, he had already been officially dead for some time. That he had ever been physically born, everyone doubted.

Suddenly, without any warning, without his name ever having been mentioned, the entire youth of the nation was urged to emulate Lei Feng by no less a personage than Mao Tse-tung himself. And equally suddenly, before this order from on high could logically have had any effect, it appeared that Lei Feng was already being emulated by fantastic numbers of young Chinese. You could scarcely open a newspaper without finding, among the spurious letters to the editors praising the "Lei Feng spirit," glowing testimonials from factory workers and farm laborers saying how much they had benefited in their work and their "political consciousness" from the study of the life and example of Lei Feng. There usually were flattering and obsequious references to Mao Tse-tung's teachings, which the writers would say had become so much easier to grasp and understand thanks to Lei Feng's object lessons in applying them to the problems of everyday life. Lei Feng's posthumous diary, from which the *People's Daily* had only just published extracts, was forever being quoted. Lei was being advertised as Mao's little red pill for young people who were still only pink.

Two things seemed remarkable about the Lei Feng phenomenon. One was that Lei Feng had, so to speak, only come into being after his own demise and that nothing had been known of him during his alleged lifetime.

The other was that Chinese Communism should have to call upon what very much seemed to be a fairy-tale character to convey its message to the rising generation. It was understood, it was known, that Mao himself never spoke. Why did such a master of the language, such a shrewd psychologist, the man who understood the mind of the Chinese as no one else could, need so shabby a dragoman to explain himself in his own tongue to his own people? Why indeed, if his writings were as luminous as it was claimed, did they have to be peddled about the country by a dead bagman? I remember, in my prewar Shanghai days, a foreign business which had taken as its slogan "Public Preference our Best Reference." A very fine advertising slogan, I thought it was, if a little incongruous, since the firm that had adopted it called itself the Shanghai Funeral Directors.

China apparently is a country where dead men tell tales and where only they can do so with impunity, as shown by the abject if compulsory self-abasement of Mao's Number One living publicity agent, Dr. Kuo Mo-jo, in 1966.

As to the Lei Feng message of over four years ago, its essential purport was that every man must give the Party full credit for his own achievements and that it is sinful to harbor personal hopes— which may be taken to indicate that there is no such thing left anyway. The glorification of this youthful paragon of Marxist-Leninist virtue was a sort of personality cult in reverse —a cult of impersonality. It turned on the life of the unheroic hero, the unwarlike soldier, an insignificant career made worthy of imitation.

The watchword "Love-and-Emulate-Lei Feng" first appeared in the columns of such papers as the *Workers' Daily* and the *Youth Daily*. Then on February 8, 1963, the official New China News Agency took it up at length in its English service. This was the first time that Lei Feng's background and life history—both, as one later learned, subject to certain alterations—had been outlined in a language other than Chinese.

"Lei Feng," the agency wrote, "was one of the family of a farmhand in Hunan province, central China. His father was buried alive by the Japanese invaders and his elder brother died at the age of twelve in a workshop accident. His younger brother was starved to death. His mother, compelled to work for a landlord, hanged herself to escape further humiliation.

"He himself started tending pigs for a landlord when he was less than seven years old. One day, he was stabbed three times in the left hand because he had beaten the landlord's dogs." Lei Feng "fled to the hills and lived on wild fruit until China's liberation, when the People's government found him, cured his diseases, and sent him to school."

He was then nine and he must have proved a remarkably apt pupil, for in no time at all we find him reading the works of Mao

Tse-tung. He doesn't seem to have ever been familiar with any other author. Subsequently, Lei Feng becomes a tractor driver on a farm, and we find him operating a bulldozer in Anshan, southern Manchuria. In January, 1960, he enlists in the army and at once begins keeping a diary; ultimately, his daily entries will total 250,000 words. He has, of course, joined the Party (November, 1960) and his unselfishness, devotion to duty, and love of the masses are now proverbial among all who know him.

Lei Feng, we were told in that initial story, was "shining with the Communist spirit." Many a time he "risked his life to aid people in distress." But what was chiefly emphasized was not his courage but his constant eagerness to help others—and the community—in all circumstances of everyday life. Thus, "when traveling by train, he helped women tend their children, old men find seats, and conductors clean the compartments."

This original brief chronicle was vague on many points and ended abruptly with the announcement that Lei Feng died "on duty last August" (1962). He was twenty-two.

There was much speculation for a time among foreign observers in Peking over the manner of Lei Feng's death, and some impious spirits suggested that this might have proved quite a headache to his official hagiographers. The possibility that he might have been killed in action was at once ruled out as there was no fighting anywhere in China, or on China's borders, in August of that year. Should a heroic soldier's death have been deemed appropriate, then Lei Feng could just as conveniently have met it two months later, on the Indian front. But it wasn't to be so. Lei Feng's death, like his life, had to be commonplace and unobtrusive as well as meritorious.

Thus it came about, in later accounts, that Lei Feng had died accidentally, while giving advice from the roadside, to a fellow army driver on how to back his truck. Through no fault of Lei Feng's, the truck crashed into a telegraph pole, which fell on Lei Feng's head and killed him.

But had it really killed him? Actually, he was coming very much to life, to the posthumous but very real life of a legendary figure. Throughout the country, tens of thousands of mass meetings were held to extol Lei Feng, essentially for the benefit of the younger generation; excerpts from his diaries were published and broadcast, tales of Lei Feng were told before village audiences by professional storytellers, and stage and screen plays were written and produced in which he appeared as the central character, an example to all.

The very figure of Lei Feng began to take shape. One could see him in one's mind's eye, always cheerful, helpful, and busy, a totally dedicated Red pioneer who never wasted one minute of the day, generous with whatever money he had but never spending any on himself, frugal in all things yet resourceful to the point of hitting upon the one novel and economical idea that circumstances called for: *viz.* patching the torn seat of his trousers with the lining of his military cap. Lei Feng was always kind and gentle, bustling about helping others, urging others to find their inspiration in the teachings of Chairman Mao; he was scornful of all creature comforts, clean of heart, mind, and body, in love only with the Party, its leader, China, and the oppressed masses of the world—half Galahad, half Boy Scout. "I can give up everything of myself," he is supposed to have written, "but I cannot betray Party, class, or revolutionary cause."

The Lei Feng campaign was an extraordinary experiment in advertising. At times, it made one think of Western commercial methods. And it was successful, too. A new utilitarian mythology was born, almost a new creed, a new form of mystical materialism. Mao, one felt, was God, and Lei Feng was his Prophet.

Throughout this intitial period, no actual photograph of Lei Feng appears to have been shown anywhere. There were artists' drawings but snapshots were surprisingly lacking. Or, perhaps, not surprisingly. If it was true that Lei Feng had led a very modest life, poor himself and among poor people, then his friends and comrades would not have been possessed of expensive photographic equipment. But suddenly, Lei Feng graduated to a face.

The first Lei Feng exhibition opened in Peking on March 19, 1963. In its announcement the New China News Agency wrote: "This squad-leader of a People's Liberation Army engineering corps unit died while on transport duty last year. His Communist style of life and work have been widely publicized in the press which described him as a 'great ordinary soldier.'"

The exhibition, organized jointly by the People's Liberation Army and the Communist Youth League, was held at the Peking Army Museum. At the entrance, still to quote the official agency, there was "a huge screen inscribed 'learn from Comrade Lei Feng!', an enlargement of Chairman Mao Tse-tung's message in honor of the young hero, as well as appreciations by Liu Shao-chi, Chou En-lai, Chu Teh, and other Party and state leaders."

It was twelve days later that the foreign press was invited to visit the exhibition under the inevitable aegis of the Information Department. It was an elaborate show. In a glass case, Lei Feng's one and only uniform, hat, musette bag, and handkerchief (unwashed) were on view. (I understand that, when other Lei Feng exhibitions were held in major cities of China, these relics were displayed at various places simultaneously.) Slogans, culled from Lei Feng's diaries, decorated the walls in huge Chinese characters. In glass cases, the diaries themselves could be seen open at those pages that were manifestly supposed to be the most significant ones and were, close scrutiny by Reuters' Adam Kellett-Long and myself revealed, the only pages that bore any writing at all.

And there were everywhere huge, almost life-size, obviously professional photographs of the hero: a chubby, good-looking, open-faced young soldier, eternally smiling, among groups of equally smiling workers, peasants, comrades-in-arms, children. Since it had been said that Lei Feng had become famous only after his death, after his diaries were discovered, one found it a little hard to credit the official claim that these were mere amateur snapshots, unposed, taken with cheap cameras by some of Lei Feng's personal chums and admirers.

In addition, drawings, paintings, and woodcuts depicted various moments in the life of Lei Feng and his family—captions somewhat at variance with the earlier New China News Agency version. Thus, one learned that Lei Feng's father had not been buried alive, but had died, as the English language magazine *China Reconstructs* later put it, "broken by the overheavy loads he had been forced to carry as a laborer for the Kuomintang army and the Japanese invaders, and by the beatings he had received at their hands." Lei Feng's elder brother, no longer the victim of a workshop accident, had been sent to work in a factory at the age of twelve to support the family and "soon contracted tuberculosis and died." Several episodes of Lei Feng's own childhood had also undergone substantial changes.

As we left the exhibition, one of the last correspondents of the Western Communist press to remain in Peking, Edward Brake of the *Daily Worker*, whispered to me: "I hope you realize, old boy, that this is April Fool's Day." He was right about the date—it was April 1—and we were unanimous in looking upon the Lei Feng story as a complete fabrication. No one believed that Lei Feng had ever lived. Yet at that moment, he was very much alive. And had been for some time. And in the weeks and months that followed, the more incredible he became, the more real he seemed.

The exhibition ran on for six months, but foreign reporters were not allowed in again. I am not even certain that it was ever possible for any individual member of the Chinese public to visit it unbidden and unshepherded. In the words of *China Reconstructs*, the exhibition was from the first "fully booked up." Factory workers were taken there under guidance, and so were university students and schoolchildren, all in properly organized groups, and so were processions of private citizens led by responsible members of their respective Street Committees.

Supplementing the exhibition, the official organ of the Chinese Communist Party, the *People's Daily*, ran Lei Feng's life history in cartoon-strip form, under the title "Lei Feng, a Good Soldier of Chairman Mao." Provincial papers followed suit. Periodicals were full of articles extolling the "good soldier's" virtues and achievements in "helping to build socialism," stressing his exemplary devotion to the Leader.

Soon, letters from converts began to appear by the hundreds in the press. Studying the life of Lei Feng, university students wrote, helped them to work with greater ardor and success. It also helped members of People's Communes to produce better crops. Factory output increased. Selflessness flourished, together with what was described as "Party consciousness." "Lei Feng classes" were conducted in every school.

Songs, often running to dozens of verses, were composed in memory of Lei Feng. One of the more widely publicized contains these lines:

> Let me be born a thousand times over
> Born in the bosom of my Mother, China,
> Let me live ten thousand years
> Within the glory of Mao Tse-tung.

The refrain goes:

What is this shout of Joy
 I hear echoing?
Lei Feng!
Lei Feng!
Lei Feng!

Another Lei Feng song proclaims:

Mao Tse-tung, you have shaped my life with your bare hands!

Mao Tse-tung himself had written: "Let us all emulate Lei Feng," and since the bulk of Lei Feng's alleged writings could be boiled down to "Let us all emulate Mao," this seemed only civil. What was Lei Feng, anyway, but a simplified Mao, the poor man's Mao?

We all speculated greatly at the time on the reasons for Lei Feng. Things were not as clear then as they have become as time passed and they fell into perspective.

Of course, in the first place, we were already aware of the necessity of an effort to stir the masses out of the apathy which was the result of the previous years' setbacks when the Party had lost much face.

Second, the sudden break with Russia made China decide to stand on her own feet. National unity, in the circumstances, was more than ever essential, and a national ideal and focus had to be found. These had to be simplified in the extreme, or the masses would not be able to follow the line.

Third, if the people of China must stand together and act together unquestioningly as one man, such things as personal ambition, pleasure, or even hope must not and could not be permitted to rear their ugly bourgeois heads. "No matter how successful you are or how much you achieve," writes Lei Feng, "you must never forget that the credit belongs, and therefore should go, not to you but to the Party."

This was not meant to be a temporary attitude but a permanent one. The Chinese must remain the Spartans of Communism. They must never grow soft through prosperity, as the despicable Russians had done. They would triumph over their enemies, the reactionaries, the modern revisionists, the neo-colonialists, and, above all, the still indifferent masses of the world, not necessarily by force of arms, but by their shining example and the inflexibility of their faith and discipline. Pride in the community and nation was the ultimate goal; nothing more was offered or might be expected. Virtue must be its own reward. Such was the moral of Mao, as simplified by Lei Feng.

Perhaps what we did not discern, and now, looking back, I am surprised that we did not, was that Lei Feng was not just the poor man's Mao, but that he was meant to be also the young peoples' Mao, not only a simplified Mao, a mentally inexpensive Mao, a Woolworth Mao, but a younger Mao, a rejuvenated Mao, speaking the language of enthusiastic adolescents.

This was of course the negative side of Lei Feng, as seen by Westerners. There was also a positive aspect, likewise created by necessity. If the Chinese were to stand firmly united, then they must learn to help each other and not just their relatives or their personal friends as they had always done. In all the inhumanity of the Mao-Lei system, there was an entirely novel element of human kindness. This paradoxically Christian view of life—"Love thy neighbor as thyself"—represented a new departure in Chinese thinking and ethics.

Of course, "thy neighbor" meant another Chinese. Lei Feng did not love foreigners. He was not a Mongol or a Manchu or any other mongrel from distant marches. He came from central China. He was a pure Han, if also a pure myth. He *was* China. His writings—the work, one suspects, of a panel of selected propaganda experts—left no doubt as to that.

The numerous lyrical pieces in prose and verse devoted to the glory of Lei Feng often show a nationalist streak. A poem entitled "Lei Feng" by K'o Yen, which appeared in the *People's Daily* of April 3, 1963, begins thus:

In our country the laughter of our children is the happiest
In our country the eyes of the young are the most shining
In our country the feelings of the soldiers are the deepest
In our country the minds of the old are the most serene.

As to Lei Feng himself—even though he writes that he is ready to "cross a sea of fire and climb a mountain of knives," that he will "never change," that "even if my head is cut off and my body cut into pieces, my heart will remain red," that his greatest desire is "to liberate Taiwan and all the oppressed and exploited peoples of the world," that he wishes he had "wings in order to fly to Cuba and to annihilate the American enemies together with the People of Cuba," that there can be "no peace before an offensive against the enemy takes place," and that finally "we must sharpen our knives in order to exterminate all imperialists and reactionaries"—he remains essentially kind, if deliberately and cold-bloodedly so.

He is an example to follow, he is the China to come, the ideal depersonalized China of tomorrow when everyone will be happy because no one will be conscious of any personal needs, and all will obey orders because it will not occur to anyone to disobey them or to question their wisdom.

To everybody's surprise the posthumous Lei Feng was short-lived and so were his disciples, successors, and continuators. The last of Lei Feng's reincarnations seems to have been a young soldier named Wang Chieh. He appeared—and disappeared—in the spring of 1966 and when, in May, the English language publication *China Reconstructs* published a picture of him, I thought, looking at it, that Lei Feng had come to posthumous life once more, so striking was the resemblance. But it did not stop there. Like Lei Feng, Wang was already dead, having been killed at the age of twenty-three in July, 1965, in, like Lei Feng, an accident. Like Lei Feng he had kept a diary and, the periodical recounts, "The entries in it revealed his day-by-day struggle, guided by the writings of Chairman Mao Tse-tung, to create in himself the spirit of a true revolutionary." *China Reconstructs* adds that Wang's diary was published in November, 1965, and that it "quickly became the most sought-after book in the country." As Lei Feng's had once been. The article is further illustrated with various "artist's views of Wang Chieh's life" showing him drying his platoon mates' padded coats and taking an old woman home in a hand-cart with himself between the shafts—just like Lei Feng. He also had at least one ephemeral disciple, one Chao Fu-lin, described as "another soldier following the example of Wang Chieh," and Chao is shown in a photograph smilingly emptying a bucket of water in the tub of an equally smiling peasant woman. There is a third equally edifying photograph: it is that of a group of female workers of the Taiyuan mining machinery plant discussing "how they can be like Wang Chieh" before a blackboard which says "Learn from Wang Chieh." Three years before, identical blackboards throughout the width and breadth of China had said "Learn from Lei Feng." Identical photographs and identical articles had been published everywhere and the very same *China Reconstructs* had sung his paean.

I read through the article, missing nothing, certain that, at some point, I should find a pious reference to Lei Feng, the true master of this unknown and spurious Wang. But no. I thought I must have missed it, and I read it all again. Still no Lei Feng. I read how Wang had lived like him, struggled like him, worshipped Mao like him, written Lei's own diaries all over again, the shameless plagiarist, and even had the audacity to die like him. Who was this low, scurrilous, impostor? Who had dared so brazenly to step into Lei's own coffin? But, above all else, *where* was Lei Feng, our Lei Feng, my Lei Feng (I knew him, Horatio!), the Lei Feng we were all supposed to emulate for a hundred years, if we lived that long? Not even his name was mentioned, he had been whisked away, "vaporized" as in *1984*. He might as well never have existed, poor Yorick! I was aghast and indignant and ready to write to *China Reconstructs* in no uncertain terms, to expose the abominable Wang.

It took me quite some time to cool down and to face again the fact that, in all likelihood, neither Lei Feng nor Wan Chieh nor the intermediate false Lei Fengs had ever been more than figments of propaganda, that in a strange way all represented a utilitarian revival of the cult of the dead, so severely condemned by Mao's regime.

Had we all been able to breathe a less rarefied atmosphere than we did in Peking, we should of course have realized that none of the successive Lei Fengs could possibly have been meant to endure and that child mortality was bound to be high among these phoenixes. We should have understood that these youths, dead before they were born, would never become the Red counterparts of the dreadful children of the American cartoon strip who for decades on end will play their daily pranks, never growing older, frozen in static time. While we naïvely imagined that Lei Feng would live his zombie life for all the eternity of Mao, we should have known that nobody but Mao was to be remembered eternally. It was indeed imperative that these young heroes should succeed one another rapidly and be in turn rapidly forgotten because, in the true Maoist revolution, the only fundamental change brought to the Chinese way of life and education is the substitution for the ancestral system based on memory of a new system based on oblivion. Such a concept as the Russian "Love-Stalin-today-hate-him-tomorrow" could not work in China. Therefore such people as the Lei Fengs could only flit across the stage, quickly disappear in the wings, and not enter again. Looking back one sees that they were but a succession of necessary but temporary links between Mao and a generation with which he could have no personal contact until that generation, by means of various stratagems, could be made to feel closer to him and to burn symbolic joss-sticks before his true effigy, instead of before that of a perpetually rejuvenated Faust.

It is clear that Lei Feng was never meant to be a Portrait of the Fuehrer as a Young Man. At no time was it suggested that Mao and Lei had been born and brought up in similar environments and circumstances or had suffered the same hardships. It would never have done if Lei Feng had been born like Mao in a well-to-do family and had had a secure childhood under the old regime. Lei Feng had to have a tragic childhood, the accepted and recommended childhood for anyone born in the old society. Moreover, there was the essential and indispensable difference that Lei Feng owed everything to the Revolution while the Revolution owed everything to Mao.

None of the Lei Fengs therefore was allowed to be remembered long. They all had to disappear rapidly, one after the other, before the face of any one of them could become fixed in the memory of the masses; and that may be the reason why they all had to look alike—familiar features, but nameless in the end, reflecting nothing but the greatness of the Leader and the humility of his people.

As to their good deeds, their unselfishness, their devotion to duty, their thrift, their blind fidelity to Mao, they would, instead of remaining the virtues of one man or a breed of men whose example the many must follow, become the basis of an ethic, as categorical but also as impersonal as the *Analects* once were when the Chinese lived by them without knowing what Confucius had looked like.

It becomes evident that the quick succession of the Lei Fengs was not only meant to implant Mao's thinking among fickle youth, but was also designed to be a sort of drill in amnesia, a political commodity in the production of which China sadly lagged behind the U.S.S.R.

31

ON SLEEPING TOGETHER

BOUND as they are by their monastic vows, the younger Party members present no problem from the moment they take the red veil and swear to worship only Mao. The time will come when they may be permitted to perform legitimate mating—I hesitate to use the word "marry"—and they may even be encouraged to do so, for they will breed the right sort of children. They will then dutifully comply, with "political affinities" a substitute for love, and later, when their offspring are old enough to go to school, a substitute to some extent for our more sentimental bourgeois relationship between parents and children. Thus will come into being the only really safe families, closely bound by common ties of political discipline and without the usual distrust between generations. Of course, the children will continue to report their parents to the school authorities, but it will be done, so to speak, in broad daylight and without any of the present secretiveness which is so humiliating to snooper and snoopee alike. I can well picture, in years to come, Comrade Wang (female, as shown by her pigtails) saying with pride to Comrade Chang (of the same hairdo) over a nice cup of hot water with the expensive tea leaves left out:

"Our little Ti-ti is so bright for his age! Why, he's only seven and he already knows over five hundred characters. Only last week, he wrote a three-page report to the Street Committee about me because he had seen me sniff when the night-soil collector came by. He thought I objected to the smell, poor lamb. Of course, my nose just happened to be itching. As if I weren't educated enough to know that vital manure smells much sweeter than a useless rose!"

"But how did you find out?" Comrade Chang would ask.

"Well, actually," Comrade Wang would blush with pride, "the Committee were so impressed that they sent someone around to congratulate us on how well our children were being brought up. Isn't it just wonderful?"

Or, in different circumstances, it is easy to imagine Comrade-Mother Yü admonishing her small daughter thus:

"Mei-mei, when Daddy and Mummy are in the next room with the door shut, a good little girl does not sit on the floor, playing with her doll. She looks through a crack and she listens, too. If I ever catch you again *not* spying on me, it will be *my* turn to report *you*. You are a disgraceful child."

The room next door indicates, of course, that we are dealing with a respectable household belonging to the upper Party middle class. Most Peking families live in one room.

Keep down the birth rate. Make sure that the young devote their entire strength to production and study (technical and political). These are the two official reasons for the campaign against early marriages. There are others, expressed by the hackneyed phrase: "A successful partnership between man and woman is based, not on love, but on shared political consciousness."

A marriage, early or not, based on love is likely, if the worst comes to the worst, to produce personal happiness as distinct from the communal happiness which the Party aims at. This is in itself unorthodox and may lead to further heresies. It is therefore essential that, when at long last young people, no longer quite so young, receive permission to wed, their minds should have been so conditioned as to preclude person-to-person affection from taking precedence over "love of the masses."

Thus does the fortnightly *China Youth* inform us that marriage itself "is of negligible importance, compared with the great revolutionary task." Moreover, to make the marriage a happy one, love is not essential, whereas "a common political attitude" is.

Also it must not be thought that husband and wife are necessarily meant to live together. "Miss" Wang, of the China Travel Service in Peking, was wed in the early summer of 1964 to a man who, quite naturally, she said, left the very next morning for Shanghai, where he worked. She hoped to see him again for a day or two in December when he would come to Peking on business. She was still incidentally Comrade *Wang*, for since the Liberation, wives no longer take their husband's name.

Free love is of course even more objectionable and indeed almost unknown, for it would represent a gesture of revolt, and revolt is the one thing that the revolution will not tolerate.

Even ordinary friendship—and that is a very sad thing indeed, for the Chinese can be the best and most reliable of friends, as I have good reason to know—is taken exception to. But such is the rule: there must be no straying from the herd.

The official attitude was already defined in the mid-July, 1962, issue of *Chinese Youth* under the heading: "Need One Still Have Intimate Friends When We Are All Comrades Together?" The article is signed by one Chi Chun-yi and is supposed to be a reply to a letter addressed to the periodical by "a certain comrade."

The author begins with an explanation of the meaning of the word "comrade," which, he says, "expresses cordiality and unity within the great revolutionary family. The relationships between comrades are of an entirely novel nature and never existed before in the history of mankind."

However, the article goes on, "individual degrees of friendship still survive for a variety of reasons. Some young men became friends when they were sharing hardships in the past or fighting the same battle side by side. There are also friendships which go back to childhood. In the case of certain others, friendship is based on the sharing of special interests. Thus can deep friendships originate. Such cases were common in the past and there was great personal friendship between Lu Hsun and Ch'ü Ch'iu-pai * and Marx and Engels.

"Thus it appears that within our revolutionary groups, personal friendships are possible apart from general comradeship. Through closer relationship and deeper mutual understanding, personal friends may in certain cases help one another particularly effectively. For instance, should you make a mistake, either in your work or in your way of thinking, then a personal friend may help you to correct it, whereas average comrades would hesitate to criticize you quite so frankly."

* Two well-known Chinese Communist figures of the 1920's.

But—the author finally makes his point—such friendship should not lead one away from the masses or the community. "To belong to the masses means that one has an understanding of the spirit of the masses and that one follows the line of the masses. Having one's own personal friends must in no way be a cause of estrangement from the masses—just the opposite."

This is still pretty mild, for the author is treading on not very firm ground. Where platonic friendship between boy and girl is concerned, the tone becomes sterner, as shown, among other examples, by an article published in the *China Youth Daily* of August 21 of the same year. Here again, it is an answer to a letter from a reader, but the original letter, emanating from a student of "traditional" medicine from the Urumchi (Sinkiang Province) medical school is reproduced. The letter, signed Pai Wu, reads:

Comrade Editor!
In our class, there are students of both sexes. Some have become "sworn brothers and sisters." They exchange notes in which they pledge themselves to help one another and to exchange criticism. They even sometimes write in a sentimental mood. Other students suspect them of being in love, and there is therefore much gossip. Is it right for boys and girls to become "sworn brothers and sisters" and, if it is, should it give rise to gossip?

The answer is very much to the point:

Comrade Pai Wu!
In the schools of our new society, close friendship exists among all comrades. They assist one another in their studies and achieve progress in common. It is therefore quite unnecessary for certain boys and girls to become "sworn brothers and sisters."
If some students in your class indulge in that sort of friendship, it may not be described as indecency, but it certainly should not be encouraged.
The spirit of comradeship represents a new element in human relationship and a great progress over the customs of the past. It promotes unselfishness, it is beneficial to all, and it favors no one in particular. If comradeship becomes especially close between two persons because their common political awareness is exceptionally keen, then it is a good thing because they can militate together in the ranks of socialism in efficient

cooperation and set a good example. But this has nothing to do with boys and girls becoming "sworn brothers and sisters" or girls becoming "sworn sisters" or boys among themselves becoming "sworn brothers," which can only lead to misunderstandings, as shown by what has happened in your class.

On the other hand, we cannot approve of making fun of "sworn brothers and sisters," for that would make them feel isolated from the others and draw them closer together. They should be shown great sympathy, treated as comrades, and given every possible assistance by all in their studies and also in political matters. They must be made to feel warm friendship around them, and thus they will be induced to abandon the "sworn brother and sister" relationship.

It goes without saying that the article so far deals purely with platonic forms of friendship. Its author, Comrade Chang Yi-hsin, winds up on a sterner note:

"Should some students," he warns, "indulge in amorous activities under the pretext of establishing a 'sworn brother and sister' relationship, then it would be highly indecent. Speaking of love when too young results in culpable squandering of one's energy and adversely affects the course of one's studies."

When the Chinese are being accused of destroying family life, they protest vehemently and quite rightly. It is true that they did attempt it in 1958, but they failed and have not tried since. What they are very actively engaged in destroying—how far they will succeed, it is still too early to say—is *private* life, which, paradoxically perhaps, is not at all the same thing. A family pattern is to be preserved, at least temporarily, but the relationship between man and wife, parents and children, is undergoing a drastic change—and I do not mean from the old, traditional, "feudal" family system, which was already on the way out in pre-Communist days and, indeed, survived in the villages alone. In order to make sure that allegiance to the masses, which means to the community, which means to the Party, is not superseded or even affected by a more personal and reciprocal allegiance, a considerable amount of prenuptial conditioning is required. The process is a lengthy one, which accounts also for the official accent on late marriages. Quite apart from strictly ideological indoctrination, it includes a general campaign against romantic love in any form and, logically, against all physical factors that may encourage it. The regime is taking great pains to make women unattractive. The almost compulsory trousers they wear are compulsorily baggy and any individual effort at being well dressed is liable to be severely dealt with. Under the Manchus, the Chinese male had to wear a pigtail. Under the Communists, the Chinese female wears two. You just cannot stop progress.

The whole educational process demands much sex segregation among the unmarried. Of course, young boys and girls work together in factories and coeducation is the general rule. It was already so under Chiang Kai-shek. But in all their activities— leisure as well as labor—privacy is almost completely out and "personal friendships" between the sexes the much disapproved exception, as already shown.

The night is spent in dormitories.

The importance of dormitories has been stressed in the Peking press on various occasions, the educational value of dormitory life being more heavily underlined each time. The earliest clipping in my possession is dated August 29, 1962. It is a lead story which appeared in the *Peking Daily* under the title: "Dormitories Should Be Organized with the Support of the Masses." It begins thus:

> If the workers can be likened to front-line soldiers, then dormitories may be said to represent the rear, for, indeed, the proper administration of dormitories in factories and government offices affects not only the life and health of the large family of the workers, but also their work, their productivity, and their studies. Cleanliness, orderliness, and harmony, in the dormitories, have a favorable influence on the morale and the will to work of those who live in them.

The author then warns dormitory dwellers that they must seek "their inspiration from the masses." No dormitory must be turned into a sort of exclusive club. Its members must never stop identifying themselves with the people as a whole. On the other hand, "Since dormitories are places of collective habitation, discipline must be observed by all so that water and electricity may be sparingly consumed and security strictly maintained." *

A fine example is being set by the employees (no mention is

---

* I have not been able to ascertain whether "security," in this instance, is meant as a warning against indiscretion in speech or as the danger of setting the place alight with a cigarette carelessly dropped on one's blanket.

made of the students) of the Peking Academy of Sciences whose dormitory, after remaining for a long time "in a state of disorder due to administrative neglect," rapidly improved in all respects once its inhabitants themselves began taking care of their own collective interests. After this dab at bureaucracy, the author points out that "to work for the general good is to work for one's own good and also for the good of the state and in the interests of social order. National reconstruction through hard work and economy must be pursued for the even more important edification of socialism. By saving water and electric power, one gives this principle a practical application. If one thinks of one's personal comfort, thereby neglecting the welfare of the community, one is due in the long run to suffer oneself."

The point is then neatly driven home:

Only a few months ago, the inmates of that particular dormitory in the Academy of Sciences had to spend much money on settling their bills for current and water. Why was that? Because most of them thought to themselves: "Why should I bother to restrict myself when others do not?" Which attitude resulted in tremendous squandering of electricity and water. Also they thought: "Why should I bother with cleanliness when the others don't?" Thus, the dormitory became very dirty. Soon, however, they realized that to think only of oneself was a bad policy and that one had not only to exert self-discipline, but also to make sure that others did likewise. Thus did conditions in the dormitory quickly improve.

Dealing as it does largely with the material aspect of dormitory life, the article makes it nevertheless extremely clear that to mind one's own business is a grave sin.

An editorial in the *Chinese Youth Daily* of March 28, 1964, goes much further. The headline is: "A Good Place To Watch Living Thought: the Dormitory," and the text deserves to be quoted in full, because it tackles China's main problem with remarkable frankness and sheds interesting light on the role played among the workers by the Chinese Communist Youth League:

Those who live in the dormitories of industrial and mining concerns are, *for the most part,** young unmarried workers.

* All italics are mine. (J.M.)

After their work, their studies, and their political meetings, they spend all their time, more than twelve hours out of every twenty-four, in the dormitories, where they rest, play, read, and talk among themselves, which all, together with the sanitary conditions prevailing, has great influence on the molding of their character. The study of the writings of Chairman Mao, the reading of Red books, the singing of revolutionary songs, healthy cultural activities, good relations between comrades can help the young to acquire knowledge, to make progress, and to accept our revolutionary education. Fanciful novels, unhealthy songs, conversations about low subjects, *unhealthy strolls*,* bad friendships are bound to weaken the revolutionary spirit of the young and cause them to choose the path of degeneration. This all means that moral and physical conditions in the dormitories are a matter of vital importance when viewed against the background of class struggle between the workers and the bourgeoisie, vying against one another for influence over the young.

Frankly speaking, the question is this: *can we or can we not form a new revolutionized generation?*

The Chinese Communist Youth League must therefore look upon the proper running of dormitories as one of its political duties. In order to perform it, it is not enough to sit behind a desk. The dormitories must be actually entered. This, so far, has not been done often enough.

The usual excuse is: we are too busy.

There are however responsible cadres in the League. These realize that the very purpose of the League is to take care of the people. Should the League forget its mission, then not only would its activities become pointless, but it would do itself harm by losing touch with the living thoughts of the masses.

There can be no better places than the dormitoris to catch these thoughts.

Let it be known that the dormitories are not just made for sleep. They are gathering places where the young study, read, indulge in cultural activities, and discuss various questions among themselves. Many words that are not uttered in the workshop can be spoken there. Of this, some cadres of the League are well aware already. That is why every year they go and spend some time in the workers' dormitories, living with the workers, taking their share of the communal chores, sweeping the floor for instance, studying the works of Chair-

* Presumably in couples.

man Mao, singing revolutionary songs with them, and speaking to them about their personal problems and their families, entering thus into personal friendship with them. Soon, the young workers automatically begin to tell the cadres about their own troubles and ask for practical suggestions.

In this manner, the cadres will acquire a deep understanding of the dormitory and the problems which may arise among the young workers. The more active the League becomes in the workers' dormitories, the greater the workers' determination to do well will become and there will be much improvement in their attitude toward their task.

Already a number of experiments have been conducted in various factories and mining concerns and from these it clearly appears that the League, working in close cooperation with the various administrations concerned, must be guided by these five considerations:

1. The thinking of Mao Tse-tung must be made to prevail in dormitories in order that ideological influences emanating from the bourgeoisie and feudalism may be eliminated. In order to achieve that, a deep study of Mao Tse-tung's writing must be encouraged.

2. New ethics and a new code of behavior must be introduced into the dormitories and old customs eliminated. Anyone who behaves in a meritorious manner must be publicly praised and his name must appear on the dormitory's bulletin board with proper honor.

3. The new culture must be introduced into the dormitories in order to eliminate the unhealthy and harmful cultural activities which are still prevalent and are detrimental to body and spirit among the youth.

4. Dormitories must be kept tidy and well run and it is the essential duty of the dormitory committees to see that they are. They will have in this task the support of the masses.

5. A system of comparison must be created whereby "Red dormitories" will become known and will be models, patterns, and pilots for others, for backward dormitories, to conform to, to emulate and follow.

And so it goes on. The China Youth League did not exist when Orwell wrote about Oceania's "Youth Anti-Sex League." It looks once more as if the Chinese Communists had taken *1984* literally, not as a novel, a fictional anticipation, but as a textbook.

32

OPERATING ON THE OPERA

       ❧❦❧❦

CHINA's Great Cultural Revolution, as it is called, suddenly made the headlines in the world press in the spring of 1966. It had by then reached a new intensity, and a concomitant purge, affecting many intellectuals and scholars, several well-known political figures, and at least one very high-ranking soldier, gave it an artificial momentousness. But very little of what is news is new, and the self-abasement of Kuo Mo-jo, President of the Academia Sinica and the Fuehrer of New China in the fields of literature and learning, the disgrace of Peking's Mayor Peng Chen, the demotion of General Lo Jui-ching, were not without precedent in the history of the seventeen-year-old People's Republic. Dr. Mao is old-fashioned: purgation and even bloodletting administered at the proper intervals will, he believes, keep the body politic healthy.

As for the Cultural Revolution, it has followed a steady course, if not an even one, for twenty-four years. It began in the Yenan period and has been prosecuted ever since with varying intensity, almost dormant during the lean years, forceful again when the people's bellies were full enough to make their minds amenable. Its aspects are as numerous as the country's "cultural" activities, which include not only poetry and literature (fiction and nonfiction), the plastic and graphic arts, the stage and the screen, education, of course, in all its ramifications, but sports and the innumerable if prudent political symposia as well. As a whole, it is part of the national thought suppression campaign based on Mao's variously expressed will that his subjects should make theirs the very un-Cartesian motto: "I am, therefore I think not."

In the fields of literature and art, due importance is given to academic perfection but what counts most is passive acceptance and active utilization of "correct" inspiration. Flights of fancy are discouraged and the artist in fact is given little choice. When I visited the Peking School of Fine Arts in the wake of a posse of special correspondents (I could not have got in otherwise), the theme on which the students were at work was the following: an old man, looking fairly prosperous, showing his already well-dressed, but apparently fastidious son the tattered rags he himself had to wear before Liberation raised his standard of living. Some fifty students, well advanced all, for their skill in drawing was remarkable, were busily doing their best to convey graphically the notion that everyone should be grateful to the Party and Chairman Mao for putting a shirt on every shirtless back and that they had never had it so good.

Incidentally, they themselves were not particularly well dressed: their blue denim trousers were much patched and their singlets (for the weather was still hot) abundantly darned, and they looked rather like youthful ghosts from the days of oppression than like members of a generation enjoying the benefits of a proletarian dictatorship. At the inauguration of Peking's new gallery of modern art, in May, 1962, to which the foreign press was invited and where there was a lot of excellent poster-style work still very much in the Russian style as well as a great amount of traditional painting, the latter mere copies of the old masters and products of skilled craftmanship rather than art, I was unpleasantly struck by an enormous canvas done in various shades of brown, the collective work of several artists who, I felt, must have studied under that master, Shih Chuan-hsiang, the celebrated night-soil shifter.

"Isn't it beautiful?" Mrs. Chen had asked, materializing at my elbow.

"I cannot say," I had cautiously replied, "that I am very fond of the colors."

"What do the colors matter?" she objected. "This painting shows soldiers of the People's Liberation Army breaking the fetters of poor people who had been imprisoned by the reactionaries. How can you say that it is not beautiful?"

"The idea is certainly beautiful, but perhaps not the execution."

"Certainly, no doubt," said Mrs. Chen, "they would have been executed if the P.L.A. had not freed them in the nick of time."

The notion that the political value in all forms of artistic and literary creativity comes before the esthetic and that talent is to be measured by the yardstick of Party conformity dates back to Mao's famous talks at the 1942 Yenan Forum, recently reprinted in a slightly modified form in which the original version's high praise of the U.S.S.R. is discreetly toned down. "Politics first" was already the operative slogan, the catchword of a campaign that, to Mao, has never ceased to be of primary importance. The basic idea, not exactly original, was that all intellectuals and artists must first of all serve the Revolution, meaning the Party, and in order to do so effectively, they must first learn, through manual labor in the fields and factories, to identify themselves with the people on whose life it would be their duty to base their professional production. Since Mao increasingly identifies the people, the Party, and the Revolution with himself, to praise Mao is to praise and serve them all.

The effects of the Great Cultural Socialist Revolution make themselves felt far beyond the various realms of intellectual culture. Directly or otherwise, it affects every form of the nation's activities. This is bound to be so, since a coal miner, a peasant, a table-tennis player, an artist, a soldier, a factory worker, a cabinet minister, a scavenger, a policeman, a writer, a midwife, a salesman (in a state-owned shop), a butcher, a cobbler, a candlestick-maker—in short, representatives of every trade, craft, and profession in China—will testify to the fact that they have achieved greater skill, proficiency, and efficiency since they began studying Mao Tse-tung's writings, understanding his message (which is more than I can do), and allowing themselves to be guided only by the "shining beacon" of His Thought in the darkness-at-noon that engulfs their country, thus deeply altering, one is told, their *cultural* outlook. It has already been gathered that the adjectives "cultural" and "political" are synonymous.

The reform of the Peking opera may be chosen as a case history for two reasons. One is that the production of a musical play-ballet combines many forms of art. The other is that the reform of the old Peking opera (and of other styles of traditional

Chinese opera which followed suit) was more brutal and less discreet than that of the fine arts and literary genres taken severally. To be precise, it can be dated from the Festival of 1964 when the opera was given its new canons.

Stage reform had been attempted before—it, too, began during the Yenan period, as we know—but this first experience may be discounted because its guinea pigs were a restricted audience within the tiny Red-held territory of China, not the bulk of the Chinese people. Immediately after Liberation, efforts were made, not to reform the traditional theater, but to supersede it and to oust it gradually by the introduction of pseudo-realistic Soviet-style propaganda plays. I watched several of them in Shanghai in 1950. All those elements of theatricals so dear to the heart of the Chinese public—the typical singing, the stately semi-ballet, the stereotyped sham fighting scenes, the gorgeous dresses, and all those conventions and symbols that made old-fashioned Chinese theater rather bewildering to the uninitiated—had been done away with. The themes were patriotic and revolutionary and strongly anti-foreign. They were matter-of-fact. They failed to arouse the expected enthusiasm. They were the new regime's first flop. They were soon given up.

In subsequent years, there took place a first reform of traditional opera, but it was technical and did not touch the essence of the old plays. The costumes became soberer, and more acrobatics were introduced (and very good acrobatics they were), and certainly the old libretti had been politically expurgated. But basically the classics were still being produced, and the crowds still liked them.

The results of this reform I saw in 1962 in Peking, and I was sorely disappointed. It was not just that the plays themselves seemed to have been pasteurized; the audience also was now deprived of all ferment, all spontaneity. The show was confined to the stage. There were no more peanut vendors crying their wares up and down the aisles with superb disrespect for the actors' exertions, no more throwing of steaming hot face towels from aisle to stall and back again. Gone were the interminable performances in which one short play succeeded another from early afternoon until well into the night almost without interruption, and fans no longer dropped in for a brief moment only to hear their favorite star utter a certain note or make a certain elaborate gesture, then break into individual shouts of applause, *hao! hao!* and leave, treading on everybody's toes amid general good humor and forbearance. Perhaps the acting had now improved. It was certainly brisker, and painstaking attention had been lavished on stage management. Attendants no longer entered from the wings during a scene to bring or remove some piece of property, which was not a very bright innovation for, in the old days, one was not supposed to see them (they were often clad in black to indicate that they were invisible) and therefore one *did not* see them with one's conscious eye. Even the applause, reduced to Western clapping, had acquired a sort of discipline and lost its informal and warm spontaneity: one was reminded of the compulsory plaudits at political meetings.

Soon there were timid attempts at "modernizing" Peking opera. New plays were produced with unglamorous, utilitarian, and highly moral plots, invariably showing proletarian virtue rewarded and reactionary sin punished, and nothing could have been more ludicrous than the sight of performers in blue denim suits or mustard-khaki army uniforms going through the almost hieratic motions of the old opera and women singers warbling about the rural commune's cows producing more milk because they were better fed since Liberation in that high falsetto that had helped to make the late Mei Lan-fang famous in those days when men played feminine roles on the Peking stage. The theatergoing public still did not take to the new formula. Nor did, from what I heard, the actors, brought up for the most part, as they were, in the classical tradition.

In order to turn the theater into the vehicle of indoctrination which They meant it to become, two problems had to be solved: make the public change its taste, and make the actors and producers alter their professional outlook. No difficulty was expected from the actual dramatists. There was only a handful of them and they were mostly rewrite men engaged in adapting and purifying old works. The theater of the future was to be essentially the result of teamwork.

The first problem was an easy one. Put a man on a starvation diet and he will stop thinking of his favorite dish but will eat out of your hand anything that resembles food. This was done, figuratively speaking. The solution of the second problem required pressure; it was applied.

In June and July, 1964, a "Peking Opera Festival on Contemporary Revolutionary Themes" was held in the capital, rather in the nature of a conference, it would seem, at the end of which Peking's then Mayor Peng Chen, member of the Politbureau of the Central Committee, made a "long speech," as the official news agency put it when it published excerpts of it on August 2.* It sounded the knell of the old opera (henceforth banned) and rang in the new. Its most important passages follow:

> In the past, the bulk of the Peking opera repertoire depicted emperors and princes, generals and ministers, scholars and beauties, lords and ladies, and their sons and daughters, prettified the exploiting classes and uglified the working people. Only a few contemporary revolutionary themes were staged. For a long time, the Peking opera stage in the main served feudalism and capitalism. Reform of the Peking opera has been attempted a number of times and revision of certain items was successful.
>
> But the present festival of Peking opera on contemporary revolutionary themes represents *a reform without precedent*† in as much as it is comprehensive, systematic, rich in content, and has such wide support from the masses. *This is a revolution in Peking opera.*

Referring to the "feudal plays," Peng Chen said that reform was "absolutely necessary." The "good plays" required "further refining." However, he admitted,

> as far as artistic form is concerned, the Peking opera is a form with a comparatively long history, rather high artistic level and rigid conventions. In this respect, reform is more difficult. . . .
>
> Literature and art must serve politics and help enhance the development of the productive forces. The society we live in is a socialist society. Should the Peking opera serve socialism, stage plays in the interest of the socialist revolution and socialist construction, or serve the interests of feudalism and capitalism? . . . How can an important opera form, one with a high

---

* According to the agency's English service, the speech was made on July 1, but the date may be a misprint, since the speech begins with the words "congratulations on the success of the festival." It is more likely that it was made on July 31.

† All italics in this and the following pages of this chapter are mine. (J.M.)

artistic level, an important legacy like the Peking opera be allowed in our socialist society always to portray emperors and princes, ministers and generals? How can such things detrimental to the socialist revolution and construction be allowed to be portrayed all the time? No. It will not do. For *that would be helping the feudal forces carry out activities for a restoration of feudalism and helping the capitalist forces carry out activities for the restoration of capitalism. Therefore, the Peking opera must be reformed. Either it is doomed or it serves the workers, peasants, and soldiers and socialism. It must choose one alternative. There is no third road.*

Pen Chen adds in the usual repetitive manner of the Party:

Should the Peking opera serve the workers, peasants, and soldiers (including revolutionary intellectuals) *who comprise over ninety percent of the population* or the landlords, counterrevolutionaries, and rightists who make up only a few percent of the population . . . which side should our writers, artists, the literary and art workers of the socialist state, fighters on the front of Peking opera, take?

One may think it odd that these "few percent" should be given so much importance and be so feared. The truth is that it is not as simple as it is claimed to establish percentages and that between a minority of true zealots and a minority, perhaps not so small, of people who consciously and profoundly dislike the regime and would actively oppose it given half the chance, there is the tremendous bulk of the passively dissatisfied who take the fatalistic view that the present dynasty will in time pass as other dynasties have done before, who submit to constant propaganda but remain unaffected by it. These are the people the Party dreads, for they represent the unpredictable mass that submitted to Manchu rule for three centuries, meekly sporting a pigtail as they do now the proletarian cloth cap, and who suddenly turned to chopping their masters' heads with considerable gusto.

The existence of this most important of all classes in China's classless society is never to be admitted outright, but it is sometimes alluded to officially in speeches or articles about an element "not yet fully politically conscious." To be politically conscious means to agree unreservedly to everything the Party does or orders. *Not* to be politically conscious could be, for instance, not to like the new Peking opera. At another point in his speech, Peng says that the reform has gained "wide support from the masses." That is another constant cliché. Whatever new venture is embarked upon, it already has, in print, such "wide support" well before the masses are even told of its launching, let alone its nature.

Peng Chen goes on to claim that the young do not like the old-style opera. "Only those over fifty or sixty and a few fans patronize it. If this state of affairs goes on unchanged, Peking opera will die out in forty years if not in twenty, in sixty years if not in forty." In fact, when Peng spoke it had already been banned.

Still, the Party does not want to do away with historical plays altogether, for

whether to depict dead people or living people is not a question just of the dead and living. It is a political question . . . we oppose the portrayal of only dead people who advocate feudalism and capitalism and who prettify the exploiting classes. It is of course permissible to stage historical plays that heighten the morale of the working people and crush the arrogance of the exploiting classes . . . but emphasis must be placed on contemporary revolutionary themes, on the portrayal of living people, of the masses and the proletariat who are engaged in the present struggle . . . reform should be made in music, singing, dialogue, acting, and acrobatics. Refusal to reform will make it impossible to depict workers, peasants, and soldiers successfully.

There are two prerequisites for guaranteeing the successful reform [Peng Chen explains]. First, the playwrights, directors, and actors must go in the midst of the workers, peasants, and soldiers, identify themselves with them, and establish living ties. This means that the policy "from the masses and to the masses" put forward by Comrade Mao Tse-tung should be implemented. . . . Second, there should be a revolution in the thinking of Peking opera artists. That is, their thinking should be revolutionized and proletarianized . . . they should have the determination to remold themselves.

Thus spake Peking's Mayor. But even before the festival opened, the ground had been prepared by numerous articles

published in a good many Peking newspapers and periodicals—
and presumably provincial papers as well—even though Hsinhua
had remained silent. The *Kwang Ming* (The Light) *Daily*, the
paper of the intellectuals, had as early as October, 1963, reminded
its readers that a number of plays "on contemporary themes" had
recently been added to the old repertoire "as a temporary
campaign." It mentioned among others a play based on the life of
Lei Feng. However, it warned, this did not mean that the "problem of theater reform" had been solved. There were still "poisonous weeds" to be eliminated. Much more outspoken than Peng
Chen was to be ten months later, it warned that "some people"
took the view that the theatrical new look was meant as a
temporary phase and were confidently waiting for the traditional
opera to come into its own again. Others "did not believe that
actresses would be as competent as actors in playing female
parts." This was all wrong. Actresses were potentially all right,
but they must "plunge deep into the life of the people and revise
their ideology." Classical opera, before it could be performed
again, must be pruned "of its lyrical tradition which is in
contradiction with the present-day revolutionary ebullience," and
scenes showing "young people becoming secretly engaged in
gardens" or "romantic young men becoming officials of high
rank" must be deleted.

That was on October 9, and on the 13th the *Kwang Ming* was
at it again, but in a much more explicit way. Playwrights, directors, actors, and actresses, it said, had "been sent among the people
and to military units to gain experience of life." One actress "went
to work in a barber's shop and put on a white gown and began to
learn how to cut hair. She was deeply inspired by the labor
enthusiasm of other young barbers, which enabled her to impersonate in a modern play a girl barber who loved her job
fervently." How the customers reacted is not mentioned. The
paper further urged "all art workers to intensify their political
studies and to take part in all political campaigns so that they can
give a true rendering of modern socialist militant workers."

On the same date, but in another article, the *Kwang Ming*
deplores that Peking opera should "lag far behind the development of the revolutionary situation" and that "in the Peking
opera repertoire, there are very few operas based on modern
themes and even the newly revised classical pieces are still much

too few." Many actors, it sadly points out, "have a conservative outlook," and to those who overoptimistically think that Peking opera has become more revolutionary, as shown for instance by "better costumes, singing, and performance than were seen in the past," the paper sternly says: "We think that these improvements had been made solely in the fields of artistic forms and techniques. What we want today is a new ideology."

It did not take the new opera long to get properly organized after the Peking festival. It was interesting to watch how any new campaign in the political field was immediately supported by appropriate stage productions. Broadly speaking, there were two main fields in which acted propaganda was active: the domestic and the foreign ones. In the first the virtues of the P.L.A., either in wartime or since Liberation in the service of the masses (the Lei Feng theme), were extolled, the Revolution at home was kept urgently alive, modern revisionism, always rampant, was denounced, and its advocates met their richly deserved doom. In the other, World Revolution was the main theme, great emphasis being laid on China's solidarity with the oppressed peoples of the universe fighting for independence and socialism. There were plays set in Cuba, in Vietnam, in the Congo.

Of the first variety, *Spark Amid the Reeds*, produced shortly before the festival was held, is supposed to have been epoch-making. It won high praise in the Party press. The Peking theoretical periodical *Frontline* claimed that it had "definitely proved that Peking opera can express modern life and can express it truthfully and movingly." It had further proved that "those people who think that Peking opera is apt only to show the lives of ancient heroes, kings and generals, scholars and beautiful women" were in the wrong.* The English language magazine *Chinese Literature*, together with the rest of the Chinese press, daily, weekly, fortnightly, and monthly, said likewise and in much the same words, but since all plays are Party-inspired and since commentaries on them are too, one cannot be quite certain that a dramatic critic is not at the same time a playwright and

---

* I must once again apologize to the reader for constant repetition of set formulas, but Mao's China is essentially repetitive and I do not feel that I can honestly suppress them all from my quotations, dull and irritating as they may be, for they may help convey the feel of an atmosphere which is, indeed, dull and irritating beyond belief.

that he is not compulsorily praising something of which he was a compulsory co-author.

I have watched a performance of *Spark Amid the Reeds*. It has scenery, which modern plays always have and the old theatrical forms had not. The costumes, of course, are those of the present day, but the acting and singing remain traditional. The revolutionary element is to be found in the psychology of the *dramatis personae* and of the actors who no longer play the stereotyped parts of yore but "strove to portray characters out of real life." Actually, in *Spark* and in all other new productions, the characters are as two-dimensional as, for instance, in any old-fashioned Western melodrama. The hero (or heroine in this particular case) is one hundred percent good and the villain one hundred percent bad. The plot is of the utmost simplicity and the happy ending sees virtue triumphant.

The action of *Spark Amid the Reeds* is set during the Sino-Japanese war, and the central characters are two women, one young and the other old. In the words of *Chinese Literature*, "the former has to bring out the noble qualities of a Communist posing as the owner of a tea house; the latter the resolution and steadiness of an old revolutionary through a housewife." Other characters include a wounded soldier from the P.L.A.,* after whom they look with heroic devotion, a Chinese traitor whom they outwit, brutal Japanese soldiery and admirable Communist patriots. After many vicissitudes, guerrillas appear in the nick of time and shoot down all the bad men and the curtain falls.

In a scene called "A Battle of Wits" (for scenes have titles in the new Peking opera) the following duet is sung by the young heroine Ah-ching and the treacherous Tiao, a stooge of the enemy:

Tiao: This is no ordinary woman.
Ah-ching: What tricks is Tiao Teh-yi up to?
Tiao: She has sharp eyes, a ready tongue.
Ah-ching: He hides daggers in his smile.
Tiao: She's neither humble nor pert.
Ah-ching: He's neither fish nor fowl.
Tiao: What is she after? Who backs her?

* Upon being wounded, the soldier does a very nimble and artistic little acrobatic dance, the meaning of which, to the experts, is that he has been so seriously hurt that he cannot walk at all.

Ah-ching: Is he working for Chiang Kai-shek or the Japanese?

Tiao: I shall sound her out.

Ah-ching: I shall have to watch my step.

This is described as "a sharp clash between good and evil" by *Chinese Literature*, adding:

> In this battle of wits both sides are vigilant, testing the other. They sing alternate lines in the style of traditional "soliloquies" and this is good theater. In actuality, Sister Ah-ching and Tiao are afraid to expose their secrets, but this method of revealing their thoughts to the audience freely is bolder, more expressive, and therefore more dramatic than the "asides" in modern drama. This is one example out of many of the successful use of traditional methods to depict new content.

Other examples of musical plays with a Chinese setting include *A Bucket of Manure*, a short piece "about a woman who wants to carry manure to her private plot but is persuaded by her husband to take it to the commune field. . . . The singing and acting in this opera are more impressive and moving than lengthy dialogue," and *Sentinels Under the Neon Lights*, based on the gallant front which the famous Nanking Road Company had put up against the temptations of lechery, opium, and perhaps even beer.

In its October, 1965, issue, *Chinese Literature* has much to say about the success of *Sentinels Under the Neon Lights*. After reminding us that "the foundation for the proletarian Chinese modern drama was laid down in 1942 when Chairman Mao Tse-tung gave his Talks at the Yenan Forum on Literature and Art" and that "since then, Chinese modern drama has been developing along the line of serving the needs of workers, peasants, and soldiers, becoming a form of art which spreads revolutionary ideas and which the general public love to see and enjoy," the article goes on:

> The theme of *Sentinels Under the Neon Lights*, for instance, was taken from the experience of a company of the People's Liberation Army assigned to guard Nanking Road in Shanghai just after Liberation. The men of this company came from

poor peasant families. After defeating the Japanese aggressors and Chiang Kai-shek they were given the task of guarding one of the most fashionable streets in a great metropolis. The issue raised here was vitally important: in this transition from the old society to the new, would those proletarian soldiers succumb to the decadent influence of the luxury and glittering neon lights around them, or would they firmly oppose these bourgeois influences and retain the simplicity and honesty of proletarian fighters? Events showed that from the very beginning they have kept their integrity in the midst of a boisterous city, holding to their fine tradition of austerity and simple living so that they become a model company. The play poses this issue and effectively answers it by means of a gripping plot and sharp dramatic conflicts.

The main political preoccupation of the day is then taken up and the article goes on as follows:

> *Sentinels Under the Neon Lights* reflects the intense class struggles in China during the early days after Liberation. Do similar class struggles exist after the cooperative movement in agriculture and transformation of capitalist industries, now that in the ownership of the means of production socialism has achieved victory? The facts prove that classes and class struggles still exist. For bourgeois influences and old habits still live on in our society. There are still people, though their number is small, who have not remolded themselves well enough, and whenever an opportunity presents itself they are liable to leave the socialist path.

Another "success" was *The Red Lantern*, and in May 1965, the same *Chinese Literature* published an interview with the director of this opera, Comrade Ah Chia, who happens to be also "one of those who helped to adapt it from the Shanghai opera version," thus reminding us that in spite of everything that has been said, tastes differ from one province to another and that the cultural unification of China is still to come. Of Ah Chia, the Peking periodical says that he is "a script writer and a brilliant director of Peking opera" and that "the year after the outbreak of the War of Resistance against Japan in 1937 he went to Yenan, the center of the revolution at that time, and joined the Lu Hsun Academy of Literature and Art to employ his knowledge of Peking opera in the service of the resistance. In the last twenty years and more, by producing and studying Peking operas, he has delved deeply into their special laws in order to make this traditional art form, which could formerly only reflect the life of the past, give an accurate reflection of life today."

The interviewer, Hung Yu, then moves on to the inescapable repetition:

> Ah Chia reminded us that for nearly 200 years the Peking opera stage was virtually monopolized by emperors, princes, generals, ministers, scholars, and young ladies. During the Twenties and Thirties of this century a few artists tried to stage operas on contemporary life but all of them failed because they could get no support from society. After Liberation the government encouraged the production of operas on revolutionary contemporary themes and this had positive results. The festival held last year [1964] was the most significant attempt to develop a revolutionary Peking opera to serve the workers, peasants, and soldiers; and *The Red Lantern* was a product of this revolutionary movement.

Lack of support from "society" obviously means lack of support from the theatergoers. The plays he refers to, it must be said in all fairness, had very little to do with the Communist revolution or they would obviously not have been tolerated by the Kuomintang authorities. They were rather poor attempts at "Westernization" of the traditional Chinese drama. And, having seen several of them, I cannot blame "society" for not thinking them supremely good.

The Red Lantern, the December, 1965, *China Reconstructs* writes, is the

> story of the struggle of three generations of a railway worker's family against the Japanese imperialist invaders. In the past year 300,000 people in several big cities have seen it as staged by the China Peking Opera Theater. The railwaymen's ordinary red lantern is not only the secret signal of underground Chinese Communist Party workers, but the symbol of light and revolution. Audiences call the opera itself a "red lantern" in the sense that it has lighted a way in today's revolution in culture by successfully dramatizing themes of present-day significance through a traditional medium. . . . After attending six per-

formances of *The Red Lantern* a seasoned Peking operagoer said: "I have watched Peking operas all my life and seen all the famous actors and actresses. But I have never been moved to tears as I was by the great heart of the revolutionary hero in *The Red Lantern*."

The opera unfolds the character of Li Yu-ho, an underground worker of the Communist Party, fearless, staunch, and of deep wisdom, qualities which today's Chinese audiences earnestly want to acquire. The story also clearly reveals the fundamental weakness of imperialism hidden behind its mask of strength—the fact that because its acts of aggression are unjust, the just spirit of revolutionaries will always be able to overpower it. The railway worker's family in the opera demonstrates this when by their courage and determination they defeat every ferocious and cruel attempt of the imperialist enemy to break them. In the political awakening of the worker's daughter, Li Tieh-mei, today's young audiences see an important truth, that the flames of revolution can never be put out, and how they themselves can carry on the revolution as Tieh-mei does.

Actor Chien Hao-liang, "the young man well known for his military roles who plays the hero Li Yu-ho," had this to say to the *China Reconstructs* reporter:

"After studying and gaining a deeper understanding of the role of Li Yu-ho, I began to see that I could use many of the traditional warrior conventions, such as the highly rhythmic, slightly exaggerated movements and the erect, statuesque carriage." Chien Hao-liang stood up to demonstrate what he meant. "For instance, to bring out the fearlessness with which Li Yu-ho faced torture, I used many of the old body movements and ways of walking. When Hatoyama, head of the Japanese military police, fails to break Li Yu-ho with bribes and threats, he orders torture. At this moment, to the dramatic rhythm of drums and gongs, Li Yu-ho rises to his full height, turns to face his enemy, calmly opens his coat, laughs in cold contempt, buttons his coat again, takes his cap and flicks the dust off it, then puts his hands behind his back and strides off the stage *with the dignified and measured steps of a hero in traditional Peking Opera*. These movements, compared with those in actual life, are artistic exaggerations, but they seem fitting because they give true expression to the spirit of the character." . . . Chien Hao-liang explained how the music of

Peking Opera is used to accentuate the noble character of the hero. Li Yu-ho remains dauntless throughout inhuman torture in prison and even as he faces execution is confident that the Communist ideal will triumph. To reveal the heart and soul of this proletarian fighter at such a critical moment, Chien Hao-liang uses a beautiful Peking Opera melody with great variation in tempo and with words typical of Peking Opera language—lyrical, concise, glowing with imagery, and highly rhythmic:

"With soaring spirit I walk to the execution ground,
Looking far toward the horizon I see
The red flag of revolution raised on high,
The flames of resistance sweeping the land.
Vain invaders, how many more days can you ride over us?
When the storm's over, a hundred flowers will bloom,
A new China, like the morning sun, will shine.
Red flags will fly over all the country.
I am filled with confidence, my fighting will is firm."

Yuan Shih-hai, "a famous actor of forty years' stage experience," also interviewed, says that *The Red Lantern* cannot be said to be perfected as yet. . . . We are going to keep on polishing this opera until it is good enough to be passed on from generation to generation."

The East Is Red was considered the masterpiece of the new style when it was staged in the Great Hall of the People on the occasion of the fifteenth anniversary of the Chinese People's Republic. It was officially called "a pageant in music and dance" and it was all of that. Its theme, in the words of *Chinese Literature*, was

the history of the Chinese revolution for the last forty years and more. . . . a compact pageant of the arduous revolutionary struggles waged by the Chinese people under the leadership of the Chinese Communist Party and Mao Tse-tung since the founding of the Chinese Communist Party in 1921, and of the mighty socialist revolution of the last fifteen years. High tribute was paid to the Chinese Communist Party and its great leader Mao Tse-tung, the General Line for socialist construction and the thoroughgoing spirit of the Chinese people. The grand finale showed the unity of the workers of the world, the unity of the workers and all oppressed peoples and

nations, the unity of all the peoples of the world in the revolutionary struggle against imperialism as, to quote from a new poem by Chairman Mao Tse-tung,
"The Four Seas are rising, clouds louring and raging,
The Five Continents are rocked by storm and thunder." *

The official "critic" put it neatly thus:

> By means of splendid dances and songs, all colorfully and *distinctly Chinese*, they [the actors] showed the people's infinite love for the Chinese Communist Party and Mao Tse-tung, expressing the happiness of life in the big socialist family of New China.
>
> [The songs were] chosen mainly from Mao Tse-tung's poems, folk songs, and the best revolutionary songs of different periods, were steeped in the spirit of their age and stirringly recalled the past revolutionary struggles. However, to meet the needs of this pageant a few songs were composed like "Chairman Mao Is the Sun in Our Hearts" and "People of the World, Unite!" These conveyed the Chinese people's enthusiasm and determination to hold high the great red banner of the thinking of Mao Tse-tung and to carry the revolution to the end; they challenged imperialism and expressed the people's convictions in *the most impassioned music of the age.*†

One is further informed that "more than three thousand people took part in this pageant, including poets, singers, dancers, and actors from many organizations from Peking, Shanghai, and the People's Liberation Army, as well as choirs of workers, students, and Young Pioneers. It marked a further step in the revolutionizing of China's music and dance."

It was certainly lavish enough and well staged and the cast made the most they could of impossible parts. Still, it left the feeling that something akin to it could have been achieved had the best troupes of the Occidental world banded together to do a charade.

The foreign-policy operas follow the pattern of the home-policy ones. Only the setting and the costumes are different. The plot never alters basically. The leading character is undaunted, invariable bullied and tortured, and, if circumstances require, put

---

* This is the poem mentioned on page 134, which Mr. Ma was at such pains to translate. After over two years of interpreting back and forth, there is now available an official English rendering.

† It must be borne in mind that the writer has never heard the Beatles.

to death cruelly. The imperialist villain is inevitably a coward at heart and shown up as one. There is invariably the misguided character who will put his trust in the very enemies of his country, but finally sees the light, repents, goes through the verbal motions of self-criticisms, and redeems himself at the cost of his life.

Of late, the two main subjects have been Vietnam and Africa. There was also Cuba, but now that Fidel Castro had been bold enough to criticize his powerful Asian *neighbor* (for it must be clearly understood that for a while one was made to feel that the two countries had a common frontier), Cuba is definitely out and I see no point in recalling here the Cuban admiration for China and the Chinese admiration for Cuba as once piously recorded by Chinese playwrights. The odds are Africa is also on the way out.

The two most significant operas staged in Peking on foreign themes are *Letters from the South* (Vietnam) and *War Drums on the Equator* (Congo, Léopoldville). Of the former's last scene, *Chinese Literature* gives the following résumé:

It is 1962. One day before dawn a U.S. transport vessel is preparing to leave a harbor in South Vietnam with prisoners arrested in different districts by the U.S.-Ngo-dinh-Diem clique because they refuse to be slaves. These patriots are to be shipped to a desolate island. At this juncture a U.S. adviser, Colonel Kent, comes aboard with orders to force a girl prisoner named Ha to disclose the names of the underground members of the Liberation Front in a certain town. This is the start of a fierce struggle.

Twenty-four-year-old Ha, who has been cruelly beaten, stands proudly before the American officer. He speaks gently and persuasively to her of the joys of youth, freedom, happiness, honor, U.S. dollars, mother love, humanism, cooperation and friendship, hoping by this fine talk to trick the girl into giving him the list of names they have tried so hard to obtain.

Ha immediately sees through his ruse and when the colonel talks eloquently about friendship she retorts, "Friendship? Let me ask you why your planes are bombing our land and murdering our people? Why are you using napalm to burn up our paddy fields and coconut groves? Why have you murdered our mothers' children, made our young women widows, our children orphans?" Pointing the finger of scorn at Kent she warns him, "Believe me, all the oppressed peoples of the world have awakened. Hundreds of millions of those who were enslaved have taken up arms to fight you. Gone forever is the age when you could slaughter the people of the world."

The abashed U.S. colonel furiously draws his revolver, but before he can shoot the girl a shot smashes his wrist. Guns on the shore open fire and the enemy is thrown into confusion as South Vietnam guerrillas launch a surprise attack to rescue their compatriots. The U.S. officer is taken captive.

Standing on the deck of the boat, Ha proclaims loudly to the world: "We shall fight on!"

China Reconstructs has this comment to add:

> The actor's art, the painter's brush, the writer's pen, the cameras of the film workers—all have become sharp weapons helping our Vietnamese brothers resist the U.S. aggressors. Writers and artists speak out clearly of the heroism of the Vietnamese people and the justice of their cause, and their works greatly heighten the determination of the Chinese people to carry out their proletarian internationalist duty to help defeat U.S. imperialism.

War Drums on the Equator tells of "disillusionment after independence . . . through the story of an unemployed Congolese worker's family whose fate is bound up with the whole struggle in the Congo. . . . Their different experiences shape their characters and give them different outlooks. A wide cross-section of life is presented, so that the play has a profound social significance." The play, *Chinese Literature* adds, "is an expression of revolutionary solidarity and conveys the profound admiration of the Chinese people for the Congolese people's armed struggle." Further bits of that periodical's review are enlightening:

> Mukania's elder son Milindi, the leader of the patriotic Congolese armed forces, hates the old and new colonialists and traitors with all his heart and works indefatigably in the mountains and jungles for the liberation of his people. He teaches his men that to create a new Congo they must learn to use strategy in their fight. Old Mukania himself at first has illusions about the United Nations, but once hard facts have made him see the truth he urges his family to go forward in the bloodstained steps of their ancestors and stride boldly to

their death from prison. His daughter Rochali is undeterred by the enemy's bayonets, torture and threat to kill her, and as she is dying she warns the American aggressors, "The women of the Congo will remember the debt of blood you gangsters owe us!" Even her teen-age daughter Berry seizes the whip from a U.S. officer's hand and uses it to beat him as hard as she can. As for Mwanka, at first he is like a sleeping lion, but once aroused he becomes an intrepid fighter. The Mukanias indeed epitomize the fine qualities and indomitable spirit of the sons and daughters of the Congo and make it clear why not all the imperialists' planes and guns can suppress the flames of revolution there.

Walco stands for certain African intellectuals who, once their illusions are shattered, come to have faith in the revolution. Wavering at first, he becomes resolute; and from first wanting to preserve his own integrity he advances to join in the collective struggle. This is how many intellectuals join the revolution.

And then there is this:

Special mention should also be made of the G.I. Warren whose part in the play although not large is highly significant. Warren is an American Negro descended from brave fighters like those described by Mérimée in *Tamango*. He represents the growing strength of the Negro movement in the United States and speaks with the voice of the Negroes who are gradually awakening to the truth, declaring that "America is my homeland, but she doesn't belong to me." His role in the play brings home to us the far-reaching ties between the U.S. Negro movement and other democratic and national liberation movements throughout the world. We are convinced that *although the United States does not yet belong to the Negroes* the day will come when it will be the homeland of all those born there.

The play itself, now published in English, is abominable theater but interesting to the student of present-day China. It contains several examples of Chinese *leucophobia*, if I may coin a word. It shows that the white man is always bad, the colored man at least potentially good. "Drive out that white general Ronson and get a black general," one of the *personae* shouts. And even though the setting is African, the whole opera is entirely Chinese, with many of the Maoist bees busily buzzing in the blue cloth cap. The United Nations, of which China is not a member, are "just another name for the U.S.A." and "old hands at subversion and coups d'état. Like a centipede with a golden head they reach out viciously in every direction" (*sic*). And, reverting to the time-honored formula, a woman character at one point shouts at a still vacillating male: "How can you take the side of the *foreign devils?*"

Neither does religion get off scot-free, for Walco sings:

> "And when to God we pray,
> God says: U.S. dollars are in power today
> And when to God we pray,
> God has belly-ache today."

It is worth knowing that the play is the collective work of four playwrights from the "Drama Group of the Political Department of the Navy of the Chinese People's Liberation Army." One of them, Li Huang, told *China Reconstructs* (July, 1965):

> Last November the U.S. and Belgian imperialists launched a murderous attack on the Congo. Chairman Mao Tse-tung immediately issued a statement supporting their great fight against the aggression [*sic*]. In China, millions of people demonstrated in the streets in protest. During a demonstration our anger was enormous, and we felt like joining the fighting ranks of the Congolese people at once. We turned to our own special weapon—dramatic art—to present their struggle and condemn the U.S. imperialists' crimes. . . . Many things happening in the Congo today also happened in China in the past. The lesson, never to be forgotten, is that the nature of imperialism does not change. Though we have won victories in our revolution, we must never forget that two-thirds of the world's people today still live in the same hell we once went through. Their struggles are our struggles.

Rochali, the leading female part, was played by actress Lu Chia-ying, who had this to say:

> Rochali breaks out from the small world of her own family and joins the people's struggle. This was also the road which many of us Chinese women took in real life before the Libera-

tion. When Rochali realizes the truth, she cries out, "Sisters, get up! We Congolese women's hands can also take up swords!" Everytime I said this on the stage, I felt as though my Congolese sisters were in front of me and that I was crying out to them.

In the same series of interviews connected with *War Drums on the Equator*, "one of the young script writers" said: "None of us has been to the Congo."

Yet no Chinese is permitted to write about China, no Chinese actor is permitted to take part in a modern play with a local setting until and unless he has lived among the Chinese proletariat, especially the peasants. "Unless you have lived among the people and shared their lives and their work, you cannot write about them" is a phrase that occurs in one form or another in all the Mao-inspired nonsense that has been published in China for years. It would seem, however, that when foreign parts and foreigners are in question, this prerequisite no longer holds good. It takes an actor much hard manual work among the peasants before he can identify himself with China's peasantry. But he can become an African patriot overnight.

Another thing worth remembering is that in the autumn of 1964, when a strict ban had been imposed on the traditional Peking opera in China, an official Chinese troupe was touring Western Europe, playing nothing but the old plays "about emperors, generals, and pretty girls" that were anathema at home.

Finally three recurring characteristics of the new "revolutionary" opera have struck me as highly significant. First, the most heroic characters are frequently women. They are more patriotic than the men, they show greater courage, initiative, and "Communist spirit." It is the regime's policy to make much of the women, to make them feel that they are more than the equals of the men, and since they did benefit from the Communist takeover much more clearly than the men, they are probably much stauncher supporters of Mao. Second, it is the old generation rather than the young who show the most ardent revolutionary fervor. That is explained by the fact that they have known pre-Liberation days and China before it became a Communist paradise. They have, presumably, been oppressed and ill treated and they have starved under the old regime, and it is of course taken for granted that they are the ones who know that "everything is better now than it was before." Also, China's leaders are no spring chickens and it is certainly in their own interest to inculcate the young with proper respect for the ancient. Third, there is never any mention of the wartime truce between the Communists and the Kuomintang, and the puppet, Japanese-dominated Wang Ching-wei regime of the war years is generally ignored. It is made evident that it was China's Red Army that defeated the Japanese, practically unaided. The audience is given to understand that the Japanese and the Nationalist government were, at least tacitly, allies, which was certainly not so even if the cooperation between the two Chinese parties remained questionable throughout and even if it is true that, once the American counteroffensive in the Pacific and Southeast Asia had manifestly turned the tide, Chiang Kai-shek became less concerned with the defeat of the invaders, now a foregone conclusion, than with the postwar internal problems which his shrewd mind was bound to foresee.

It goes without saying that there are no love scenes in present-day Chinese drama.

All things considered, despite claims that are still made, the general reform of the various forms of theatricals was only partly successful. It falls very short of its aim which is a total break with tradition. This is admitted in the already quoted article in the November, 1964, number of *Chinese Literature*. The writer, Wang Chao-wan, "a well-known art critic born in Szechuan in 1910," candidly writes that "as these are Peking operas, if they were too different from traditional operas, the audience would not enjoy them." It is the old story of the horse that can be taken to water but not made to drink. It is indeed the whole problem of the regime: how to make the pill less bitter. The answer has not so far been found. The patient does take the pill and then spits it out, with proper Chinese discretion, and politely behaves as if it had taken effect. The only result of its administration is an increasing distrust of the doctors who prescribed it, and everybody knows it, and that is the great tragic joke of China's Third Reich.

33

MAO—AN IDENTIKIT PORTRAIT

THE LIFE of Mao Tse-tung up to his accession to the Throne and even afterwards has been told in quite a few books. I have read some of them. To me, they are neither entirely satisfactory nor entirely convincing. Not that I doubt the good faith of their authors. It is rather that they quote Mao on Mao a little too often, that too much of their material seems to have been obtained straight from the horse's mouth, and that I am not altogether convinced of the horse's veracity.

In the main, Mao's career as a public figure is known, as well as the stepping stones he used, and it is further known that in using them he was not always surefooted. Some episodes, both personal and political, which he related himself lack corroborative evidence but must at least be given the benefit of the doubt and thus accepted as the possible if not as the established truth. It is the man himself who fails to emerge as a clear-cut figure and leaves one wondering. He remains enigmatic. He may have moved his biographers to admiration. Through them and their admiration he looks a little too admirable to be true.

As to his own prose writings, his *Selected Works*, four volumes of which have so far appeared in Chinese (and also in English) are a collection of essays, pamphlets, lectures, and proclamations. They do not amount to *a book*.

Mao may be a magnificent calligrapher. He may be an outstanding poet (even though none of his verse shows profound or original poetic inspiration in the various foreign translations available). As a speaker, he appears to have been mediocre always and to have addressed comparatively small audiences mostly, strange as it may be to the Western mind for a leader to be able to achieve victory, whether martial or merely electoral, without a command of eloquence.*

As a political writer, Mao displays the rural shrewdness of a well-to-do farmer's son turned guerrilla chieftain. But he is no Karl Marx and he is no Lenin. On the podium, he never was, again, a Lenin or a Fidel Castro. Or, for that matter, a Khrushchev. Or a Hitler. If he fires the masses, he does so by proxy.

The sum total of his writings and recorded addresses, when all is said and done and published (if such a time may come), will prove, I think, rather barren on the ideological plane. This revolutionist is no great innovator and most of his catchwords and watchwords, far from being the products of his own genius, are culled from the Chinese classics, which he studied assiduously first at Changsha in his early youth and later at Peking University where he held the post of assistant librarian.

He comes into his own, however, when he deals with the strategy and tactics of guerrilla warfare. This forte of his does not bear discussion; his principles and methods have been tried with decisive success in his own country and, since, elsewhere. Some say that they were really Chu Teh's and that Mao merely took the credit. I am no judge of that. Whoever fathered them, they are brilliant and officially his and it is quite possible that, had they not been evolved and applied, the Communists would have been crushed. This consideration would be enough to explain the continuing fidelity of his old comrades-in-arms.

Hard as it is at this stage to imagine that Mao can be conscious of his failings in other fields, he still proclaims himself primarily a soldier. War, he has often proclaimed, is the highest form of class struggle. National salvation is the responsibility of the army and the army is endowed with his mandate to spread his gospel, to

* Yet, in his *Red Star Over China*, Edgar Snow who interviewed him exhaustively in Yenan described Mao as a "good speaker." But then Snow also wrote that, in those days, Mao seemed to be "quite free from symptoms of megalomania." It may well be that Mao gave that impression, or that the symptoms had not yet developed. And when Snow further writes that he "never met a Chinese Red who drooled 'our great leader' phrases," a statement the accuracy of which I have no reason to dispute, I can only point out that the times—and Mao—have changed.

Moreover, as will be seen, Agnes Smedley, the author of *China's Red Army Marches,* thought little of Mao as an orator and less of his speaking voice.

preach it and practice it and set the whole country an example in all things. That is perhaps why Lei Feng and his successors *had* to be soldiers, why everyone, in or out of uniform, is urged to be a "good soldier of Mao Tse-tung," why his regime is, in the final analysis, a military dictatorship (all high-ranking Party and government officials are war veterans), why it is inconceivable that the Revolution should ever become fully triumphant once and for all—for that would mean peace and Mao does not want to be demobbed. Now that he is the most exalted personage in the land, I can imagine him in his rare moments of leisure looking back with nostalgia upon the war years and even on that grueling year-long, immensely costly but successful retreat known as the Long March. They were the good old days when one took one's life in one's hands every day and fought for one's cause, not in an office with a pen, but under the sky and on God's good earth and with a rifle, and when the day's fortunes were assessed in terms of *li* covered, won or lost, and enemy dead and one's own. There he sits (perhaps) sipping the maotai he is so fond of, disillusioned, unduped by the dupery of his present fake greatness, a very sad and bitter man, a sort of Asiatic Alexander sighing for more Chinas to conquer. For, as a civilian, he is not at his best.

I do not know Chairman Mao personally. I have seen him at closer quarters than most of his subjects but I have never spoken to him.

Apart from his infrequent appearances at Peking Airport and at the Banqueting Hall, he customarily appears in public only once a year on the First of October, New China's national day, when he takes the salute from the rostrum of Tien An Men and thousands march past in a parade that lasts well over two hours and is almost entirely civil in character, the army being represented only by detachments from the local militia, male and female. With minor variations, the elaborate floats are the same year after year, and the same huge, hollow, papier-mâché statue of himself is paraded in front of Mao. It has its right hand extended in a sort of fascist salute and since that is the time chosen for the release of hundreds of gas-filled toy balloons of many colors, the figure seems to be reaching out for them. Afterwards come, striding at the double, schoolchildren, students, factory workers, artists, intellectuals, civil servants, members of national minorities and religious groups including talapoins in saffron robes and grim-faced Western and Chinese nuns from the one remaining convent school where Peking diplomats send their children to learn how to read and write and which is being permitted by the regime to die of old age, all replacement being banned.*

The whole show is impressive when you are new to it. After you have seen it several times, it becomes monotonous and unimaginative. The only new float the 1964 parade (the last I witnessed) could boast of was a cardboard Himalaya on wheels over which the Chinese flag flew. This was because of the recent success of a Chinese mountain-climbing expedition, prior to which there had been, so to speak, no official Himalaya.

When I say that Mao, on that particular day, is seen by his people, it is not strictly so. Only the huge but still carefully selected and privileged crowds that fill Tien An Men Square get a glimpse of him. Others will line Changan Avenue and watch the progress of the parade, but they will not get even a fleeting glimpse of the Leader. The great majority will simply stay at home, happy to have a day off and making the most of it.

As seen from the square, the living Mao is a tiny speck, just visible above the huge picture of him that hangs below the rostrum, and hardly identifiable; almost anyone, you can't help thinking, could stand in for him. What is very real is the overenlarged, flatteringly rejuvenated portrait. Of course, on the screens of the communal television sets and the few private ones, comparative close-ups of the mortal Mao will appear. I say *comparative* for, no matter on what occasion, his face never actually fills the screen. He always seems to be at least several feet away from the camera. Despite the batteries of powerful tele-photo lenses trained on him from below, the pictures stay remote.

Mao remains silent throughout, for he does not speak in public any more.* He has never been heard on the radio, and I believe that there exists no obtainable record of his voice.

* This was written before the Red Guards closed the school in August, 1966, when the foreign nuns were expelled as "spies" and the Chinese nuns simply vanished.

* The formal address from the rostrum preceding the parade used to be delivered by Peking's Mayor Peng Chen, who stood next to Mao. He has now fallen from grace. On October 1, 1966, it was the Defense Minister Lin Piao who spoke.

Why is Mao silent? People who have met him reasonably recently remark that his elocution is difficult, but apparently it has always been so and he never could rid himself of his native Hunan accent. That would hardly explain the fact that he seldom writes nowadays and that nothing much has been added, almost since Liberation, to his published works. Yet it all seems to hang together, with nothing fortuitous at all. To his people, he is almost invisible in the flesh. His voice is not heard. Even his renowned brush has become almost idle. What matters, what he hopes will last for generations and generations, is the picture. It is the picture, the two-dimensional proxy, that counts.

This picture and others, Mao's effigy, his statue in death-white plaster, are everywhere and you cannot escape them no matter where you go or turn. There is always Big Brother, not really looking at you because he is not much interested but merely looking vague.

Self-idolatry, narcissism, is not original in dictators. Others in our century have suffered from it. Their names no doubt will go down in history which, to use Mrs. Chen's favorite phrase, will judge them by their deeds. But even if they themselves did not question their own greatness, it seems that, in the final analysis, what they all wanted to be remembered by was their features no matter how ugly, and that was, of course, because of the actor in them. It is odd that they should have been anxious to preserve above all, in the most literal sense of the phrase, appearances. In the case of Mao, the Chinese, it would be too easy to say that traditionally he wanted to save his face. It would be a bad paradox because one form of art which is conspicuously absent from Chinese painting is that of the portrait. If we happen to know what the late Empress Dowager looked like, it is only because photography had been invented in her lifetime and she had her picture taken. Indeed, Mao and she have certain points in common.

Perhaps from the practical point of view of a dictator who wishes to be remembered not just as a historical abstraction, no matter how tremendous his conceit, but as someone future generations will be in a position to look at as well as look up to, the idea of turning oneself into an icon is not so stupid: there can be no hero worship without a hero. And a hero, even posthumously, must have a face, distinct from all others. Mussolini is a jutting jaw (actually, the picture of him that sticks in my mind, the last one taken, is unrecognizable and upside-down). Hitler is a Charlie Chaplin mustache and a lock of hair. Stalin is also a mustache, but of the luxuriant variety. Lenin's mustache is nothing much but it goes well with his goatee. As to the fathers of socialism, Marx and Engels, their piliferous magnificence is a challenge to all comers, and if their beards are so identical that they look like one single beard which they wore in turns because they couldn't afford two, it does not matter since they both signed the *Manifesto*. Mao, even though his name means "the Hair," is at a considerable disadvantage with his receding hairline and clean-shaven face. Why then does he shave? Because, I submit, if he grew a beard it would hide the Mole. Mao has a mole on the right side of his chin, and it is extremely distinctive. If I can trust my memory, the mole was absent from the 1949 official picture. Now it is there, and it seems to be growing bigger and bigger all the time.

Long after Mao has ceased to be read he will be remembered by his mole. But then, who but the specialist can today quote a single phrase from the Duce's Palazzo Venezia balcony speeches or from *Mein Kampf*, or from Lenin and Stalin? Or, for that matter, from *Das Kapital?* Even Mao, in the latter instance, might find it difficult because he does not know his Marx as well as is generally assumed.

I am absolutely positive on the subject of Mao Tse-tung's relative ignorance of Karl Marx's works. Of course, Mao Tse-tung knows some Marx, but he cannot possibly know all of it. When I left China, *Das Kapital* was still in the process of being translated, and no mystery was made of that. Nor was any made of the fact that Mao Tse-tung has never mastered any foreign tongue whatsoever.*

At the time the Chinese Communist Party came into being in the French Concession of Shanghai in 1921—Mao was not

---

* Though Mao is an accomplished Chinese scholar, he cannot conceivably be a Marxist scholar. His limited knowledge of Marxism is not such as to be a counterpoise for his classical knowledge. It may in fact be suggested that whatever he knows of Marxist philosophy he has learned in the light of the Chinese classics and that the Party tenet (which means Mao's own official tenet) that everything, including the classics, must be viewed in the light of Marxism-Leninism is a bit of a paradox. Perhaps if we compared Mao to a tree we could say that his roots go deep into the soil of China and that his socialism is merely the foliage that he is now shedding in this very winter of his discontent.

there—only those comrades who knew a Western language could possibly have read Marx's chief work. This is a point worth remembering. Not so many years afterwards, it was announced, in the name of Mao himself, that Marxism was being adapted to Chinese conditions and needs. That was indeed cleverly and neatly put, for then any divergencies from the orthodox Marxist line would appear to be deliberate and well thought out and not put down to sheer ignorance. This must not automatically be thought a Chinese trait. I have met a great many Frenchmen who prided themselves on their Cartesian thinking but who had never read Descartes, highly readable as he remains. Or, for that matter, foreign missionaries in China, in the old days, hardy Flemings of peasant stock, who were extremely brave and successful in their work in faraway Szechuen and who could account for many converts, but they could hardly tell Solomon from Adam. On the subject of Marx, Fishface told me once that he had been a leader of the Paris Commune.

I do not wish by this to imply that the early Chinese Communists were bogus. They had an ideal rather than an ideology, or perhaps just ideas. The fact that they were not very strong on Marxist theory was not even a handicap. Nor must it be inferred that the missionaries whom I have just mentioned, even though they did not know the Holy Writ by heart, were not genuine Christians.

As I said before, I have never spoken to Mao Tse-tung. During the war years, which were the years of truce between the Communists and the Kuomintang, it was comparatively easy to organize a trip from Chungking to the Communist headquarters at Yenan. The Nationalist authorities did not encourage one to take it, but they would not stop one either. I had neither the time nor therefore the possibility to visit Yenan, which I have always regretted. In the China of those days, I mean of course Kuomintang China, the Chinese Communists were held in high esteem by foreigners generally. The Chiang Kai-shek regime was highly unpopular, perhaps unjustly, because, now that things can be assessed up to a point, it would seem that, on the whole, the Nationalists did very much more for their country than they are usually given credit for. Be that as it may, people who returned from Yenan were uniformly full of praise. The Chinese Communists were *wonderful*. They looked and sounded positively like saints in armor. Mao Tse-tung was a great man. Surprisingly enough, the only discordant note came from a woman, a Communist herself, who lies buried in the plot reserved for the Heroes of the Revolution in Peking.

What Agnes Smedley told me about Mao Tse-tung I must quote from memory because I no longer have my notes with me. Of her answer to my question: "What is Mao Tse-tung like?" I can remember very clearly and indeed word for word a few phrases because they were quite unforgettable. The gist of what she told me I have not forgotten, but I could not reproduce it literally. I am taking the liberty here of putting what she told me in the first person, singular. Most of it is perforce paraphrased. The sentences which are italicized are those which I am sure I have memorized almost verbatim:

"I saw Mao Tse-tung on many occasions in Yenan," said Agnes, "either in the cave where he worked or elsewhere. *I found him at first physically repulsive.* It was difficult to meet his eye and he would answer my questions *in a roundabout, impersonal way.* There were times when he would not answer them at all and give me the impression that he had not heard them. He seemed somehow unsure of himself, even though his popularity and authority were not to be questioned. I attended several public meetings at which he spoke. They took place in the open air and the audience was enormous. His elocution was not good. *He spoke as if his mouth were full of hot congee and his voice did not carry well.* He was certainly aware of this and expressed himself in *short, clipped, simple sentences, but slowly and with many pauses, during which those listeners in the front rows relayed his words to those further back who had not been able to catch them.* A general murmur of approval then went through the crowd and Mao waited for this to die down before proceeding. He would begin his speeches very quietly, keeping his hands still. Then, gradually, he would start gesticulating and his elocution then grew worse. It didn't matter much because that was precisely when those close to him began to clap their hands and of course the clapping was taken up by everyone present. It was rather impressive because it gave one the feeling that no matter what Mao said, *he was the spokesman* of his very audience."

I asked Agnes Smedley what her impression of Mao had been

when she had shaken hands with him, which of course she must have done many a time. "*I disliked it and tried to avoid it as much as possible. It was limp. He neither grasps nor shakes your hand, but takes it in his own and pushes you away.*"

This remark I remember very distinctly because it reminded me precisely of the handshake of a Kuomintang official whom I saw almost daily in Chungking.

In January, 1964, a French parliamentary delegation, headed by M. Marie François-Bénard, had come to China at the invitation of the People's Congress, Peking's very consultative parliament. Their visit coincided with the establishment of diplomatic relations between France and China and therefore the delegates were received by Mao Tse-tung. According to the usual pattern, it was merely reported that Mao had had a "friendly talk" with French *députés* and no time or place was mentioned. The interview in fact took place in Peking and I saw the leader of the delegation within a couple of hours after it had ended. He gave me his account of it. It was then confidential, but as he made it the subject of a press conference immediately upon his return in Paris, I shall break no secret if I quote him now. Here, therefore, is a literal translation of the notes I took in French on January 31, 1964. They add a few strokes to the picture I am trying to draw. Mao, of course, spoke only Chinese and the conversation took place through an interpreter:

"Mao Tse-tung sits deep in a deep armchair. There is a nurse standing behind him who goes through the motions of helping him up whenever he wants to get up. He waves her back with an impatient gesture.* His delivery is not clear. He speaks, according to François-Bénard, 'rather through his nose, like an American.'

"François-Bénard points out that the interview lasted an hour and a half and that Mao's audiences (so he has been told) usually last only forty minutes. Mao is very much relaxed. When he speaks of Chiang Kai-shek, he invariably says: 'our Generalissimo.'

"He begins with a diatribe against America, which François-Bénard calls 'the usual phonograph record.'

"Mao Tse-tung then goes on: 'I began by saying that the Kuomintang and the Japanese were paper tigers. I have been

---

* I was quite surprised by the "she." The nurse who normally stands by Mao is a young man. But M. François-Bénard was positive.

proved right. Later I said that the Americans were paper tigers. I
have been proved right. Now I am saying the Russians are
paper tigers. And when you have paper in front of you, what
do you do?'

"From the depth of his armchair, Mao violently stabs the air
with his forefinger and says:

" 'You drive right through it.'

"Mao says: 'I went to Russia twice, but I shall never go there
again. These people tear up the treaties and they've no respect for
their own commitments. I will not go to them again. The Russians have landed us in the dirt.'

"At this point, Mao's own interpreter turns to the head of the
French delegation and says apologetically, 'The Chairman actually used a much stronger word.'

"About France, Mao has this to say: 'France is a great country.
She proved it by rejecting American domination. France has
given birth to many great men. The one I admire most is Napoleon. I have read everything he has written, everything that
was published about him.'

"Mao Tse-tung goes on: 'Not only the Communists are against
America. Even some capitalists are against America. Take Mont-
gomery, for instance. I know Montgomery. I have seen him.
He came here. He is a capitalist. Still, he is against America. As
for me, when we parted, I advised him to go and see De Gaulle.
I hope he did so. Did he do so? Tell me.'

"On the subject of the Common Market, Mao says: 'You did
well, you Frenchmen, to keep Britain out of it.'

"On England: 'England has fulfilled two of our conditions out
of three. She has recognized us. Good. She casts her vote in our
favor in the United Nations. Good. But she remains an agent of
the United States. She wants to have an Ambassador in Peking.
We do not need a British Ambassador here. If an exchange of
Ambassadors between China and Britain takes place fifteen years
from now only, it is of no concern to us.'

"François-Bérnard then quotes Mao as follows: 'I tell you
about things as I see them. I am not a diplomat. I am a soldier. I
fought for twenty-two years. Is General de Gaulle a soldier? He
must be one since he is a General.'

" 'We must create a Third Force and bring Britain into it. We
must bring England into it but first she must get a divorce from

the United States. It would be a beautiful thing to have a London-Paris-Peking-Tokyo axis.' At this point, François-Bénard chips in with: 'It would have to pass through Moscow.' Mao does not seem to have heard."

The head of the French delegation also told me that Mao struck him as "very tired, but certain of his own infallibility."

The conversation, or rather the monologue, I have just quoted I discussed shortly afterwards with other members of the delegation. Three things had struck me as novel: the references to Napoleon, to Tokyo as the Eastern terminus of an Euro-Asian political axis, and to Chiang. They said these had puzzled them too.

Napoleon seems to have exerted a strange fascination upon the Chinese leaders of modern times. Already Yuan Chih-kai, in whose favor Sun Yat-sen, now known as "the Father of the Revolution," abdicated as provisional President of the Chinese Republic in February, 1912, publicly likened himself to the late French emperor. As for Mao Tse-tung's own admiration for "Na Po-liu," it seemed to be confirmed shortly before I left China, when it was announced that French film producer Abel Gance was coming to Peking at the personal invitation of Chairman Mao. In the late Twenties, well before the invention of the wide screen, Gance had created quite a stir by making a film which was projected on three standard-size screens, set side by side, on which three different sequences of the same production appeared simultaneously, with one battle seen in progress on the righthand screen and another on the lefthand screen, and in the central screen, very properly, was a close-up of the emperor, looking both thoughtful and triumphant. The whole thing, otherwise unremarkable as far as I can remember, was unpretentiously entitled *Napoleon as Seen by Abel Gance.* Later, I heard, but this was not officially stated, that Abel Gance had been commissioned to do a film about Mao Tse-tung's life. Whether the film was ever made, I do not know. I have not heard of it since.*

His reference to Japan as an eventual partner seemed fairly logical. Hints in that direction had already been dropped by many Japanese visitors, official or otherwise, and it stood to reason that a Sino-Japanese alliance would be something rather

* In 1954, Mao gave the Field Marshal's baton to ten of his generals—another Napoleonic touch which, I think, was not mere coincidence.

formidable. But perhaps Mao's wishful thinking was running away with him once more. No such alliance can of course materialize unless and until the Japanese Communist Party comes into power, which is unlikely to happen as long as the Americans are there with their vested strategic and economic interests—and further encouraged to remain by the present ruling class in the country.†

"Our Generalissimo" was no doubt spoken in jest. Still, there must have been some quite serious if erroneous thinking behind it. At that time, it was generally believed in Peking's diplomatic circles, and that belief seemed based on sound information, that there were still contacts between the governments of Peking and Taipei. I had it from Soviet-bloc sources that, should Chiang Kai-shek choose to make his way to Peking, he would at once be given the post of Vice-Premier. It was then said to be a standing offer and I think that it has not been withdrawn. I am confirmed in that by the welcome extended to General Li Tsung-jen in 1966, a welcome certainly not justified by the fact that Li, for a brief period, fought not a military but a political rearguard action on the mainland after Chiang's own flight to Formosa. Li Tsung-jen has certainly not always been a Kuomintang zealot, but he has been even less of a Communist sympathizer. He and the late Pai Chung-hsi were for many years the two strong men of Kwangsi Province and were treated with due respect by Chiang Kai-shek, only finally siding with him during the war against Japan, when they had indeed little choice.

Li, to Peking, should have remained what the Chinese Communists are supposed to hate most: a feudal warlord.* He had not been kindly disposed toward them at the time of the Long March and they had very carefully avoided his territory, where they knew they would have had to fight a well-trained and equipped, if provincial, army. Li Tsung-jen and Pai Chung-hsi were not in those days on very friendly terms with Chiang Kai-shek, but

† There were signs in 1966 already that the Japanese Communist Party, long Peking-oriented, was breaking away from the Communist Party of China, possibly as a result of the unforeseen Chinese political fiasco in Indonesia, and that its relations with the Communist Party of the Soviet Union are improving correspondingly. The break actually came to pass, to all intents and purposes, in 1967.

* But then, what was Mao in Yenan but an ambitious warlord with a political excuse?

they had no intention whatever of allowing the Communists to enter their province. But this is now of no consequence. The body of the Church is there for all repentant sinners to join. All they have to do is acknowledge their guilt, make a full confession, beat their breasts, and promise to be good. They can all come in. Once they are in, getting out again may prove more difficult. According to as good a source as one is likely to have in Peking, Mao was convinced that, someday, Chiang would see the light and make his way to the Mainland, not as an invader, but as a convert. He had pointed out before foreign witnesses that it would then become very difficult for the Americans to hang on to their Formosan "aircraft carrier." Mao's guests had remained skeptical.

During the rest of the year 1964, a good many more delegations came to visit China and were received by Mao Tse-tung. They were of various nationalities. Some were extremely secretive; others not quite so. Others still were so open in their revelations that a grain of salt suggested itself. But on one very important point, all their reports tallied: that was Mao's profound distrust of the rising generation.

There was a contradiction bordering on schizophrenia in a man who expected his teachings to be transmitted, honored, and obeyed for centuries to come and who at the same time had no confidence in the youth of his own country. He made no mystery of this lack of faith in those whom he described as "the bourgeois of the Revolution." In fact, it recurred again and again whenever he received foreigners.

His distrust of the young seemed to have reached the proportions of a constant obsession. This not only I but many others gathered from the delegations of various countries which he received during my stay in Peking.* The very subject moved him to the verge of anger. When he received a Western trade delegation in Hangchow in the autumn of 1964, he once more voiced his skepticism about the future of Chinese youth, which means, after all, about the future of China.

* On the whole, Peking journalists agreed, it is better to interview Mao through someone who is not connected with the press and who is not a writer, for then Mao will speak his mind, or at least some of it, as he would not for publication. Not that any *resident* correspondent ever had a chance to speak to him. Still, this view was not altogether a matter of sour grapes.

When one delegate pointed out that he had visited the Peking University and that all the students to whom he had spoken (through an interpreter) had unanimously assured him that they worshipped Mao Tse-tung's thought and had a deep knowledge of Mao Tse-tung's writings, Mao replied: "Of course, they are bound to say so."

Another delegate then mentioned that he had been shown through the Polytechnic University at Chungking, from which he had just returned. He himself, as he pointed out, had studied Mao Tse-tung's writings in translation, and he had found the students well versed in them.

Mao Tse-tung replied: "They have to be. That doesn't mean a thing."

"But," the foreigner insisted, "they all said that they agreed with you in everything, that you could be wrong in none, and that they would be forever guided by your thinking."

Mao replied: "What else could you have expected them to say?"

Does it mean that at times Mao himself may wonder whether after all he is infallible? It is most unlikely. Mao certainly believes in his own mission and in his own message. The question is: can China receive and understand both? Will the Chinese of tomorrow have the guts and the heart and the proper inspiration to carry to a successful end the task that he—the continuator of the emperors, the restorer of the ancestral tradition of China's greatness, of China as the center of the world—has begun? When Mao says that he has no faith in his eventual successors, what it means is that he at least suspects that the youth of China has no faith in him, or the question would not arise. So that, if the young cannot be made to *understand* and if the task is nevertheless to be carried out, then they must be made to *believe*.

Western intellectuals have often been appalled by the naïve character of the propaganda, not just handed out to them but handed out to the Chinese population in general and especially to the younger element.

After all, it is not intelligence or reason that moves mountains, but faith. The difference between that book of ethics known as the Analects and the Koran is that Confucius kept to this earth and that Mohammed, the Prophet, promised the faithful great pleasures of the flesh after their flesh should have dissolved. On the strength of this probable fallacy, the Arab hordes swept through North Africa, Spain, and half of France. Had the Arabs questioned the divine character of the Prophet, they would have stayed in Arabia, waiting for oil prospectors from the U.S., the royalties they would provide, and for the opportunity to sell dirty pictures to tourists at Jeddah. This would, of course, have deprived them of the profits of an immensely prosperous trade in slaves which they carried out in Africa for centuries until suppressed by Western imperialism.

But I am sure that Mohammed was an honest man and I am sure that Mao Tse-tung is an honest man. All honorable men. If Mao Tse-tung has dared to upset the twenty-five-century-old Confucian way of life and thought, it was because he felt sure that it had outlived its usefulness and equally sure that he could replace it with something better, more practical, equally profoundly national, and something that would also survive for centuries and centuries.

34

THE FAMILY ALBUM

༺✦༻

IN THE preceding chapter I mentioned that the only new float in the 1964 National Day procession had been a cardboard Himalaya. There was, however, in that celebration, something else that was novel. On such an occasion, newly composed songs are sung and these previously had been in praise of the national effort in various fields, achievements in production, the heroism of the People's Liberation Army, the coming world revolution, the wisdom of the Chinese Communist Party, the greatness of China, and Mao Tse-tung's never-erring leadership. Such songs are shrilled in unison, one after the other, by various youth organizations as they march past the Leader, by schoolchildren, students, members of the Communist Youth League, and the red-scarved Pioneers. On the First of October, 1964, all these subjects were dropped but one: all the paeans we heard were uniformly and without one single exception in praise of Mao Tse-tung. The one sung with most fervor was called "We Shall Never Change" and it contained these two lines:

> The sun rises and the sun sets,
> But Mao Tse-tung has risen and will never set.

It sounded silly and it sounded pathetic. Yet you could not help wondering whether the children were altogether wrong in their nursery rhyme.

That was the question I asked myself again some eight months later in the summer of 1965. At that time, Mao had not been seen in public for several weeks or, as far as one knew, received anybody. He was out of the news and the usual rumor went about that he was seriously ill, perhaps dying, perhaps already dead. I had been asked by *The New York Times Magazine* to write an article about his possible successors. As I went through my Peking notebooks hunting for material that was not too hackneyed, I found an entry which I thought was very much to the point.

Shortly before I left Peking, I had had an unusual conversation with a reasonably high Chinese official, the head of one of the state corporations which deal with those Western industrialists and capitalists who periodically come to China in their numbers to hold exhibitions and to sell China technical equipment which she will eventually use in her struggle against the countries whence they came and the social class which these salesmen represent. The conversation was unusual in that it took place at all, contacts between Chinese officials and foreign correspondents being, as already stated, few and rare. But I had been invited to a small banquet which the exhibitors were giving for members of the corporations they had just done business with, and the food had been good, and much fiery maotai had been drunk. Faces were flushed and tongues somewhat loosened, not, however, to the point of indiscretion. Most of the Chinese present spoke English or French or German, others Russian no doubt, and even though official interpreters were present to deal with formal speeches, their services were mostly dispensed with. The man I was sitting next to appeared to be in his late fifties and had keen intelligent features. I had been told by one of the hosts that he was remarkably competent in his own field. I put him down, not as an old Party member, but as a genuine patriot who had made his choice and decided that the regime was what China needed. He approved of it and served it well.

A group of foreigners had recently been received by Mao and had reported that he was mentally alert, but in questionable physical condition. I asked my neighbor whether he had heard that Mao was ill.

"Chairman Mao is perhaps a little tired," I was told. "He works very hard."

"He is no longer a young man," I said, bluntly adding, "Who do you think will replace him when he dies?"

Then came the plain, one-word answer: "Nobody."

"You mean to say that the Party will have to do without a Chairman."

"Oh, no. Of course, there will be another Chairman."

A pause. A thoughtful one. And then, very softly: "But not another Mao."

"Well, then, who will be the next Chairman?"

There was another pause, a rather longer one. A friendly hand came to rest on my shoulder. A pair of brown slanted eyes gave me a surprised look and the same soft voice said: "It doesn't really matter. Someone on the Central Committee. Someone reliable. They are all reliable, or they wouldn't be there. . . ."

A third pause. ". . . or the Party at all.*

"You don't think that Chairman Mao has already appointed his own successor at the head of the Party?"

"Of course not. He couldn't do that. There will have to be an election. But it is rather an administrative matter."

My own reactions to this conversation I had also jotted down and here they are for what they are worth: "It is really quite impossible to know for sure how ill or how well Mao is. The only thing that is certain is that he is over seventy and has had a hard, exhausting life. The inner sanctum of the Party must of course know, and Mao's life expectation is bound to have been envisaged and discussed, with Mao himself probably in the chair. He might be suffering from a long illness with a predictable

---

* This tenet that no one in the Party can possibly be untrustworthy, that the Party is a flawless monolith, was a familiar refrain. Yet, there had been several purges in the CPC before and since Liberation and it was admitted that "mistakes" had been made. But the "mistakes" remained vague; they would not be specifically mentioned, or the names of their perpetrators. Unless, of course, one went back, for instance, to the Mao-Li Li-san divergences of thirty-five years ago—but Li was still a member of the Central Committee—or the post-Liberation (1953) Kao Kang "conspiracy" which resulted in Kao's suicide (if it was suicide), but the latter, all things considered, was not a traitor. He was, which is worse, a man who *disagreed*, much as Li had done before at a time when the Party could not afford terrorism. Had Li disagreed in the Fifties, he might not be alive today. Had Kao disagreed as early as the early Thirties, he might be in the Party's top drawer.

No past *purge* was ever referred to as such and the "mistakes," ill defined as they remained, were turned into something like a national, collective, anonymous responsibility with the constant implication that they would never have been committed had Mao Tse-tung's thinking been better understood and respected and more carefully applied to general policies and everyday tasks.

The more brutal and open methods of the Cultural Revolution are not as revolutionary as the name implies. They indicate a crisis much more than an actual break with political tradition. They are more disorderly but far less drastic than those used in 1953, the Year of Fear.

course. Or, as has been suggested on and off, his heart may be weak, in which case his sudden demise would be a definite possibility. All eventualities must have been provided for and all pertinent arrangements made in advance with the full knowledge and approval of the prospective corpse. Should it be felt convenient, Mao's death could be kept secret for a long time, and in any case the passing away of the Son of Heaven will not be heralded to the world at large by a mad scramble for his succession. China is not Russia, and jockeying for power among the senior Party members is quite as unthinkable as a palace revolution in the Forbidden City of 1964 Peking. As to Mao himself, he has been actively participating for quite a few years already in his own embalming. His pronouncements, relayed with proper respect by his high priests, are the words of an oracle, not of the mere living man, no matter how exalted and unique his position. So the thought that now springs to my mind is this: *if Mao died, would it make any difference?*"

As to the suggestion, often made in the West, that either a counterrevolution would be sparked off or that a "softening" of the regime along Khrushchevian lines would gradually take place once Mao had breathed his last, I found them too preposterous to "make a wise man smile," as the Chinese say. There might have been at one time such possibilities but now everything pointed to the fact that they had been taken care of at the appropriate moment or moments and no longer existed. Indeed, why should it be assumed that Mao's career would end with his death? Had Marx's? Or Lenin's? Or for that matter had the career of Confucius?

My dinner-table conversation I mentioned, in the days that followed, to several foreign diplomats and journalists of various nationalities and discussed it with them, as we did whenever a Chinese told us something, no matter what. Together, we brought up the names of a good many possible candidates and eliminated most, some because we thought them too old—the average age in the Central Committee is sixty-five—or because they were holding jobs too vitally important to be relinquished, or else just did not seem to have the required stature. We all agreed that there couldn't be "another Mao."

As we examined the careers of Mao's hypothetical successors, we felt as though we were looking through an old album of photographs showing the same group of people posing together at various stages of their lives. There they stood in their serried ranks, all getting older together, all flatfooted Long March veterans, all dyed in the wool but not mothproof.

But would the succession really be "rather an administrative matter" as my fellow-guest had said? *

In the affirmative, it was generally agreed, the man to be selected would obviously be the present Head of State, Chairman of the Republic Liu Shao-chi, already a Vice-Chairman of the Central Committee, and a member of the Standing Committee of the Politburo, a native, like Mao himself, of Hunan province (a true Han!) and his junior by five years. The Chairmanship of the Communist Party could technically be taken over by Liu without his having to resign from that of the Republic. Mao once held both.

Liu of course has a fine revolutionary past, not only, as seems to be thought abroad, as a Marxist scholar and a trade unionist, but a man of action as well. As early as 1922—the Chinese Communist Party was just one year old and its total membership still negligible—he led a railway strike in Kiangsi province. In 1927 he was at the head of the mob that wrested from the British their Hankow concession. He is of course a Long Marcher. During the Kuomintang-Communist truce of the war years, he was among other things a political commissar with the Communist New Fourth Army and later Vice-Chairman of the Chinese People's Revolutionary Military Council. The important posts he held after the Liberation, including that of Vice-Chairman of the Republic under Mao, seemed to indicate the Leader's confidence in his old comrade-in-arms, even though Liu could have been thought to suffer under the increasingly burden-

---

* If I again pick up the old pictures now and turn the most important figures in them into close-ups, it is because no new faces have as yet appeared. Some have receded from the first row to the third, and one at least, Lin Piao, has come forward. But Lin Piao has only risen in the hierarchy of the Imperial court. His official post of Minister of National Defense he has held for many years. He has not actually been officially promoted and one cannot but feel that his present importance on the Chinese scene is essentially due to the fact that the complicated figures in Mao's opera-ballet have brought him closer to the footlights and the orchestra pit, and so to the audience. The fact that he has been given a leading position in the Cultural Revolution and is now described as "Chairman Mao's close comrade-in-arms" means that great honors are being heaped upon him, not that he has been formally promoted.

some handicap, as Sino-Soviet relations kept deteriorating, of having been educated at Moscow's Far Eastern University and of having joined the Soviet Communist Party shortly before returning to China.

Within the Chinese Communist Party, if not elsewhere, he is also deservedly famous for the lecture he gave at the Yenan Marxist-Leninist Institute in July, 1939, on "How To Be a Good Communist." This was soon released in booklet form and remained for many years a sort of Communist *vade mecum*, an ideological précis which Party members could conveniently carry in their pocket and consult for guidance when in doubt. It had long been out of print in 1962 when the official organ of the Party, the *People's Daily*, published a revised, expurgated as well as enlarged, version of it, without, however, troubling to inform its readers that the original text had been tampered with. A comparison of both versions is rewarding in the extreme. It very clearly shows the evolution of the Party's attitude toward not only the U.S.S.R. but Marxism itself, and the trend toward "National Communism." In the *People's Daily* revamping, most quotations from Lenin *and even Stalin* have been replaced by quotations from Mao, the names "Marx, Engels, Lenin, and Stalin," repeatedly used in that order as one single phrase in paragraphs devoted to the history of Communism, become just "the initiators of Marxism and Leninism," with a careful avoidance of personalities. Chinese Party members are warned that Marxism-Leninism cannot be accepted in its foreign "standard" form, but must be rethought to fit "the characteristics of China." The new version is particularly important in that it actually lays down a new set of rules, and all publications on "correct" behavior and thinking which have appeared in China since 1962 draw their inspiration from it. Thus brought up to date, it remains, the "good Red Companion" which the old text was meant to be twenty-six years earlier.* More important still, some observers claim, it represents, as far as Liu himself is concerned, not only a thorough piece of self-criticism—if only apparent as such by comparison with the 1939 original—but actually an irreversible commitment to Mao, almost an oath of allegiance.

I am personally disinclined to share this view unreservedly. It is

* It was replaced in 1966 by an epitome of Mao's writings, bound in red plastic, a slim volume distributed gratis, fitting snugly into everybody's pocket and, it is hoped, into everybody's mind.

of course quite possible, if not probable, that in 1939 Liu would have been expressing his own thoughts and that, during the Yenan period, he and other high Party officials enjoyed greater latitude than now. On the other hand, there is nothing, not even in Mao's own prose of the same period, to indicate that, in the first version, Liu was not toeing the Mao line just as faithfully as in the 1962 version. As late as 1949, Mao was still writing: "Follow the path of the Russians." †

Be that as it may, it seems to me that Liu Shao-chi's eventual accession to the supreme leadership of the Party cannot be taken entirely as an administrative development.

Liu Shao-chi is not much to gaze at. His face is lined and flabby, his nose bulbous. While most other Party leaders look reasonably trim in their well-pressed Sun Yat-sen uniforms, Liu sticks to his blue denim suit, which always looks distressingly slept-in. Others will mostly go bareheaded in fair weather and sport extremely luxurious fur hats in winter, but Liu will not part with his proletarian cloth cap. Still, up to the middle of 1966, in the Party's living pantheon, he undoubtedly ranked among the major saints. A saint in a peaked halo.

An alternative heir apparent to the Party throne whose name automatically suggested itself was Premier Chou En-lai. Chou, too, is a strong man, but they are all strong men (or they would not have survived to this day), yet another Long March veteran and therefore another military man (with the rank of General) —but again, they all were, at some time, military men and they all fought in the civil war ("the highest form of class struggle"). Chou's career, however, has been essentially political and diplomatic and his influence within the Party chiefly felt in matters of concrete policy. Ideological niceties were never his chosen field. He is both a brilliant negotiator and a man of action. Although a former political commissar, he is by no means a theoretician. In a practical sense, he is probably far more intelligent than Mao, without quite the latter's acknowledged talent for military leadership. He can be urbane and even suave. It is still evident that he was once very carefully brought up in a very un-proletarian family. With his regular, if exceptionally strongly marked features, his keen, rather large eyes under bushy eyebrows, he was

† "On People's Democratic Dictatorship," a pamphlet now included in Mao's *Selected Works*.

in earlier life strikingly handsome, and even now, despite his sixty-nine years, his present poor health, and his slightly crippled arm, he is still referred to by a good many feminine members of the Peking diplomatic corps as the "Party's pin-up boy."

Chou was born in 1898 at Huaian, not far from Shanghai. He was educated at the Nankai High School, Tientsin, where in 1919 he edited a very left-wing students' newspaper. He was imprisoned after the "May 4th Movement," staged in Peking and Tientsin as a protest against the decision of the Paris Peace Conference to cede vanquished Germany's "Treaty Rights" in Shantung province to allied Japan. After spending six months in jail, Chou was released and went to Paris to study. There, in 1922, together with other Chinese students, he founded a Communist Youth Group. Back in China in 1924, he became an instructor at the Whampoa Military Academy near Canton, where Sun Yat-sen had just set up a new Revolutionary government. (The Whampoa Academy, which was founded in May of that year with Soviet backing and help, had Chiang Kai-shek as its Dean. It is worth noting that at the time the actual membership of the three-year-old Chinese Communist Party was only three hundred and that by 1927, just before the split with the Kuomintang, it had risen to almost forty-eight thousand.)

When the "Northern Expedition" set out in July, 1926, Chou, who had risen to Head of the Political Department at Whampoa, went with it, as a political commissar with Chiang's First Army, a post he doesn't seem to have kept for long, as, early in 1927, we find him in Shanghai, busy organizing strikes and armed workers' uprisings. When the Kuomintang-Communist split occurred in April, the pro-Chiang forces of Kwangsi warlord Pai Chung-hsi crushed the workers' movement at Shanghai, and Chou was taken prisoner. He escaped and joined the Communist Revolutionary Committee at Nanchang where he was one of the leaders of the August military rebellion and one of the founders of the Chinese Red Army. 1927, however, was fated to be a sad year for the Chinese Communists and their new army, and their various attempts at mobilizing the masses at the time of the autumn harvest ended in failure (Mao himself was unsuccessful in one of these and severely criticized by the Party, temporarily losing his seat on the Politburo). The Communist army, which was making its way back to Canton, suffered several reverses. Chou was with it and, when the year ended on the fiasco of the "Canton Commune," he had to flee the city for the comparative sanctuary of British Hong Kong.

He did not linger there, though. In 1928, he traveled to Moscow as a Chinese Communist Party representative on the Komintern. Next year, he is in Juichin, in South Kiangsi, where Mao Tse-tung and Chu Teh are engaged in "organizing" the countryside, not always without antagonism from the peasants themselves, and in recruiting a motley army. Chou is put in charge of the vital Party Organization Bureau. He obviously enjoys the full confidence of the two leaders, and will prove himself worthy of it when, spurning both the "Soviet faction" and the "International faction," he sides with the "native faction" and with Mao, who faces a large measure of opposition within Party ranks, at the first All-China Communist Congress, out of whose labors the "Chinese Soviet Republic" is born. I have been reliably told that it was Chou's personal influence that tipped the scales in favor of Mao and Chu Teh, the former emerging as President of the newly formed state.

By 1933, Chou is the Vice-Chairman of the People's Military Affairs Commission and concurrently political adviser to the headquarters of the Commander-in-Chief, Chu Teh.

I have laid considerable stress on Chou's early career and reviewed it at some length because it already shows two significant characteristics of the man: a constant fidelity to Mao and an almost total lack of original contribution to Party theory. Chou is at all times a good organizer and a man of decision. But when he is not engaged in some active, physical task such as the promotion of labor uprisings or, indeed, leading an army, he will content himself, as a political commissar or adviser, with seeing that the ideological law is properly understood and obeyed. He does not attempt to lay it down himself, or to modify it.

In 1936, Chou En-lai came into his own as the most brilliant diplomat and negotiator of the Party. This was the time of the "Sian incident" when Chiang Kai-shek was put under arrest by the "Young Marshal" Chang Hsueh-liang, whom he had entrusted with blockading the Communists in China's northwest, their new post-Long March territory, with Yenan as it capital.

The shaky alliance which ensued between the Kuomintang and the Reds, looked upon, from its very inception, as a mere truce by both, was to become official nine months later and to endure, not without friction, until the middle of 1946. The Communist Party had by then grown to a membership of 1,200,000.

After the fall of Nanking, in December, 1937, Chou had been stationed at Hankow, China's first wartime capital, as Yenan's representative to the Nationalist government. Foreign journalists found him extremely approachable, cooperative, and informal. I used to see him often in those days. He was a lean and cheerful man of forty, alert and fit, never at a loss for an answer, always ready to laugh at a joke. I met him privately for the last time in Nanking, late in the summer of 1947, shortly after the fall of Yenan to the Nationalists, who were then on a short-lived offensive. Although hostilities has been resumed, diplomatic relations, so to speak, were still unbroken, which accounted for Chou's frequent trips between the Communist-held areas and the Nationalist capital. When there, he lived in an old-fashioned Chinese house in a small street, not unlike the Peking *hutungs*. I had not seen him in the past seven years and I noticed that he had put on quite some flesh. "This comes," he grinned, "of living like a capitalist." He was not in the least dismayed by the Communists' recent reverses when I mentioned them, but merely said with a shrug: "They mean nothing. We know we shall win. Our real problems will begin with victory." How right he was!

"Liberation" made him and the other Communist leaders rather inaccessible. They were no longer struggling revolutionaries, eager to secure favorable publicity for their cause through the international press. They had stiffened into the aloof Cabinet Ministers and high officials of an established sovereign state. You had to resign yourself to the already known fact that Communism, once it has achieved power, cannot be out-bourgeoised by any other regime.

During my last stay in Peking, I met him at occasional formal functions, usually seeing him from a distance only, and we never did more than say *"Nin Hao"* (How do you do) and shake hands, except on one occasion when I was invited to dine with him and Vice-Premier Chen Yi by former French Premier Edgar Faure who had come to Red China to discuss its recognition by France. Even then we merely exchanged banalities, and that through an interpreter. When I mentioned Hangkow and Chungking, Chou smiled and said: "That was a long time ago." Again, how right! And in more ways than one.

Nowadays, Chou receives privileged special correspondents only, who never stay very long in the country and to whom he tells, in the course of exclusive interviews, precisely what unprivileged permanent correspondents have been reading for weeks or months in the columns of the *People's Daily*, which Chou invariable points out. But then the V.I.P.P.'s do not read the Peking press.

Chou En-lai is at present not only China's Prime Minister (Premier of the State Council is his official title) but also one of the five Vice-Chairmen of the Party's Central Committee and of the Standing Committee of the Politburo. In the CCP he ranks second only to Mao. It is unlikely, however, that Mao has chosen him as his political heir. There are reasons.

To begin with, Chou remains irreplaceable as China's number one public relations man at the highest level. His usefulness in that particular field is such that indeed, for a very long time now, he seems to have served his country essentially as an ambassador at large and a diplomat of unique standing. Of all the Chinese statesmen he is the one who knows best how to handle foreigners and how to spread goodwill. His Western education is certainly an asset; also he is a much-traveled man, used to negotiations abroad. As the leader of the Chinese delegation to the 1954 Geneva Conference on Vietnam, he gave one of his most brilliant performances, presenting his country in the light of a moderator in Far Eastern politics and a factor of stability, a champion of nonintervention in other countries' affairs, at the very moment when China was providing discreet but nonetheless positive military assistance to Ho Chi Minh's Vietnam and, if less successfully, to the all-Chinese Red *maquis* in Malaya. In the summer of the same year, Chou visited India and Burma, convincingly preaching nonalignment and, incidentally, winning Jawaharlal Nehru's confidence and friendship. (I was told in New Delhi recently that China's breach of faith in 1962, for which Nehru held Chou personally responsible, proved such a shock and bitter disappointment to "Panditji" and so deeply affected him that "it did more than anything else" to precipitate his death.) "Nehruism," however, had already been bitterly denounced in Moscow, two years before, by the disquieting Teng Hsiao-ping.

At Bandung, China's "Five Principles of Peaceful Coexistence" were again expounded and elaborated on with proper effect.

More recently, the results of Peking's diplomacy (apart from the establishment of formal relations between Paris and Peking, of which China seems to be the chief beneficiary) have not been so gratifying. The 1962 invasion of India by large forces, chastely described by the Chinese press as "frontier guards acting in self-defense," had been carefully prepared, exactly timed, and was carried out to its planned conclusion: the Chinese "one-sided cease-fire" and the spectacular "spontaneous withdrawal" which followed it. The operation was actually a "diplomatic" one, meant to impress the world at large with victorious China's moderation, disinterestedness, selflessness, and generosity. It miscarried. The "it-hurts-me-more-than-it-does-you" touch was wasted on India, whose own Communist Party in the main came out strongly in support of the government and where foreign aid (including Russian aid) began pouring in. The West was shocked, the Soviet bloc made uneasy, and even the nonaligned countries of Asia and Africa, wooed by China as they were, began to wonder what that friendly country would be up to next.

Self-centered China's top politicians are often guilty of gross miscalculation where foreign reactions are concerned. But normally, *not Chou*. It is quite inconceivable that China's Prime Minister should not have foreseen the far-reaching consequence of his country's Indian venture, the distrust it was to breed, the loss of "face," by far outweighing the doubtful military kudos of an unequal show of force. I have it indeed from a source I consider very reliable—not a Chinese source, but also not, politically speaking, a "Western" source—that he attempted to oppose it repeatedly in the Central Committee and was still trying in June, 1962, only four months before the Chinese offensive, with the support of his Foreign Minister Marshal Chen Yi. Both men were overruled by superior authority, Mao's and Liu's, as well as by an overwhelming majority of mostly China-educated, jingoist tough boys. The utilitarian honeymoon between China and Pakistan, on the other hand, is said to have his warmest support, and so has the mutual back-slapping with France, both being, among other things, part of China's anti-SEATO game.

Chou's tour of Asian and African countries in 1963–64 was far from being the "triumph" claimed by the Chinese press, and his clamors that the new African states were ready for revolution did not impress his audience altogether favorably. It was generally assumed abroad that he was then voicing his own opinion, personally arrived at in the course of this fact-finding tour. Actually, he was repeating word for word what Mao himself had said before and what the Peking newspapers and speechmakers had been printing *ad nauseam* for a good many months past. When he made exactly the same pronouncements in Zanzibar in the summer of 1965, drawing a sharp rebuke from Kenya's President Jomo Kenyatta, he again acted strictly as Mao's unhappy spokesman—and certainly failed to win extra support for China's stand at the supposedly forthcoming Algiers Afro-Asian Conference, which was the very purpose of his journey.* Among the forlorn missions entrusted to Chou, one may also remember his trip to Moscow after Nikita Khrushchev's summary dismissal in October, 1964, when Mao fondly expected the Kremlin to make proper atonement for past revisionist errors and revert to the "true" Marxist-Leninist tenets as preached and practiced by China. Still, no one else in China could have undertaken all these thankless jobs with half of Chou's chances of success, meager as they were, for, if he cannot always convince, he is always worth listening to. He is like an outstanding actor doing his utmost to save a poor play by dint of superlative performance, spurred on by tremendous loyalty to the author.

Chou En-lai's complete allegiance to Mao is unquestionable. It is strongly and deeply rooted in the past. It is also a complex allegiance, made up of personal loyalty to the old comrade-in-arms, of Communist loyalty to the Head of the Party, and finally of the traditional Chinese ministerial loyalty to the Throne. Of all this, Mao is well aware, or Chou would not be where he is. Yet it can be wondered exactly how far and in what respect Mao trusts his Prime Minister.

While Chou's devotion to the Leader, to the Party, and to China is above suspicion, the way his mind works, perhaps, is not. Actually, as people, Mao and Chou are poles apart. Mao has left his native land officially twice only for brief journeys to Moscow and, possibly, once, very early in his career and strictly incognito, to go to Hong Kong. He speaks no foreign language and has a peasant's instinctive distrust of foreigners, reinforced by tradi-

* The "Algiers Bandung," for which the Chinese had been fighting tooth and nail, they decided not to attend after it had become clear that they might not succeed in keeping the U.S.S.R. out and that, come what may, China would not be permitted to rule the roost. The "second Bandung" failed to materialize and, if my guess is right, it never will.

tional Chinese hatred of everything foreign, *including Marxism*, which must be turned into Maoism before it can prove wholly acceptable to China as a national doctrine. To him, China is still the Middle Kingdom, the Center of the World, the land of the Chosen. Chou knows that China is not. He has traveled far afield and has a perception, an appreciation, and an understanding of the West which Mao does not share. Mao's horizon is narrow, Chou's is wide, and it is difficult to put one's entire confidence in somebody who sees farther than oneself. Moreover, Chou has often offered good advice which has not been followed. He is said to have warned Mao that the Hundred Flowers movement of 1956 was premature (which did not prevent him from playing an active part in it once Mao spurned his counsels) and that the Great Leap Forward of 1958 was out of proportion with the nation's possibilities. Mao doesn't like to be told of his mistakes, either before or after he has made them.

Why, then, have not the two men fallen apart? Probably because Mao needs Chou's intelligence to deal with the barbarians, because, in their long association, loyalty is not entirely one-sided, and because Chou can be relied upon to obey orders and to be a faithful and yet adroit follower, even if he cannot be considered an unquestioned disciple. And, on the other hand, Chou knows that he is immensely useful, that, without him, Mao's constant self-willed breaking of shells would even more often result in scrambled political eggs than in the hoped-for masterly omelets. He has moreover a sense of political consequence, which Mao lacks, and knows that, no matter how hard one tries to unscramble the scrambled, Humpty-Dumpty cannot be put together again.

Perhaps Marshal Chu Teh should be Mao's successor. Yet he cannot, as such, be taken into consideration, the inescapable objection being that he is already over eighty. Both men once ranked as equals, and I remember that, in the days of the Kiangsu Soviet Republic and of the Long March, one spoke of Chu Teh and Mao Tse-tung more often than of Mao Tse-tung and Chu Teh. A soldier essentially and a more than outstanding guerrilla strategist, Chu is credited by many with being the true originator of Mao's ever-successful military doctrine. I have heard it said by an old Party member that "Mao learned the art of war at Chu Teh's knee." Chu himself, the son of a well-to-do family, is a native of Szechuen province where he, too, studied the Confucian classics at an early age. Later, he attended the Military Academy at Kunming, Yunnan province, and perfected his military education in Germany. After his return to Yunnan as an army officer, he became provincial Police Comissioner, but joined the anti-Manchu movement together with other young officers, in 1911, just before the dynasty was overthrown. He joined Sun Yat-sen's Kuomintang in 1921, went back to Germany, became a member of the Communist Party there, was expelled from that country in 1925. He toured several European countries, including the U.S.S.R., prior to his return to China. After that, his career follows the same pattern as that of most other Party veterans. He is to be found in Canton toward the end of 1925, embarks upon the Northern Expedition in 1926, takes a leading part in the Nanchang uprising of 1927 and in the founding there of the Chinese Red Army. He becomes Commander-in-Chief of the somewhat nomadic Communist forces in 1930, organizes the Kiangsi stronghold with Mao, whose trusted *alter ego* he already is, victoriously repulses the early Kuomintang offensives against it, and later plays a leading role in the Long March. During the Kuomintang-Communist anti-Japanese alliance, he is in command of the main Red force, renamed the "Eighth Route Army." After the Liberation he is concurrently Commander-in-Chief of what has now become the People's Liberation Army and a Vice-Chairman of the People's government until 1954, when he becomes Vice-Chairman of the Republic. In 1959, at the age of seventy-three, he replaces Liu Shao-chi as Chairman of the National People's Congress, a post which he still holds. He is, naturally, a Vice-Chairman of the Central Committee and a member of the Standing Committee of the Politburo. He ranks first among China's ten Marshals. He remains Mao's closest friend * and has never disagreed with him or criticized him. He is a figurehead, he may be the Grand Old Man of the Revolution, but his usefulness is a thing of the glorious past. And so is that of many of the old guard. There is no need to mention them all.

The "young" guard are themselves no spring chickens.

The National Defense Minister, Marshal Lin Piao, is their

* This was written before Lin Piao became Mao's "close comrade in arms."

youngest member, born as late as 1908, but before his 1966 revival he was hardly considered a likely successor, and even in 1965 when I tried to suggest likely candidates in *The New York Times Magazine* article, I gave him only a few lines. During most of my stay in Peking, Lin had not been seen anywhere and, as is usual in such cases, it had been bruited that he was in disgrace. In fact he was ill, very ill indeed, and old-timers remembered that this was not his first disappearance and that he had been suffering from TB for a long time. When he resumed his official duties, he looked so frail and worn that a strenuous future seemed for him entirely out of the question. That was the only reason that made it so, but it seemed an irrefutable one. Otherwise Lin might indeed have proved eminently eligible. He is everything Mao could wish his successor to be.

Lin is a native of central China, Hupeh province to be precise, he speaks no foreign language, and, as far as I know, has never left China. Moreover, he is said to be a remarkable strategist and to have invented what is known as the "short attack" tactics and to have used it against the Kuomintang forces with great success when he himself led the Communist First Army corps, the command of which he had been given in 1932 at Juichin. Like so many others, he began his military career at Whampoa Military Academy under Chiang Kai-shek, and upon graduation was given the rank of captain. In 1927 at the time of the Northern Expedition, he had been promoted straight away to a generalcy in the Kuomintang Fourth Army, from which he defected together, one is told, with his entire regiment after the Nationalist coup when he joined the Communists, now the open enemies of the Kuomintang and due to remain so for ten years. He too then took part in the apparently fashionable Nanchang uprising. He further distinguished himself during the Long March seven years later and in Yenan was made President of the Red Academy. He has always been a close follower of Mao Tse-tung and is indeed a man after Mao Tse-tung's heart, but even now that Western opinion, as usual a little too eager to oversimplify and to jump to conclusions, sees in him Mao's heir apparent, his latest photographs in the Peking press are those of an emaciated rather than of a robust man. I, for one, do not at all see him in the light of a possible successor to Mao. He may be a Benjamin among the veterans; there is nothing, to be quite blunt, to suggest that he will outlive them.

If it is indeed so, then what China has to face is not just the eventual demise of Mao, but the disappearance of the entire generation that made the Revolution and made it victorious. Red China, the youngest world power on earth and the most ambitious, is run by old men who have no confidence in the truly young, indoctrinated and regimented from childhood though these be, and who look upon them, with a touch of senility, as too "soft," too politically spoon-fed. Such an attitude has had a sterilizing effect on the regime. Since the Liberation, not one single new personage of any caliber has appeared on the political scene. China, with its population of seven hundred million, suffers from a distressing shortage of *men*.

However, Red officialdom will give you to understand that the masses are strong and reliable, and that the "thinking of Mao Tse-tung" will live on for ten thousand years, that the problem is, not to find Mao a worthy successor, nor even a continuator, but to set up a first *team*, to be replaced by others in the course of years and centuries, of "perpetuators," all thinking, feeling, and reacting precisely, not as Mao did, for no one can think like Mao, but as Mao would have them think, through Mao actually, forever leading the nation along the path he chose and showed. Such, indeed, is Mao's own will.

That body of men whose essential duty it will be to perpetuate the cult of Mao will be in the nature of a college of church dignitaries.

It may still, despite present appearances, include Liu Shao-chi and, of course, Chou En-lai and Chu Teh (if he is still alive), and Vice-Premier and Foreign Minister Chen Yi (also a brilliant diplomat and soldier, but like Chou and, for the same reasons, no longer active in the shaping of policies), and (if such a college comes into being in the near future) National Defense Minister Lin Piao and a good many others. There will be no new faces, but up to the summer of 1966, it looked as if there would be those of three more comparatively young men: two Party politicians, Teng Hsiao-ping and Peng Chen, and one general, Lo Jui-ching.* All three are still in their early or middle sixties and therefore belong to the "Young Guard." In point of fact, one would look in vain for anyone much younger than these three in

* The latter two were demoted in the early stages of the Cultural Revolution, but they are not certain to be out for good and they will still be worth a look at if and when they reappear on the political scene.

the Party's higher spheres, except Lin Piao whose life expectancy is short.

Central Committee Secretary General Teng is short, broad, and wiry. His hair is black and his face almost unlined and nearly as wide as it is long, as if at an early age he had been constantly carrying a very heavy weight on his flat head. It sits squarely on his collarbones, apparently dispensing with the luxury of a neck. Surprisingly enough, he manages to look like a ferret. You wouldn't, from his appearance, put his age at anything over fifty. He looked fit when last seen by me; he is probably still tough.

He was also a member of the Standing Committee of the Politburo and a Vice-Premier under Chou En-lai. When the latter was away from China, Teng was given the post of Vice-Prime Minister. This was notably the case when Chou went on his long Asian and African tour in 1963–64. Many people suspected then that Teng held that post permanently, to all intents and purposes, whether the Premier was in Peking or not. This was certainly an exaggeration.

It is not uninteresting to compare the careers of the two men. They are almost lifelong comrades. Whether they are also lifelong friends is another matter.

Their respective birthplaces have the whole width of the country between them, Chou being a native of East China and Teng of the western province of Szechuen. They met in Paris when they were students. Both were in the group that started a Chinese Communist Youth movement in the French capital, both found themselves in Canton in 1925 and, the year after, on the Northern Expedition. They were together in Juichin from 1928 to 1934. But while Chou's progress can be followed throughout the prewar period, that of Teng Hsiao-ping is unclear during the Long March and the Yenan years that followed, which does by no means signify that it was necessarily undistinguished. But whereas, in 1949, Chou's fortunes were reaching their peak, Teng's possibilities—and ambitions—as a public figure were just beginning to take shape.

In 1953 he emerges from comparative obscurity to be appointed a Vice-Chairman of the Committee for Financial and Economic Affairs. This is an important post, and the Committee needs able men to take care of the country's food and development problems. Teng does well. Promotion rapidly follows. In

1954, almost simultaneously, he becomes Vice-Premier, Finance Minister, Vice-Chairman of the National Defense Council, Secretary General to the Central Committee. A man of many parts. Finally, in 1956, he is made a member of the Standing Committee of the Politburo.

Chou is, by nature, a statesman and a diplomat. Teng, despite his numerous Cabinet jobs, is a Party man. If he is a government man as well, it is due to his position within the Party, to his "correct" line of approach, from an ideological point of view, to national problems—Mao approves of him.

I do not know how far Teng reciprocates. To his pragmatic mind, Maoist mysticism must remain foreign. But if Mao is not his god, Mao remains a sound investment, and moreover, Teng undoubtedly believes in China's glorious destiny and in the necessity of enforcing Spartan discipline if national greatness, not to say world hegemony, is to be achieved. In this, he sees eye to eye with Mao and disagrees with Chou En-lai.

When Teng went to Moscow early in July, 1963, as the head of a Party delegation for patch-up talks with Russian Communists (talks which were broken off very quickly when Teng walked out and slammed the door), he had, as his second-in-command, the Mayor of Peking, Peng Chen, senior to him in age by one year.

Little is known, at least to me, about Peng's past, apart from the bare facts that he was born in Shansi province, that he spent six years in a Kuomintang prison, became a member of the Politburo in 1945, and was engaged in some sort of secret service activities in North China for some time. Details are lacking. He, like Teng Hsiao-ping, only really breaks surface at the Liberation. He soon joined the Municipal Government of Peking, in which he reached the highest office in 1951. Ten years later, he added to this post that of Secretary General to the Standing Committee of the National People's Congress, which endowed him with still wider powers and greater authority in Red China's capital. It goes without saying that he was a member of the Party's Central Committee like everyone else who was anybody at all. He was also a member of its Secretariat, which placed him directly under Teng.

Such was the picture up to the 1966 purge. Until then, Teng and Peng enjoyed considerable influence in the all-powerful

Central Committee, and, through it, exerted a large measure of control over the Communist Youth League (of which Peng Chen, who reportedly joined it at the age of twenty-one, still happened to be a member, age no matter—or so I was told). The Youth League, a country-wide organization devoted to the study of Mao Tse-tung's works, general indoctrination among the workers and peasants, and snooping in Communes, factories, schools, universities, and dormitories of all sorts, operates in fact as part of the thought-police.

Physically, Peng Chen and Teng Hsiao-ping are as dissimilar as two men of the same skin hue can be, for Peng is tall, thin, and frail-looking. His head, his chin line and hairline, his nose, his hand, which I once shook, are respectively: egg-shaped, receding, long, limp. He droops. His politics then did not. He was considered another of Mao's more lethal pets.

Like Teng, Peng Chen in pre-purge days, was a frequent and venomous speaker. The Peking diplomatic corps considered them both sinister and strongly disapproved of their manners. Peng was particularly unpopular at the Soviet embassy where he attended the November 7 National Day reception in 1964 and gave the "modern revisionists" a piece of his or Mao's mind in the course of a totally unexpected speech. "A gross breach of etiquette and hospitality," a member of the embassy commented to me with proper protocoletarian stiffness.

The then third Musketeer, Lo Jui-ching, Chief of Staff of the Armed Forces, Vice-Premier, Vice-Minister of National Defense, etc., was the youngest of the trio. And, possibly, the most dangerous.

Another Szechuenese (the Szechuenese consider themselves the brightest people in China, despising all others, and are in turn, together with the Cantonese, despised as mongrels by all proper Hans), the General, born in 1907, got his military education at Whampoa. His early record conforms to the usual pattern: Northern Expedition, Nanchang uprising, etc. Though a military man, his career is otherwise largely political. It can quite easily be followed almost year by year, and it is eloquent in itself.

In 1934, Lo is on the Executive Committee of the 2nd Sino-Soviet Conference; in 1937, a political commissar at Yenan's Anti-Japanese University. Later, he operates in the same capacity in the Shantung Military Area. He joins the Central Committee and becomes Director of the Propaganda Department of the 18th Army Group, in the early 1940's. In 1944 he is back at the Anti-Japanese University but as Vice-Director this time. In 1949 he joins Peng Chen in organizing the Peking city government. For him also, the year 1954 is one of quick results: he sits on the Committee of the Party's Central School for Political Leaders, represents Hopeh province (Peking) as a delegate to the National People's Congress, and is a member of the Council for National Defense. In 1955 he is made a General of the People's Liberation Army. He attends the 8th Communist Party Congress as a member of its Committee in 1956.

In 1959 he is appointed Minister of Public Security, which means head of the Secret Police, civil and military, Deputy-Premier, Chief of Staff of the Armed Forces.

Actually, due to Lin Piao's illness which in 1962–63 kept him away from public affairs, Lo was, though unofficially, the acting Minister of Defense. In that capacity, and in that of Chief of Staff, he controlled the Armed Forces. He further remained, if no longer formally, in control of the Secret Services. He, too, was on the Central Committee's Secretariat and, in association with Teng Hsiao-ping and Peng Chen, one of the *de facto* leaders of the Youth League. As a former political boss of no mean standing, he thus held considerable sway over the ideological trend. He was considered an orthodox Maoist theoretician and he seemed to enjoy Mao's full confidence in so far as Mao's confidence in anyone is ever full. His successive promotions, coming unusually fast on top of each other, certainly pointed to that. Physically, he looks like any staff officer in any regular army, tall broad, erect, with a rather round face. From the back, he was still slim and athletic. Seen from the front, he also did. A side view revealed a slight pot belly.

These three "young men," it seemed, might well play the leading roles when Mao, through his demise, added the final touch to his well-calculated, carefully timed, gradual apotheosis, and the first "Mao-forever Committee" took charge. But no one of them would try to set himself up as a second Mao. For one thing, it could not be done. To supersede Mao, dead or alive, would be like removing the keystone from China's Red arch. For another, everyone will have to keep his feet firmly on the ground; becoming another semi-abstract deity wouldn't do. For still another

Mao must remain China's guide and his immortal teachings the common national bond. And, finally, it is too much of an onus for any mere man to take over from a myth.

Apart from expediting current affairs of Party and state and dealing with problems and emergencies as they may arise in various fields, the main task of the post-Mao governing body will be to make sure that the teachings of the Leader stay clear to all, and that all remain faithful to them. There can be no question of altering the official doctrine. If, to the Russian leaders, the very theory of Communism can change with the times, to Mao, at least, Maoism is to be eternally static if forever alive. His purpose is to make sure that the Chinese remain both the Spartans, as I have said elsewhere, and the Puritans of the Red world, and do not become its Athenians.

Should a contingency arise for which the writings of Mao do not provide, then these could very easily be added to as required, another communal bit of homework which his perpetuators may have to do. There is in fact no reason why, dead or alive, Mao should ever cease to write. In the years after his actual demise, scholars—if the regime endures—will certainly "discover" and bring to light the necessary amount of posthumous guidance. That is why, whoever succeeds Mao as the formal head of the Communist Party of China actually matters little. When the time comes and someone takes over the still warm seat in front of the controls, the automatic pilot will already have been switched on. China's course is mapped and set.

Thinking of these three men, I wrote for *The New York Times Magazine* in July, 1965, as follows: "If in years to come, there is a change at all, it will be in the sense of a further tightening of thought control, discipline and austerity. . . . China will become increasingly hard, nationalistic to the point of racism, ambitious and ruthless. Dogmatic, too, for she must not follow in the revisionists' suicidal footsteps."

This had indeed come to pass, and much sooner, or rather more suddenly, then I had expected. But the orders came straight from Mao, not from the now dismembered trio.

I do not for a moment suppose that either Peng Chen or Lo Jui-ching ever indulged in "anti-Party" activities or had become the tools of the "revisionists." I have before my eyes, as I write this, two texts: a speech by Lo and an article by Lin Piao, both bearing the same date—September 3, 1965. It is impossible to tell which of these two documents paraphrases the other. Yet the author of one is in disgrace and the author of the other has become Mao's "close comrade-in-arms." Again, the opera-ballet.

What strikes me as probable, however, is that the Teng Peng-Lo combination looked at least potentially a little disquieting to Mao and that he broke it up before even a flash and a bang could be stolen from his thunder.

Still, the two purgees of the trio, bitterly criticized and removed from office as they have been, do not in the least look as if they were about to face trial—or even an informal firing squad. One feels that, essentially, they have been put on the shelf, filed, so to speak, for later use.

Should Mao disappear while they are still under an official Party cloud, they might prove to be, after resuming their association with Teng, the very men to attempt an eventual anti-Mao reaction. Having fallen from grace would then be a powerful asset. For it must be realized that if Mao were already the people's worshipped idol, there would be no need for the present all-out effort to turn him into just that. A new Confucius? No. Rather Confucius worse confounded.

Indeed, in spite of everything that is done and planned, I do not believe that the present "line" will endure unwaveringly for fully as long as the Peking hard core fondly believes. Even in China, perhaps not quite as fast as elsewhere in the world, ideas are bound to change as men do. And the men at the top will change, and they will do so with increasing speed. No one, at least among his own age group or thereabouts—and, again, one sees no new faces on the Chinese screen—can last at the head of the Party for as long as Mao will have done for the inescapable reason that Mao started being the leader much younger—well over thirty years ago. No sooner will someone technically succeed Mao than the problem of succession will again arise. China's ruling body will get more and more stricken by advancing years, with replacement waxing increasingly problematical. The end will come, either through simple wear and tear and the insufficiency of available human spare parts or as a result of another series of major international blunders or even eventual defeat in war, when chaos would follow.

35

FISHFACE UNMASKED

AFTER thirty months of Peking, I had asked to be replaced. My successor had been appointed, had proved acceptable to the Waichiaopu, and had been granted a visa. He would soon be coming out. It stood to reason that my residence permit, press card, and cable card, all about to expire shortly and simultaneously, would not be renewed, even if my replacement was detained. I would thus be expelled, but it would be only a gesture that would not have been made, even symbolically, had no one in Paris volunteered to take my place. *Persona non grata* that I was, the formal expulsion of the French news agency's correspondent in Peking might, by way of retaliation, have adversely affected the activities of the several Hsinhua correspondents in Paris, all actively engaged in the promotion of Sino-French cultural relations on a basis of equality, reciprocity, and one-sided gentle subversion.

It was tacitly understood that, although I was no longer officially accredited or even officially permitted to live in China, I would not be interfered with in any way, either personally or professionally, and that, even after the arrival of my successor, I could continue as before, albeit technically illegally, until I had shown him the local ropes to his and my satisfaction and had handed over the office. Whereupon, I would request permission to leave the country, which would be given together with a retroactive extension of my residence permit, to make everything legal again, valid up to the day, which I was to name myself, when I should cross the border at Shumchun. I daresay that, had I asked for an exit permit immediately upon being told that I was no longer a welcome guest, it might not have been obtainable, and I should have found myself in the position of being forbidden both to go and to stay.

Things had not yet come to any crucial pass, however, and my credentials were still valid for some weeks when I was invited to attend the traditional banquet on the eve of Red China's National Day. It was to be a very special National Day, being the fifteenth anniversary of the proclamation of the Chinese People's Republic, but China's position in the Communist world had become somewhat parlous and her prestige abroad was already on the wane. The Soviet Union might not be eligible as a participant to the planned forthcoming "Second Bandung," but Moscow's influence within the rather theoretical Afro-Asian community, based on concrete technical and financial assistance (hand in glove with American imperialism, as Mrs. Chen would have said, had she not recently disappeared from the scene and, presumably, been sent to the countryside for a bucketful or two of political re-education), was very much outdoing China's largely platonic encouragements and showing them up for what they were: signs of impotence. In spite of the perfunctory, exaggerated gong-beating, this very special celebration was not announcing itself as a day of triumph and glory. The guests of honor who had arrived by air the day before were few in number and comparatively negligible in standing. And now we were about to attend the eve-of-National-Day banquet. I had arrived early at the Great Hall of the People, climbed the red-carpeted stairs, entered the Banqueting Hall, only just beginning to fill, and there was Fishface.

The guests of honor and the heads of the foreign diplomatic missions were in another room with Liu Shao-chi and Chou En-lai and the other hosts, and we were drinking the traditional maotai.

"I understand to my regret," said Fishface, "that you have expressed the wish to leave us."

"I have indeed, and it happens to coincide with the wish of the Information Department to see me go."

"But we hope to see you again very soon. You are not saying ah-dee-you but merely oh-ree-voo-ahr."

"I hope so. But there is always the troublesome formality of a visa. I am in bad odor, I understand, and shall be leaving under a cloud."

"The stench will drift away with the cloud," said Fishface, "as the East wind prevails over the West wind, as Chairman Mao has said. Besides," he added, "you will be sitting on my right hand at dinner tonight."

"It will be an honor, but still I cannot see that it will bear on the issue."

"There are," Fishface said darkly, "wheels within cogs. Many wheels."

"But I have been repeatedly accused of having slandered the Chinese people, the Chinese government, the Chinese Communist Party, and therefore Chairman Mao as well."

"So you may have. You have written many objectionable things about China. You have been telling the world terrible lies about China."

"Pin me down to one."

"Way back in 1962, you described our frontier guards repelling Indian aggression as 'troops' and even as 'forces.' At times, you accused us of engaging in subversion, and when we said we were sure that the masses and true Party members in the Soviet Union were our friends and that the day would come when they would shake the yoke of their present modern revisionist leadership, you wrote things that were even worse, thereby again slandering the Chinese People, the Communist Party of China, and its great leader, Chairman Mao."

"What," I asked, "is slander?"

"The General Line," said Fishface, "is always correct, as you, an old China hand, are bound to know."

"It is perhaps easier to toe than to follow."

"I will put it for you in a nutshell. It is one of the Three Red Banners which we are holding aloft."

"Together with the People's Communes and the General Line."

"You see," nodded Fishface, "you know! Now, how can you plead not guilty? When you suggest, against your own better judgment, that the General Line is not correct, then you commit slander. But you were, of course, acting upon orders. After all, you are an official."

"I am not!" I protested.

"All journalists are. Even," Fishface added magnanimously, "even Chinese journalists. Would you like another glass of maotai?"

He deftly removed two from a passing tray and offered me one.

"By the way," I asked, "what has become of Mrs. Chen?"

"You mean Mrs. Shen."

"I mean Mrs. Chen, the head of the foreign section of the Waichiaopu's Information Department."

"You are thinking of Mrs. Shen. There she is," said Fishface, pointing to a perfectly unknown woman.

A visiting French correspondent was hovering nearby. I went over to him.

"Who is that?" I asked.

"You should know," he said. "You warned me against her. You were quite right, by the way. I had a frightful row with her this morning."

"But who is she?"

"Mrs. Chen, of course, of the Information Department. Need you ask?"

"No," I said firmly. "This is Mrs. *Shen*."

"That's what I said," he said, and after a look at my maotai glass, still half full, he went off, shaking his head.

"Foreigners," said Fishface who had caught up with me, "often experience difficulty in pronouncing Chinese names correctly."

"I hear," I said nastily, "that there has been more trouble on the border."

"Border?" said Fishface. "What border?"

"Your own. Sinkiang—Soviet. Boundary stones being shifted back and forth. At dead of night."

"*They*," said Fishface, "shift them under cover of darkness deep into Chinese territory, thus infringing upon the national integrity of the sovereign People's Republic of China hand in glove with the American Imperialists. *We* put them back in broad daylight. We already know and we have publicly stated that the Soviet Union is in illegal occupation of large tracts of our territory, but we have also made it clear that we would not press our legitimate claims for the time being. China stands for peace."

"But Sino-Soviet relations are a little strained at the moment."

"At the moment, yes," said Fishface airily. "But the time will come when the Soviet People and the Communist Party of the U.S.S.R., having brushed aside the Khrushchevian modern-revisionistic, great-power chauvinistic clique, will revert to the true path of Marxism-Leninism. Then will China and the fraternal Soviet Union surely become again as closely united as the teeth and the lips."

"Which, if I may ask, is to be the teeth?"

"It is merely an old Chinese expression. A figure of speech."

"But suppose, just suppose, that before that happy day can dawn, the modern revisionists at the Kremlin put it into their great-power chauvinistic heads to liberate the Tartars?"

"Tartars?" Fishface voiced astonished ignorance. "What are Tartars? What do you mean by liberating the Tartars?"

"Just a figure of speech. Suppose that the Russians decided to invade Manchuria, Inner Mongolia (you are of course well aware of the fact that the People's Republic of Mongolia would give them free passage and could not possibly refuse it), and also Sinkiang. Where would you be then?"

"Our frontier guards would repulse the aggressor on every front, just as they did in the case of the Indians. Besides, it is quite inconceivable that a socialist country should attack another."

"You must not underrate great-power chauvinism."

"Imbued with the spirit of the glorious October Revolution, the great Soviet people would certainly oppose it."

"I doubt that. And, frankly, if I may say so without disrespect, I am not altogether certain that the People's Liberation Army would be quite a match for the Soviet Red Army, with its powerful air force and equipment. . . ."

"As Chairman Mao has often said, wars are won by the masses, not by the force of arms, not by guns, or napalm or atom bombs, but by the indomitable will of the people. Also, we have friends."

"You have no friends," I declared, transmuting a fresh dose of maotai into venom.

Fishface almost choked over his own glassful. "No friends?" he spluttered. "No friends! It is not for you to say that so shortly after China and France have established normal friendly diplomatic relations based on equality, reciprocity, and cultural exchanges, and we are buying such a lot of essential machinery from France as a token of goodwill . . ."

"Never mind that," I interrupted unpardonably. "The incontrovertible fact is that not one single nation in the world is prepared to sacrifice Soviet friendship and, in the case of some, including your closest geographical and ideological neighbors, Soviet assistance, on the Chinese altar. Not even North Korea."

"In Korea, we inflicted disastrous defeat upon disastrous defeat upon the American Imperialists against overwhelming odds and so helped the Korean fraternal People's Republic to retain its hard-won independence and consolidate it along the lines of true Marxism-Leninism."

I had it on the tip of my tongue to suggest to Fishface that he compare two maps of Korea, a prewar one and a postwar one, before assuring me again that the boundary between north and south had been greatly altered by China's "crushing" victory. Or I might have mentioned to him that the whole tussle, after putting China heavily into debt and taking a fantastic toll in human lives, chiefly Chinese, had finally been fought to a standstill, much to the relief of all concerned—but I forbore as suddenly I realized that my improvised rigmarole, inspired as it was by a mixture of exasperation and strong spirits, was having an effect on Fishface. It was making him visibly uneasy, and the possibility that something very much like my argument had already been put forward and seriously discussed in those circles where he moved struck me with the startling suddenness of an unexpected pat on the back from someone unknown, and made my brains reel.

"Remember," I went on, "that in order to fight in Korea, you had to buy Soviet arms. At no cut price, as has officially been complained of in Peking."

"You are," said Fishface pallidly, "sowing the poisonous weeds of wishful American propaganda. You are deliberately making too much of a temporary difficulty. We have certainly been betrayed by the revisionist Khrushchev clique, and moreover, the cause of the world Marxist-Leninist revolution has been betrayed, but the great Soviet people and the great Communist Party of the U.S.S.R. cannot be hoodwinked forever, only some people sometimes, as Lenin has said, and there is a bright future still for Sino-Soviet fraternal friendship. An armed conflict is out of the question, no matter how strained relations may further become."

"It is only my own hypothesis. Let us accept it for the sake of argument. Who would conceivably sell you arms to fight the Russians with?"

"As I said, this is all a regrettable and preposterous notion. Also, we are no longer living in the early Fifties, and our own

weapons industry has developed on a scale that would astound
you if it were not a military secret of which I have no knowledge. It is a striking feature of our Great Leap Forward."

"I know that you will soon have the atom bomb. In fact, everybody expects it to go off tomorrow * and the news to be
broadcast during the celebrations. But it will be a bomb much in
the nature of the first French one—a matter rather of social
standing than of military significance."

"Let me assure you that we can manufacture a thousand atoms
if we put our minds to it. Perhaps we have already. It is also a
military secret."

"But let us go on supposing. We have the Soviet in control of
Manchuria, Mongolia, and Sinkiang. At the very gates of Peking.
Your atomic testing grounds in Sinkiang . . ."

"Who told you where they are?" asked Fishface aghast.

"Nobody. But it is everybody's deduction. If not there, where
else?"

He said nothing, looking militarily secretive.

I went on: "Your testing grounds in Sinkiang are in the enemy's hands. The heavy industry in the northern provinces is
also. Incidentally, you are cut off from Tibet with all of Sinkiang's key positions occupied. And Tibet, I may tell you, will
not be slow in de-liberating itself. Szechuen, the richest province
in China, the birthplace of some of your most distinguished
statesmen, soldiers, and scholars is threatened."

"I myself," said Fishface unexpectedly, "am a native of
Szechuen."

"So is Marshal Chen Yi, for whom I have the greatest respect.
A great military leader. But he cannot be on every front at once.
And you would have a front several thousand miles long."

"So would the enemy," said Fishface, falling in with my
fancy.

"Yes, but think of armor, of air power! And think of the uprising in the south!"

"Uprising? In the south? Why?"

"*Fishface*," I said, calling him for the first and only time by the
nickname under which I knew him (but it went by unnoticed),
and speaking earnestly for once, "believe me. As soon as you have
serious trouble in the north and west, the whole of Kwangtung

* It was actually exploded a fortnight later.

province at the very least will rise against Peking. I mean that."

Fishface said nothing. His lips were firmly pressed together and his eyes, though still slanted, somehow almost frighteningly round. Never had he looked so strikingly like a fish. But he had become, if such a thing is conceivable, an intelligent fish, deep in thought. Another tray of drinks was proffered and he waved it aside and even I was not tempted. This was a strange moment. There was the immense banqueting hall all around us, with its numberless round white tables still unoccupied and little groups, numberless also, sipping and chatting and growing imperceptibly impatient because dinner was late, later than usual on such occasions, when it is proper to keep the minor guests waiting in order to give greater face to the guests of honor who were in a separate room drinking with their hosts, Liu Shao-chi and Chou En-lai and Chen Yi, and Teng Hsiao-ping and Peng Chen. I felt that the delay was deliberately longer tonight to make up for the comparative mediocrity of the distinguished foreign visitors come to do China proud on that fifteenth anniversary of the regime. And there we were, Fishface and I, aware of this, aware of the beginning of a decline, aware that, in the state of China, a deep rot had set in that had nothing to do with the corruption which the preceding regime had been so freely charged with, a rot that attacked, not the bone structure of the nation, but its very marrow. There was a palpable swindle going on. People were no longer encouraged to sell their souls for profitable, if unethical, returns—that was plain—but they were physically compelled to give them away, to forsake them blindly, theirs and those of their children, and no believable hope was held out to them, not even the hope that someday there would be hope.

Yet there had been at first, I remembered, very much more than hope: there had been confidence. Now, even a systematically hoodwinked observer like myself knew that confidence had gone and that resignation had taken over, the frighteningly deceptive resignation of the Chinese. (Who can tell a gunpowder keg from a harmless barrel of mild beer until it explodes?) So often in history, after perhaps centuries of patience and stored-up wrath, the Chinese had burst into destructive, blind, and bloody violence. When would that point come? When would the new suppression become even more odious than the oppression of old? And how had it happened that the truly noble pride of the early days and the honest faith in a better and happier future had been so shamelessly distorted by a self-seeking prophet no longer speaking for himself, but leaving it to others, to his bound liegemen, often his betters, to ascend the soapbox and thump the tub for him? When and how had the prospects of true greatness, so credible fifteen years before, given way to false pretenses? Would it not have been better for the political Promised Land had the Chinese Moses never entered it, but met his Sinai on the way like that other illustrious Long Marcher whose dealings with the Red Sea had been conducted in a much more sensible and profitable way?

The future of China had never seemed to me more obscure or more frightening. What was there to see in the picture that the day offered? Failure at foreign policy key points. On the home front, a tremendous waste of human courage and effort; that also was already visible. Otherwise, a cancerous proliferation of propaganda, in itself a sure sign of disease; merchants coming from all parts of the world, eager to sell their wares but indifferent to the use these might be put to; other foreign professionals trying hard to make the Maoist cause marketable abroad; the faithful Old Retainers, still happily bamboozled. And, amid general indifference, seven hundred million people made to wail "mao-mao-mao," as babies do in their cribs all over the world, without being taught but likewise signifying nothing.

Well, what was it to me? I was neither a Chinese nor a Communist. I was a journalist, nearing the end of a difficult assignment and glad of it. Of course there was China, where I had spent more years of my adult life than in any other country. But if I could wax sentimental over China, why should I feel sorry for Mao when I realized to the full that, in his *Ein Reich, ein Volk, ein Fuehrer* society, the whole country had to go officially gaga when the Leader became senile, or mad if he showed signs of insanity?

As I stood there, silent and wondering, Fishface did what he had never done before: he looked me straight in the face, and perhaps it was what he saw there that made him smile a smile that was totally human and understanding. Why? I thought, why? I could understand him, but no longer myself. He had served with loyal devotion, I had no doubt, a regime which I heartily disliked and a master no longer admirable. Why should his sorrows be mine? Heine's wistful *"Ich weiss nicht was soll es bedeuten, dass ich so traurig bin"* flashed through my memory. I put it all down to the maotai.

Very soon, Fishface brought us both back to earth by asking a matter-of-fact question, and then our masks were up again, and we were once more at our usual semi-grotesque, semi-serious fencing.

"What do you mean," he wanted to know, "when you speak of a possible rebellion in the south?"

"I am not going to refer to the Hong Kong rush of 1962. It was carefully hushed up here, the papers never mentioned it, and you, therefore, cannot possibly know about it. Also, it doesn't apply. But you, who always speak of class struggle as a permanent world reality, which it is *not*, why can you not see something that is far more genuine and much closer to you, and that is now alive as much as ever in your own very country: provincial pride? On what grounds have you kept the Cantonese systematically away from the high posts? Think of Sun Yat-sen. A Cantonese. Look at the Kuomintang, at Chiang Kai-shek, whose full name is still even here pronounced Cantonese fashion, at the Soong family. All Cantonese. Remember that the Northern Expedition started from Canton, remember the Whampoa Military Academy, the *true* birthplace of the Chinese People's Liberation Army, whether you like it or not; the Hong Kong strike, organized from Canton; the Canton Commune, what else? Was not the leader of the Taiping rebels born in Kwangtung? Canton and its province consider themselves to be the cradle of Chinese Revolution. And what do you find now in the Peking government and at the head of the Party? People from Hunan, like Chairman Mao himself and a good many others, and many Szechuenese. Hardly a Cantonese worth mentioning. Do not forget that the Kwangtung people are not *Hans*, but very susceptible nonetheless. Also, they are close to Hong Kong and cannot so easily be made to believe that everything is better now than it ever was before. And even apart from Kwangtung, none of the southern coastal provinces is loyal. Fukien, facing Taiwan, is quiet because it is full of troops, all drafted from North China. No doubt: a military secret. But certain things still become known."

"The people of Taiwan," protested Fishface, playing his part again, "are only prevented from joining hands with the motherland by the American military occupation."

"I am glad you brought in the Americans. I was about to do so myself. Once the Russians begin invading China, what do you think the Americans will do?"

"I will humor you," said Fishface, "and allow you to continue with your preposterous assumptions. What will they do?"

"Probably nothing. They will be of two minds, happy to see China defeated . . ."

"The People's Liberation Army, as I told you, is invincible."

". . . and worried to see the Soviet power expanding further eastward and seizing, along the way, the resources of your industry and of your soil. Unless . . ."

"What is this 'unless'?"

"You know," I went on, "there is a disquieting precedent in recent history. That of Poland. Do you recall that, when Germany invaded Poland from the west in 1939, the Russians invaded her simultaneously from the east? Now suppose again . . ."

"This is contrary to regulations," said Fishface somewhat belatedly. "We are not supposed to suppose. You know our discipline."

"In that case, let me suppose for you and make myself more explicit. I, then, suppose that the Russians are attacking Manchuria from the north and the west across the Amur River. Another column breaks in, also from the west, but at a lower latitude, across the People's Republic of Mongolia. Yet another crosses the border from the east, that is from the southern tip of the Soviet Maritime Province. Your chaps around Manchuli are kept busy and their retreat is soon cut off by the pincer movement from the west and east. Harbin falls while mopping-up operations are conducted in Heilungkiang and the Soviet offensive develops toward Peking. Meanwhile more Russians, also coming through Mongolia, with old Tsedenbal cheering them on, or pretending to, have entered Jehol, also dangerously near Peking, on the one hand, and Sinkiang on the other. Do you follow me?"

"I do not understand strategy. Do you?"

"I do. Every military attaché in Peking is eating out of my hand." *

* With due apologies for this blatant lie, to them all and particularly to my dear old friend General Jacques Guillermaz, of the French embassy.

From his looks, I gathered that Fishface was taking all this seriously, and continued, much cheered: "Meanwhile, the Nationalists *and* the Americans, with Japan's unquestionable blessing, land in the southwest, all along the coast between Kwangtung and Chekiang. The rest of the world looks on, but, mind you, doesn't stir. Now, *you* tell me, what next?"

"A war between the Soviet Union and the United States, fought on Chinese soil, if I accept your theory. But it is unacceptable, because if such a thing as you suggest ever came to pass, the People's Liberation Army would fight both enemies to the bitter end."

"To the bitter end of the People's Liberation Army. Not so bitter, perhaps, because I guess that the number of defections, especially to the Chiang Kai-shek side, would far outdo that of the casualties. Poetic justice, in a way."

"We do not recite poetry in the People's courts. Not even Chairman Mao's."

"I remember the victory parade of the People's Liberation Army in Shanghai in 1949. It was a very grand parade, which I watched from the windows of my office. That show of military power was made the more impressive by the fact that every weapon displayed, from the heaviest tank to the smallest submachine gun, was of American make—nothing Russian, mind you—and apparently unused and brand-new."

"Taken from the cowed enemy on the field of battle."

"No, but simply handed over by the dispirited Nationalists who, as you know, deserted en masse to your side, not just during the last few weeks or months of the civil war, but actually since 1948. The reason was that it is wiser to be on the winning side than on that of the manifestly doomed. Caught between the Russian offensive and a Sino-American one, I do not think it unlikely that your own troops, equally dispirited in their turn, might do likewise, some because they could easily, in the circumstances, be made to feel that Communism in China had been betrayed by Mao Tse-tung, others because the American-backed Nationalists would present themselves as the true liberators of their motherland."

"This is nonsense," said Fishface hotly. "The Chinese people would rise as one man to repel the invaders, no matter on how many fronts. They would never stand for a return to the corrupt feudal regime of the Chiang clique, the running dogs of neo-colonialism and of Wall Street capitalism. You wrote as much yourself, once."

"Not quite in those words, and that was well over two years ago. I agree that at that period, and only as far as I could judge with the scanty means left at my disposal to form an opinion, the Nationalists did not seem to be missed and there was no visible evidence of any opposition to the present regime. I am not sure that I should be of the same mind today. 'There are tides . . .' and all that. It is my feeling, only a feeling of course, that the bulk of the people are no longer as happy with Communism as they were earlier and that the prospect of felicity through hard-ships and lack of personal freedom does not appeal to them quite as much as it is expected to. Moreover, if I may again remind you of the Polish precedent, it is quite conceivable that a preliminary agreement would have been made between the Russians and the Americans. I expect that the U.S.S.R. would be relieved at the prospect of not having to cope with the whole of your enormous country and that its forces and those of the other side would meet along a prearranged boundary with expressions of mutual goodwill."

"Peaceful coexistence," said Fishface bitterly after a moment of silence. "What you have just said proves us right when we say that the present leaders of the Soviet Union and the United States are working hand in glove together as accomplices in a great plot against the World Socialist Revolution."

"I believe that the slogan 'peaceful coexistence' between na-tions of different social systems was first coined at Bandung in 1955 and that it had China's fullest support."

"We never supported peaceful coexistence with the enemy but only between the peoples of Asia and Africa deeply united in their common struggle."

"In my opinion, the U.S.S.R. and the United States are no longer potential enemies but merely active competitors. They must come to a *modus vivendi* if a third World War, far more destructive than the first two, is to be avoided."

"We do not share the ideas of those who consider that such a war would annihilate mankind. We have said so and we have written so in one of our letters answering the slanderous so-called open letter which the Soviet Communist Party had the arrogance to publish on July 14, 1963. We made it clear that we were optimistic and did not think that more than fifty percent of mankind would perish. There would then be the brightest hopes for world socialism and for future universal happiness under the guidance of Chairman Mao Tse-tung's immortal thinking."

"I think I see what you mean, and I am not far from agreeing with you. If you explode your first atom bomb tomorrow, or in a month, or in a year, you will still remain for a very long time a minor nuclear power. In a modern war, a pushbutton war without battlefields, your 'human sea' tactics would be inapplicable. You would be as negligible as an enemy as you would be as an ally and you might therefore be left out of the fray altogether. But you would certainly not be negligible as survivors. Is that what you are thinking of?"

At this point Fishface burst into loud clapping which I took to be a startling tribute to the brightness of my deductions. Then I realized that everyone else in the banqueting hall was clapping also because the doors had been thrown open and the usual procession of V.I.P's, led by their hosts, had begun its progress among us and that the time had finally come to sit down and partake of the feast and speeches.

As Fishface had told me, I found myself sitting on his right hand. Mrs. Shen, who was playing hostess at the next table, was explaining to visiting correspondents, as they informed me later, that she had known me for years. Fishface and I were rather silent, both doing our hardest, with different ulterior motives, to consign to memory what had just passed between us. Still, after the cold cuts, the shark's fins—made more abundant if less delicious by the addition of sea slugs—and the duck had been disposed of, Fishface joined in the general small-talk by saying with a sweet-and-sour smile: "Mr. Marcuse was just telling me that he would expect the Soviet Union to launch against us a treacherous and unwarrantable aggression."

"One may expect anything of Khrushchev," said another nameless Chinese official, while a Soviet-bloc correspondent grew redder and redder in the face as this was being translated into Russian for his benefit by an obliging person.

"Mr. Marcuse even said," Fishface went on, "that they might succeed in invading our Northern Provinces."

This was greeted with visibly mixed, if unexpressed, feelings and I hastened to interpose: "But you did not let me finish. I was about to add that you would certainly be saved by a surprise Cuban landing at Vladivostok."

Fishface roared with laughter. "Now I know," he gurgled, appearing vastly relieved, "that you were joking all the time!"

The meal ended amid the usual mild pleasantries. It was indeed a grand occasion, and I noticed that, for the very first time, there were name cards, in Chinese of course, before everyone's plates. The one in front of Fishface fascinated me: there lay within my grasp the answer to a question that a great many people had been asking themselves and one another fruitlessly, for quite a few years.

So when we finally rose and were saying our good-byes, I said to Fishface: "Isn't it strange? We have known each other for so long and still we have not exchanged our visiting cards."

I promptly whisked one of my own from my wallet while Fishface was pretending to pat his pockets.

"I fear I haven't one with me," he said apologetically, knowing as well as I did that visiting cards were banned in China.

"Never mind," I said, deftly picking up his name card from the table, "this will do just as well, if you don't mind."

"By all means," retorted Fishface blandly.

This card I have kept and cherished to this very day. It is spattered with many sauces. The characters on it I had translated for me the next morning. There was a name all right but Fishface's rank was disappointingly put down as "vice-director." Vice-director of what, I still do not know. And the name I shall withhold until a certain foreign power makes me an offer. And even then, unless of course I am tempted by such a sum of money as I may retire on (and it would be cheap at the price), I shall perhaps still keep it to myself because of that fraction of a moment when Fishface had given me what I have never received from an official of Red China, a genuine look of human warmth and understanding with no ulterior motives whatsoever attached.

36

CONCLUSION INCONCLUSIVE
A Postscript

꧁꧂

SINCE I left China, things have happened that were not altogether unpredictable. And when this book was in its last stages other developments took place which could and should have been foreseen by the author had it taken him less time to re-dirty his washed brain.

The Chinese foreign policy fiasco, not only in Africa, but in Asia, and especially (from a Chinese point of view) the Indonesian catastrophe, was already predictable by the end of 1964. All was the result of overconfidence—an overconfidence which is not only typical of Mao, but traditionally Chinese. China cannot deal, despite the claims made by Chou En-lai as early as 1949, "on a basis of equality and reciprocity" with any nation. China is either top dog or underdog, never a partner. When China is, or thinks she is, top dog, there are no limits to her arrogance. When she is obviously underdog, as in the days of the Unequal Treaties, she will submit to her victors with an affected humility that never destroys her belief in herself and her future. She will bear indignities of the worst kind with a dignity of the best. She still is the very navel of the world, and time does not matter, and the temporary character of her vicissitudes and tribulations is never forgotten. The day will come when the universe will *again* pay tribute to Peking, when *again* the sun will never set over her Empire. Yet at no period in history did the whole world pay tribute to her, nor did she ever rule over an empire that enjoyed round-the-clock sunshine, weather permitting. But then, China's universe was always limited. And so, toeing the line of the past, the revolutionary but untraveled Mao has caused it to remain to this day. Indeed, because he is a *parvenu* and by birth a rural petit-bourgeois with the ambitions of his class, now that he has become the owner of all China, he cannot see clearly beyond the limits of the country he possesses, even though his greed may extend farther—toward the foreign lands over which China once ruled. China's imperialist tradition is clearly acknowledged even by so faithful and truly honest an Old Retainer as Epstein in his *From Opium War to Liberation* when he candidly writes: "In 1885, after further fighting * *China gave up all her rights in Vietnam.*" †

Mao, precisely because of his mistaken and essentially ignorant *Weltanschauung*, narrower perhaps than China's ever was, has made himself guilty of precisely that Great Power chauvinism which he so readily denounces elsewhere. It is a bad thing for a man in his position to suffer from both a megalomaniac superiority complex due to ignorance—especially when it is inextricably combined with an inferiority complex due to unwilling but still inescapable observation—and an utter lack of any sense of historical perspective—and of humor. Thus there is to my mind a certain psychological link between the absurd Chinese reaction to the harmless *Tribune* hoax ‡ and the tragic miscarriage of the Chinese-inspired Indonesian putsch, a miscarriage that caused the death of about half a million members of what was known as the most important and numerous Communist Party outside the Communist-ruled world. Oversusceptibility in the first case and overconfidence in the second indicate crass misconceptions of the non-Han world.

The damning contradiction lies in the fact that, while China is convinced in her heart that the world at large has everything to learn from her and that, as sung in the opera *The East Is Red*, "in China is born the Communist Party," by encouraging and multiplying foreign industrial exhibitions on her own soil and demanding of the Western exhibitors that they lecture Chinese students as no Chinese professor could, she reluctantly acknowledges also that there is much that is still beyond her ken. How does she get away from this apparently inescapable contradiction? Simply in the safe knowledge that she would never be so naïve as to impart to potential enemies any sort of potentially dangerous savvy

* Between the French and the Chinese *Pavillons Noirs* in Tonking.
† My italics. (J.M.)
‡ See pages 82–83.

which they would have been too stupid to think of unaided. (I have just read in a letter to an English newspaper that the Chinese, having invented gunpowder, were too humane to apply it to warlike purposes. I humbly submit that, having indeed invented gunpowder, they simply failed to invent the cannonball also. I do not think that merciful considerations came into it at all, for they had in those days brought the art of torture to such a degree of perfection as to put the rest of the civilized world to shame.) The fact that Chinese atomic scientsts were all trained in the U.S., the U.S.S.R., or Western Europe and that at least one of China's reactors was built by Soviet engineers is never mentioned.

When the Communists came into power in 1949 there was about them a pride and an honesty that has given way to vanity and opportunism. But then what can be more absurd than the Opposition once it has sunk its buttocks in the government saddle and is still calling itself the Opposition? Or the Revolution, having achieved the complete turn that the word implies, still going round and round, orbiting around itself, its own purposeless satellite, until the law of gravitation takes over again? In all fairness, on the other hand, one may well ask at what point the revolutionary leader, the man who has made his revolution and has been made by it, can gracefully admit that the revolution is finished without having to confess that he is finished himself?

∽⟨⟩∾

The purges of 1966 were inevitable after the setbacks suffered by China in her Asian and African outposts of political empire. These could easily be concealed from the masses (who could not have cared less in any case) but not from the comparative few who, by their very positions, were automatically bound to know and bound to wonder, and perhaps to criticize. Things had to be explained away, mistakes acknowledged, scapegoats found, and at such a high administrative and Party level that the mistakes would take the appearance of criminal negligence bordering on deliberate treason.

Under a regime that had made self-criticism part of its way of life, mistakes had to be perpetually confessed. And such confessions had to be taken, and were by many, as tokens of good faith and as genuine humble breast-beatings. If the Old Retainers may be quoted again, Anna Louise Strong's letter number ten, dated July 26, 1963, may prove revealing. Referring to a "memorable talk" she had had with an important Party official, she quoted that exalted personage as saying that even though the Chinese Communist Party had always been heroic, "many mistakes were made by the leadership in getting experience. They were costly mistakes and they taught us to avoid such mistakes later." Mrs. Strong adds: "This entire approach was new to me. In America we were always 'God's country,' qualified to liberate and improve the world. In Russia there was always the 'perfect system,' spoiled till now by some personal devils. In China they 'made mistakes,' suffered by them, acknowledged and studied them, thus planned victory."

It was Lu Ting-yi, then head of Propaganda, who was being quoted by the venerable pythoness. She got from his lips, so she writes, the history of the Chinese Communist Party. Lu Ting-yi happens to be one of the victims of the most recent purge. Another mistake.

Both the necessity and danger of acknowledging mistakes were already plain to Mao Tse-tung in 1958 when he offered his unrejectable resignation as Chief of State and so became, passing the onus of future blunders onto Liu Shao-chi's bent shoulders, the mere spiritual leader of the country. He gave up nothing of his powers, however, since he remained at the head of the Party and since the Party is above the Administration; but he could no longer be held responsible for anything that was bungled at government level. Others could be wrong, not he.

Everything from then on was to be done in the light of his Thinking. If things miscarried, it was either because his thought had not been correctly understood or applied to the problems at hand, or preferably because it had been deliberately distorted and, with himself used as a screen, the Revolution wilfully betrayed. It was at that point, and at that point only, that, hey presto! he restored absolute monarchy in China and set himself up as the Miscreant Emperor by divine right.

The reader may wonder why I have devoted a whole chapter to the reform of the theater and disposed briefly of the 1966 purges.

One reason is, of course, that I was on the spot at the time of the theater reform and no longer in China when the purges started.

Another is that, of these two political developments, the first is the most important in that it affected the life of the people while the other did not.

The stage revolution is something positive, if unpalatable. We can follow it through its successive phases. We know when it started, we know of its vicissitudes, we have seen the new operas and most of the libretti have been published in foreign languages; the revolution there, for once, represents a genuine change and an adventure embarked upon with very clear ideas as to its aim. At the same time, we know that, up to the present, it has had to stop at a compromise which discloses at least some passive resistance on the part of the Chinese public. It was in a way a confrontation between the political driving force and the Chinese audiences and it has been admitted that very reluctant but real concessions had to be made at the top. Entirely political and utilitarian as the new China theater has become, it remains theater. The final result of the reform is new plays produced in new settings and, up to a point, according to a new technique, and written for the sole purpose of indoctrination, but in which real actors still perform on a real stage before a real if somewhat constrained public. The 1966 purges, far from being real theater, were a puppet show held *in camera*. Indeed, the opera purge was infinitely more genuine than the subsequent purge opera.

The latter may have answered a necessity of the moment but it was also a matter of routine. The political purge is a standing institution, like the People's Congress or the Party Plenum. Both meet at irregular and unpredictable intervals, they are dormant more often than not, but always potentially there. So is the purge, the perpetual possibility of it, the fate of all hanging by a thread, the purge of Damocles.

But what does it mean for a Chinese to be "purged"? It may mean total physical disappearance and it may mean just a temporary political eclipse. Or any of a thousand different gradations between these two extremes. A great many people whom one might have considered to be purged *ex officio* and for good, having shown repentance, having re-educated themselves, have been, with more or less honor, received in the bosom of the Maoist High Church.

There is the typical example of Henry Pu Yi, the last emperor of China when a baby and later the first and only emperor of Japanese-dominated Manchukuo—a puppet from childhood on. Pu Yi has now been rehabilitated, he does not hold any post that is in any way prominent, but he is a human showpiece: he represents the converted traitor who has made a full confession, has broadcast his past sins and beaten his breast in the approved manner, thus in fact remaining true to his vocation as a stooge. I have not seen him and I made no attempt to (I think that even a permanent correspondent could have managed it), but he had been made to do his number so often already before V.I.P.P.'s that I did not see any point in repeating the process, or in forcing upon him once more the ordeal of an interview.

I have already spoken of the reception of the prodigal warlord Li Tsung-jen at Peking and of the bright future that awaits "Gimo" Chiang there. And I have witnessed past purges. The only really bloody purge was that of 1951 in which several million people lost their lives. But its victims were former Kuomintang officials, reactionary and bourgeois elements and "Westernized" Chinese; in brief, it was not a Party purge. The first Party purge took place in 1953, following the "Kao Kang Conspiracy" and there was another one after the Hundred Flowers experiment. It was the first to be aimed specifically at writers, artists, university professors, and intellectuals generally. It was bloodless, but over one million men and women were "sent to the countryside" to learn the facts of socialist life.

As to the 1966 purge, what strikes one is that it affected, not only comparative small fry, but eminent personalities such as Peng Chen and General Lo Jui-ching, in whom Mao had for years placed his trust. What does it mean? Did they really manage—and over such a long period of time!—to hoodwink the great man, to take advantage of his candor, to fool the unfoolable, to ridicule that infallible mind whose thinking is the shining beacon of seven hundred million people, to turn into a monkey the venerated Chairman, now invariably called by all Chinese publications "Our Great Teacher, Great Leader, Great Supreme Commander, and Great Helmsman"? If so, then Mao's judgment of men is certainly not to be relied upon. And if so, how come these abominable traitors have not been more severely punished than by mere demotion? But—is it so?

I cannot help feeling that there is a farcical element, after all, in that particular purge. The need for *a* purge may well have been there, but where its victims are concerned, I will not, at the risk of being branded a cynic, refrain from offering the suggestion that either lots were drawn in the Forbidden City or the matter was quietly and amicably settled over a nice cuppa.

I have made it a point not to mention the Red Guards in connection with the purge. The Red Guards are not funny.

Their sudden appearance, overnight and from nowhere, came as a complete surprise not only to the outside world but by all accounts to the Chinese themselves. Yet the *hung wei ping* materialized at their appointed hour and entered the stage upon their cue. They had been waiting out of sight for quite some time, and the fact that foreign observers, including myself, utterly failed to sense their presence and so to follow the plot makes poor dramatic critics of us all.

The Red Guards phenomenon could and should have been foreseen as logical and inevitable. By which I do not mean to imply that it was planned years ahead or that it is a good thing for China—or for Mao. Far from it. But it had to happen. Various factors had gradually been leading up to it, like lines converging toward the same given point.

Watching the activities of the Red Guards before looking at the Red Guards themselves, one is reminded of that epitome of all other Maoist slogans: "Everything is better in China than elsewhere; everything is better in Mao's China than it ever was before." The obvious corollary is "Everything foreign is bad; everything old is bad." And so we find the *hung wei ping* on the warpath against all foreign influences and against all influences from the past. Both the xenophobe and the anti-traditionalist trends were there well before Mao's hooligans had come into being.

It is odd to reflect that nothing that the Red Guards do would have met with Lei Feng's approval. The various Lei Fengs that rapidly succeeded one another between 1962 and 1965 were all *good boys*. The *hung wei ping* are *bad boys*. Yet there was a time when Mao, after keeping himself graphically to himself for a long time, had written in his magnificent hand: "Let us all emulate Lei Feng." Now he urges everyone to emulate the young vandals conjured up by himself. The East wind, which, Mao claims, prevails over the West wind, has become an ill wind that will not blow even its blower any good.

The sudden creation of the Red Guards cannot but be the result of a counsel of despair. With them and his covenant with them, and his official sanction of the brutalities and wanton destruction committed in his name, Mao has repudiated himself. We need not read far in his *Selected Works* to find recurring again and again the theme that the masses must be won over, not antagonized. The eight-point proclamation of April, 1949, to quote nothing else, orders the People's Liberation Army to "protect the lives and property of all the people . . . , all public and private schools, hospitals, cultural institutions . . . , the lives and property of foreign nationals." In its last paragraph, it says: "The People's Liberation Army is highly disciplined; it is fair in buying and selling and is not allowed to take even a needle or a piece of thread from the people." Hooliganism in Red China proper was unknown before the Red Guards. It was the very thing Mao would not have tolerated for it would have set the people against the Party and against himself. But it was an outstanding feature of the "liberation" of Tibet in 1959.

In the late summer of 1966, the *hung wei ping*, in the cause and the course of the so-called "Cultural Revolution," indulged in the very acts for which foreign troops, when they occupied Peking in 1860 and again in 1900, were rightly blamed, with the exception of looting, perhaps, for the Red Guards, caring as little for art as for personal profit, seem to have indulged solely in an orgy of destruction and beastliness. But when they so enthusiastically burned the old classics, they burned those very books to which Mao constantly referred in his various lectures and essays and which he has so freely plagiarized. For instance, in one single paragraph of his pamphlet "On Contradiction," he mentions in turn the *Book of Mountains and Seas*, one of the oldest classics going back to the era of the Warring States; an old legend recorded as far back as the second century B.C.; a sixteenth-century novel, the *Pilgrimage to the West* (turned a few years ago, with its hero, Sun Wu-kung, the monkey god, into an excellent animated cartoon which I imagine would be banned now); and the *Strange Tales* of Liao Chai, a seventeenth-century collection of fairy tales. The very authors from which Mao drew his own peculiar culture, the very representatives of a civilization that he so far professed to cherish as establishing the antiquity and richness of the Chinese heritage are now being destroyed as the remnants of feudalism. If they are that, then so is Mao.

The question is: why the Red Guards? They are actually hacking away at the plinth on which Mao's very statue stands. They are shaking the pillars of his self-erected shrine and he is running the serious risk of being smothered under the debris. But then, even though his name means literally "the Hair," he is no Samson and the temple that is about to fall in ruins about his ears is not that of the enemy but his own. Then why the *hung wei ping?*

The explanation from Chinese and pro-Chinese sources is that the younger generation, filled with the enthusiasm that is kindled in the breast of every man by the mere study of Mao Tse-tung's thinking, could no longer put up with the continuing presence in China of a bourgeois, reactionary, and possibly neo-revisionist element, and that they *spontaneously* took steps to put an end to this shocking state of things, to the betrayal of the Chinese Revolution and that it was only *after* they had come into their mysterious being that Mao himself gave them his stamp of approval.

I find this quite incredible. The reactionary elements, so-called, could effectively have been dealt with in past years by the ever-watchful Street Committees, Factory Committees, University Committees, and other such committees—there is no shortage of them—that are in fact the regime's auxiliary thought-police. When I was in China, it was admitted quite openly in official circles that discipline was the backbone of the nation and that personal initiative could not be tolerated, no matter how well-meaning. And that, I know, was true. I have watched dozens of carefully organized demonstrations of spontaneity with the participants marching down Peking's streets and screaming slogans and waving banners, and the people on the pavement not even turning their heads to look at them and paying no attention. It was not only that they were patently indifferent, but also that they were not on political duty on that particular day, which they might have been the day before or might be the next, and moreover that taking the liberty of stepping off the sidewalk and joining the crowds in the streets would not have been quite the thing to do.

The notion that a spontaneous movement can have taken place in China is to be discarded as utterly absurd. The Red Guards came into being throughout the country pretty much at one and the same time, going into action with remarkable synchronization. If we accept the preposterous thesis that this nation-wide movement, which must have been carefully organized, had been brewing for at least several months, then we are bound to accept also the equally preposterous theory that any underground movement can be organized in China, unknown to the police of the state and of the Party. It would mean, in other words, that the time-honored secret societies of China were still in a position to act freely while hoodwinking the authorities in the early stages and defying the forces of law and order in the later ones. If such a thing could have come to pass it would have done so long ago and it would have taken a very different course from that of the Red Guards.

Another theory that has been suggested, by anti-Mao sources this time, is that there was a certain amount of dirty work to be done and it became convenient to entrust it to an apparently genuine youth movement whose good intentions could not be questioned, and which indeed meant so well that, in spite of their excesses, they deserved no more chastisement than a stern finger paternally shaken in their faces. The notion that the younger element of the nation could have been moved to such explosive frenzy through a careful study of Mao Tse-tung's *Selected Works* is totally inacceptable to anyone who has experienced their strictly sedative properties. I am fairly conversant with the writings of New China's Foundering Father and I must confess that, apart from the strict line of professional duty, I resort to them only to fight insomnia. They are far better than counting sheep or taking pills and I can guarantee that anyone will be sent to sleep in no time at all by the repetition of such pearls of wisdom

as "to be subjective means not to look at problems objectively
. . . to be one-sided means not to look at problems all-sidedly
. . . ," etc.

The question remains: why the Red Guards?

The answer I think is not only political but also psychological
—a matter of mass psychology plus the psychology of one
man.

Mao, it is now a well-known fact, had no confidence in the
rising generation which he often described as the bourgeois of
the Revolution when he unburdened himself to foreign dignitaries. He was only too well aware that they were paying him no
more than lip service and that indifference toward himself and
general frustration were growing fast among the young, in the
universities particularly. It had become essential to shake them
out of their torpor and their resentful sulks. They had to be made
to feel that they were revolutionaries, and active ones at that, and
even violent ones, even if an entirely fictitious revolution had to
be staged for the purpose. That is precisely what was done, the
guiding principle being, I suppose, that there is no better way to
make an indifferent citizen feel that he is a useful member of
society than to provide him with a very long and sharp knife,
urge him to use it freely on his fellow-men, and of course assure
him of impunity. Also, physical violence and political hysteria
represent an excellent safety valve for sex frustration.

But then, who will be the ultimate victims of the Red Guards?
Their immediate victims, we know: harmless people arbitrarily
accused of being anti-Party elements; shopkeepers whose signs
were thought bourgeois or reactionary; some professors and
teachers; some foreigners such as the Sacred Heart convent sisters
in Peking. People have been humiliated and beaten; others have
disappeared. We know more or less what happened in the capital,
in Shanghai, and in Canton, because foreigners live in the first
two cities and foreigners pass through the third. What took place
in the rest of China is anybody's gruesome guess. When I learned
that actvities of the *hung wei ping* had extended as far as Tibet, I
shuddered as I thought of the 1959 atrocities.*

---

* Old Retainers A. L. Strong and Israel Epstein have published glowing
accounts of the new Tibet, but I am rather inclined to put my faith in the
two reports of the Geneva International Commission of Jurists whose
members have carried out exhaustive inquiries into the 1959 events and the
"liberation" of Tibet which the *People's Daily* described as "peaceful" and

These, as the two successive reports of the Geneva International Commission of Jurists revealed, had been essentially anti-religious in character under the pretext of being anti-feudal, and mass murder of the most revolting sort had been committed, the "excuse" being that the people had to be made to see that lamas could be butchered with impunity and that "the gods could not come to their rescue." Some priests had been put to death with boiling water poured on their heads, others had been disemboweled, others still, crucified or buried alive. This latter form of execution is an old Chinese Communist practice of which I heard for the first time (not from Kuomintang sources) in 1940. As late as October, 1966, the religious news agency K.I.P.A. reported that several Chinese Catholic priests had recently died that atrocious death (at the hands, I presume, of the Red Guards) in Tientsin,

---

Mrs. Strong as "relatively bloodless." It has been argued that members of the International Commission never crossed the Tibetan border. This is quite true. They applied in writing for visas at the Chinese embassy in New Delhi, but their application was returned "after about one hour" with the curt message that the Ambassador was "not willing to accept it." This is quite an unusual procedure, for normally such applications submitted by foreigners are referred to Peking and weeks, months, or even years may elapse before an answer, positive or negative, is given. It would seem that the Chinese embassy in the Indian capital had already received standing instructions not to let the Commission in and that impartial observers were not welcome at Lhassa. Evidence obtained by the Commission from thousands of Tibetan refugees however led to the conclusions:

  a) that the Chinese will not permit adherence to and practice of Buddhism in Tibet;
  b) that they have systematically set out to eradicate this belief in Tibet;
  c) that in pursuit of this design they have killed religious figures because their religious belief and practice was an encouragement and example to others;
  d) that they have forcibly transferred large numbers of Tibetan children to a Chinese materialist environment in order to prevent them from having a religious upbringing.

These conclusions are set forth in the second report of the Commission (1960) which further states: "These four facts reveal, it is considered, an attempt to destroy the Tibetan part of the Buddhist religious group by two methods which fall specifically within the terms of Article II of the Convention for the Prevention and Punishment of Genocide, and are also considered to represent a crime under international law independently of that convention. . . . The evidence available from Chinese sources themselves reveals an intention to put an end to the ancient religious practices and institutions of Tibet and to allow only that degree of freedom of religious belief which would be compatible with complete acceptance of Communism, in short, none at all."

which is no more than 85 miles from Peking. What may have happened still farther away from foreign eyes, one can only guess. In Peking, Shanghai, and Canton, frightening as their behavior may have appeared to some, the Red Guards were still held on a tight rein. But in their activities, restricted as they were, a familiar pattern appears: the desecration of temples and cemeteries, the humbling of priests and "bourgeois," the burning of books. All of this strikes a chord in one's memory because it all happened in Tibet only seven years ago. There, too, religious symbols were plastered with pseudo-Communist slogans, by youths motivated no so much by the thinking of Mao Tse-tung or any understanding of Marxist-Leninist thumb-the-seam discipline, as by a sudden sense of their own importance.

Still, the real victims of the *hung wei ping* are ultimately bound to be the *hung wei ping* themselves.

They will last no longer than Lei Feng or his successors did. Once they have played their assigned part they will be sent to the country both to learn from the people and to teach the people and they will be swallowed up and not heard of again or they will be incorporated, willy-nilly, in the P.L.A. They will have served their purpose, destructive as it will have been.

Yes, the Red Guards will become their own victims. But these victims will include a very illustrious person: Mao. And that is why I said that only a counsel of despair could have prompted Mao, or perhaps his deputy, his "close comrade-in-arms" Lin Piao, whose very violence is that of a very sick man with nothing much to lose, to conjure up the Guards. For if there is something that the Red Guards are *not* doing, it is spreading goodwill and pouring out the milk of human kindness by the bucket. And since they are doing everything they do on Mao's official behest, it is unlikely that the old Leader's popularity will be enhanced or that the shining beacon of his thought will acquire greater candle-power.

It is a strange picture that rises before my mind's eye at this juncture: old and sick Mao and younger but sicker Lin Piao standing together on the rostrum of Tien An Men. Night has fallen. They are alone. They are breathing maotai into each other's face, for they have just finished dinner. From the city, ill lit but for Changan Avenue at their feet, comes, not the sound, but the silence of fear—for fear is noiseless. And silent they are, too, and it makes them a little uneasy. And they watch, just to do something, the water cart below that sprinkles the macadam, while the rainclouds, unseen, gather in the black sky overhead.

A final word. I have shown various chapters of this book to various friends and acquaintances and have had various reactions from them.

The V.I.P.P. tourists thought I was being too flippant about a country which is so expensive to visit. They could see, they said, that I had not paid for my airplane ticket out of my own pocket.

A young European Communist of one of the pro-Peking splinter groups told me the book was sheer sacrilege. He had never been to China and Karl Marx was just a name to him, but he worshipped Mao and hoped to see the day when, thanks to him, mankind would find justice and happiness under the dictatorship of the proletariat. After which he said good-by rather stiffly and drove off in his red (*proletariat oblige!*) sports car, a present of his parents on the occasion of his coming of age.

Some people suggested that Fishface was a fictitious character, which hurt me. If my most solemn word is not enough, I am prepared to produce witnesses who knew him as I did and wondered for years who he was—as I did—and who will bear me out. Adam Kellett-Long, of Reuters (to name only him), is one of many.

Others accused me of being deliberately unkind to China and the Chinese. That hurt. Very much.

It was never my intention to be unkind. Or kind. People like Mrs. Chen or the moronic interpreters of the China Travel Service I described as I had seen them, and I quoted them, with the help of my notebooks, as accurately as I could.

I have spent many happy years of my life in China. I have a great love for China and her people. I have many Chinese friends and indeed owe my life to some of them.

It may sound odd, coming from the lips of an "Old China Hand" like myself who for a very long time enjoyed the one-sided advantages and amenities provided by the Unequal Treaties, but I will still say it: I do not like to see the Chinese humiliated.

And I do not like the regime that humiliates them, much as I still admire some of its leaders for what they did in the past and for what they still are today.

But when, to the odium of totalitarian dictatorship and brainwashing, I find added comic and self-important imbecility, I see no reason to deny myself the relief of a chuckle. And if others will join me, so much the better, for I no more enjoy laughing alone than drinking alone. Therefore: *Kampei!*—bottoms up!

Much very serious nonsense has been pompously written about Red China, some honest, some not, disinterestedly or with "ulterior motives." Out of it all, there emerges the picture of a nation, fired with enthusiasm and fervor, waking up every morning to face an ever better day, looking forward to a future of bliss and even freedom. It is, to say the least, a very carefully retouched portrait, not unlike the ubiquitous official portrait of Mao.

If, between the covers of this book, I have attempted to demystify China, it is not because I do not like China, but because I dislike a certain type of mystification and abominate a social system that founds its strength on the deliberate and forcible vilification of the dignity of the human person and which it is now fashionable to overglamorize, overfear and generally overrate.

INDEX

A